Effective Writing

Improving scientific, technical and business communication

SECOND EDITION

Christopher Turk
Senior Research Fellow
University of Wales
College of Cardiff

John Kirkman
Consultant on Scientific and
Technical Communication

London   New York
E. & F.N. SPON

First published in 1982 by E. & F.N. Spon Ltd
11 New Fetter Lane, London EC4P 4EE
Reprinted 1984, 1987
Second edition 1989
Published in the USA by E. & F.N. Spon
29 West 35th Street, New York NY 10001

Typeset in 10/12 Palatino by
Acorn Bookwork, Salisbury, Wiltshire
Printed and bound in Great Britain by
T.J. Press (Padstow) Ltd, Padstow, Cornwall

ISBN 0 419 14660 1

British Library Cataloguing in Publication Data

Turk, Christopher
  Effective writing: improving scientific-
  technical and business communication –
  2nd ed.
  1. English language. Writing skills
  I. Title.   II. Kirkman, John
  808'.0665021

ISBN 0-419-14660-1

Library of Congress Cataloging-in-Publication Data

Turk, Christopher
    Effective writing: improving scientific, technical, and
  business communication/Christopher Turk, John
  Kirkman.
      p.   cm.
    Includes bibliographical references and index.
  ISBN 0-419-14660-1
    1. Technical writing.   I. Kirkman, John (Alfred John)
  II. Title, T11.T75   1988
  808'.0666021--dc19   88-18703
                                                  CIP

Effective Writing

Contents

Preface

Modern technology has changed the process of writing and the methods of producing text, but the electronic revolution has not yet found a way of removing the need for clear and careful thinking during drafting and revising. To be effective, writers must still reflect carefully on their aims, audiences, and contexts, and then make shrewd choices of what to say and how to say it. So most of the advice in this book remains unchanged. We have taken the opportunity to extend the range of topics covered, and to reinforce some sections of the text.

We acknowledge with gratitude the comments sent to us by readers of the first edition. We should welcome feedback on the usefulness and practicality of this extended edition.

Christopher Turk
John Kirkman

About the authors

Christopher Turk is a Senior Research Fellow at the University of Wales, College of Cardiff, UK. He has lectured widely on aspects of communication in the UK, Belgium and Sweden. He was a Visiting Faculty member at Yale University in 1983–84, and a Visiting Fellow at the University of Geneva in 1985. He was Paul Mellon Fellow at Yale in 1986. His other publications include several articles on computer-aided writing, *Effective Speaking* (E.& F.N. Spon, 1985), and *The Computer and the Scholar* (Abacus, 1988). He has a special research interest in the processing of natural language by computer, a branch of artificial intelligence.

John Kirkman was formerly Director of the Communication Studies Unit at the University of Wales Institute of Science and Technology, Cardiff (now University of Wales, College of Cardiff), UK. Since 1983, he has worked full-time as a consultant on scientific and technical communication. He has consulted for more than 200 organizations in 16 countries. He has been a Visiting Lecturer in Technical Communication at the University of Michigan, USA, and a Visiting Fellow in Linguistics at Princeton University, USA. He has published more than 70 articles, and has written, edited or contributed to 10 books, including *Good Style for Scientific and Engineering Writing* (Pitman, 1980). The Society for Technical Communication (USA) gave him its Outstanding Article Award in 1974, and an Award for Distinguished Technical Communication (shared with Peter Hunt) in 1987.

Writing is 1
communicating:
revising basic
assumptions

Writing is a skill; like other skills, it can be learnt, and like most skills it is not inborn. For example, few people lack the basic equipment to learn to ride a bicycle (balance, strength, sight), but most become skilful cyclists only after much practice. Confidence is the main necessity, and having the courage to get on and try. The same is true of writing. Most people have the basic equipment (tact, experience, language), but like riding a bicycle, writing is a skill that must be learnt by doing it. No amount of reading, or absorbing rules and advice, can substitute for practice. So as we offer advice and give examples, our main aim is to reassure you that early 'wobbly' efforts at writing are quite normal. Don't be discouraged by the writer's equivalent of grazed knees. Practice will bring co-ordination and control that will change writing from an apparently hazardous exercise to an efficient means of getting somewhere.

We start from the assumption that thinking about writing can improve it, and that everyone can learn to write well. Most people, in reality, are better at writing than they fear. They can write successful letters to friends and effective complaints about faulty goods. These writing tasks require the same basic skills as long reports, detailed instructions, or complex letters or memoranda. Judgement of what the audience needs to know, tact in assessing which way to present this information to them most usefully, and the resources of language to do the job exist in everyone. We all develop a basic storehouse of skills. It is drawn on to tell successful jokes at the bar, to shout at the other driver, to persuade a friend to do something with you. This book sets out to encourage a more conscious use of those skills.

Writing as communication

The first task is to encourage the right attitudes to writing. An instructor teaching timid old ladies to ride bicycles would soon find that getting them to take a positive and confident view was a major step towards success. Few professional scientists busy with research projects, rushing their results on to paper for impatient managers, would like to be compared with 'timid old ladies', but they might recognize in themselves some of the same fearful hesitation when they put pen to paper. Writing is often felt to be a nuisance; frequently it is something which is secretly dreaded, rarely is it looked forward to as the climax of research.

This hesitation is the first problem. Like mathematical techniques and specialized knowledge in the subject, writing skill is basic professional equipment. Professional scientists or engineers spend up to one third of their working time writing, reading and talking, and paper is one of the major products of all industrial and research organizations.[1] Many engineers think that a sound education in writing is as important as education in technical subjects such as metallurgy or business management. By making the writing task easier, we hope to reduce the burden on the reader, and thereby make the communication of information more effective. We should start by emphasizing that writing is an essential professional skill in which we can take as much pride as we take in experimental technique.

To improve this writing skill, we need first to consider our experience as readers. Everyone is aware of the huge amount of written material to be dealt with; much of it is verbose, far too long for the job it has to do, and – what is worse – confusingly organized. By thinking of our irritation as readers with the inadequacy of many writers, we can learn to be more professional writers ourselves. Read, for instance, this passage:

> The principal advantage that the soft contact lens offers over the conventional hard contact lens is increased comfort. The associated benefits of rapid patient accommodation and extended wear times with minimal overwear syndrome are also superior to hard lens experience. However, experience has taught us that maintaining the soft lens in such an ideal, comfortable state for the patient requires the daily maintenance of a satisfactory care regimen. Of prime importance in such a regimen is cleaning.
>
> Cleaning is even more important for maintaining comfort in soft contact lens wear than in hard contact lens wear. A study

of the physical and chemical nature of the soft lens aids us in understanding why this is true.

Soft lenses possess an intricate internal structure with a tightly entwined micropore meshwork and a pore size distribution estimated at 5–50 angstroms, indeed the tightness of the pore meshwork is demonstrated by the relatively slow uptake of water by the lens in becoming fully hydrated from the dry state. In addition, tests in our laboratories have also indicated that – in completely clean lenses – an external solution exchanges slowly with the internally held lens solution.

The subject may be unfamiliar, but that is not the only cause of discomfort. Readers are on the rack as they hang on grimly through interminable sentences such as:

Soft lenses possess an intricate internal structure with a tightly entwined micropore meshwork and a pore size distribution estimated at 5–50 angstroms, indeed the tightness of the pore meshwork is demonstrated by the relatively slow uptake of water by the lens in becoming fully hydrated from the dry state.

They are irritated by the pomposity of:

. . . requires the daily maintenance of a satisfactory care regimen.

They are repelled by the windy self-importance of:

The associated benefits of rapid patient accommodation and extended wear times with minimal overwear syndrome are also superior to hard lens experience.

These features make reading the passage seem like wading through a quagmire. The feeling is depressingly familiar; but the passage is neither unusual nor untypical. Text-books, journal articles, reports and memoranda too often have the same uninviting style, the same indigestible content. Yet such passages can be written in another way, making them easier to read and therefore more communicative:

The main advantage of the soft contact-lens is that it is more comfortable to wear than the conventional, hard contact-lens. Also, patients get used to it more rapidly, and are able to wear it for longer with only slight adverse effects. However, to keep the soft lens ideally comfortable, the lens must be cared for daily. Cleaning is particularly important – even more important for maintaining the comfort of soft lenses than of hard lenses.

Soft lenses have an intricate internal structure. They have a tightly entwined micropore meshwork, and pore sizes estimated at 5–50 angstroms. The tightness of the meshwork is demonstrated by the relative slowness with which a dry lens takes up water and becomes fully hydrated. Also, our tests have shown that, if the lens is completely clean, an external solution changes places with the internally held solution only slowly.

The difference between these two passages lies in the way language is used, since the technical content is the same in both. They show that it *is* possible to make the reader's task easier, by using different writing tactics.

Causes of poor writing

Why is so much technical writing so difficult to read? If we are to improve writing, it is worth spending time diagnosing the sources of this all-too-familiar failure. The main blame for the poor quality of much technical writing probably lies with educators. The last time most writers were taught about writing was at school, but the ideas of style which the English teacher inculcated in poetry lessons had more to do with long words and roses than with using language to communicate information. Many engineers and scientists were left with the conviction that 'English' was not for them. When they chose their careers, they thankfully gave up English for the clearer and more precise worlds of physics and chemistry. And the distaste for 'English' often persists into adult professional life.

The legacy from school English lessons includes half-remembered advice about style; such rules as 'never repeat the same word in a sentence', or 'long and unusual words are elegant and interesting'. These maxims are inappropriate to the task of communicating technical information. Yet because writing has not been thought about subsequently, they survive in writers' subconscious minds and creep out unexpectedly. Bad teaching has a lot to answer for. We should review the rules of style learnt at school and re-think the whole process of communicating.

Another problem survives from education. Writing at school or college has a different audience and a different purpose from the writing of a professional scientist or engineer. During full-time education, laboratory reports, essays or examination papers are written to be read by people who *already know* the information. The readers are concerned with assessment, and writing is a process of display; students aim to impress with their sophistication and knowledge. The natural tactics are to use as much information as possible, to embed it in sophisticated language with complex structures, and to use recondite (!) vocabulary. There is nothing wrong in these tactics; they are the inevitable result of a system where learning and assessment go hand-in-hand. But the result of having no other training in writing is that most students emerge from full-time education with a writing style designed to impress rather than to communicate.

In professional life, the aim and audience for writing are different. For the first time, the new professional scientist or engineer is writing for people who *do not know* the information. The readers do not want to *assess*, they want to *learn* and *use* information for their own purposes. But usually no-one warns young writers that their tactics must change. What is needed is simplicity, not sophistication; the minimum, not the maximum of information is best. Most writers carry on writing in the way that brought rewards before, and this seems to us a major reason why so much professional writing is less effective than it could be.

Technical writing is often poor because writers are frequently not given a clear enough brief for the job. Asked to 'write a report on production', they may not be told for whom, why, and for what purpose. Is the report for technical staff, or line management? Is it for record purposes, or for some important board-level decision? How much detail is going to be needed? What facts are important? All these questions will affect the tactics adopted in writing the report. Without this information, only an approximate and confusing report can be written. Vague and inadequate specifications invite poor reports.

Some writers feel that the manager's blue pencil is hanging over them. Over-editing is discouraging for writers, and makes them afraid that their careful judgements about content and tactics will be wasted. We often find writers discouraged about the finer skills of writing because they know their well-thought-out choice of words will be butchered by hatchet-men higher up

Authority and tradition

the hierarchy. We suggest that you discuss a synopsis with the person who commissioned the report, before drafting the full text. This will usually remove distrust and misunderstandings about aims. But when you, the writer, are in the manager's chair yourself, be aware of the effects of over-editing on your staff.

Another reason why writing is often poor is that scientists and engineers tend, when writing, to take cover in a familiar and 'traditional' style. It is odd to think of the scientific community doing anything because it is traditional, rather than for good reasons, yet when it comes to writing, it is often tradition and not reason that prevails. A modern scientist, describing the atomic structure of matter, might write:

> It is hypothesized by the present writer that in essence the initial format of material substances was relatively dense, massive in weight, durable, and particulate in form; the extreme manifestation of hardness being displayed by resistance to diminution in size due to abrasive processes and by counter fragmentation systems.

Science was not always reported like this. The passage is, in fact, a 'modernized' version of a sentence from Isaac Newton. In the 17th century Newton wrote:

> It seems probable to me, that God in the beginning formed matter in solid, massy, hard, impenetrable, moveable particles; . . . even so very hard, as never to wear or break in pieces.[2]

The 'tradition' of verbose writing is a modern one. It has been pilloried often enough, but many writers still turn to it. Newton did not feel the need to obfuscate his meaning with inflated style; the simple language of clear thinking was exciting enough without decoration. Too many modern scientists and engineers seem to need to wrap up their meanings. We presume they think it makes their writing more impressive; but every writer knows how depressingly easy to write – and how meaningless to read – such a verbose style is. Writing is often poor because of thoughtless use of a 'traditional' style.

A final reason for the poor quality of much scientific and technical documentation is that some writers do not want their style to be transparent, or their meaning easily understood.

> A major psychological obstacle is fear of authority – of being fired, of not being promoted, of being disciplined, of displeasing a supervisor.[3]

When presenting the case for clear and simple expression to seminar groups on writing in industry, we are frequently surprised at the resistance. Outspoken members of the seminar often say that clear writing lets the manager see just where things went wrong, and what mistakes were made. Wrap it up in flowery language, and managers will not notice the defects of the work. This argument is a sad underestimate of the quality and intelligence of those who have been promoted, and is a sign of a depressing lack of professionalism.

Such an attitude is not confined to engineers and scientists. In many other spheres, language is used for protection rather than for communication. Complex slang which confuses the outsider is one example. Cockneys talking in rhyming slang use language to identify themselves in their group, and to confuse outsiders. Language can be a wall as well as a window, and scientists and engineers sometimes use it in this way. It becomes a badge of group identity and a way of preventing the rest of the world getting into the magic circle. As one personnel manager said:

> hoarding of information . . . by responsible people enables them to create for themselves positions of extraordinary power as they are then the only authority on a particular subject.

Or, as an industrial relations manager graphically expressed it:

> Specialists like to hold information to them like a hot water bottle.[4]

Wrong attitudes, then, as much as poor skills are at the root of much of the indigestible writing from which we all suffer. Misunderstanding of the importance of communication, lack of confidence in the use of the language code, half-remembered and misdirected education, discouragement from managers, protectiveness in the face of probing readers – all these result in thoughtless adoption of a traditional, verbose and long-winded style. Traditional attitudes and tactics must be rethought because they are inefficient. They waste time and energy for the reader, and in the modern world the reader has less and less time and energy to waste. As Magnus Pyke wrote:

> There is too much published and the pebbles of information are lost in the shingle . . . Printing was a long time coming; but now it has started, like the Sorcerer's Apprentice, there is no stopping it.[5]

First In order to bypass the traditions, misplaced attitudes, and
principles confusions which lead to the all-too-familiar poor writing, we
want to go back now to the first principles of communication.
Decisions about tactics, choice of language, style and vocabulary
can be made easily and confidently only if the writer has a clear
strategy, based on first principles. Most of this book is practical,
and discusses specific examples, but in this first chapter we
want to analyse what a writer is trying to do when he or she
communicates information. What are the basic constraints
which apply to any form of communication? What can we learn
by thinking afresh about principles?

The first observation (which is so obvious that it is usually
overlooked) is that the job of a paper or report is to communicate
information. Too often, the reason why papers are difficult to
read is that the writers have forgotten that they are *communicating* and think that they are just writing. It is so easy to think that
when an experiment is completed, or the information has been
dug out of journals and reports, the work is finished. The
writing seems like a secondary process. Put the information
down as marks on paper so that it is 'available' to others, and
the job is done. But the purpose of writing is to transfer
information, not just to make marks on paper. The whole
process, including the labour of obtaining the information,
might just as well never have taken place if the ideas and
information do not in the end get into the head of the person
who needs them. If they are merely written down in such a
verbose and disorganized manner that nobody wants to read
them, the work is wasted.

Many writers wrongly think of the marks on paper as the end
product. Because they think no further, their writing is inconvenient for the reader, who has to complete the forgotten parts of
the process. Such writing is like Christmas parcels, done up
with yards of resistant Sellotape, or like parcels of biscuits
mummified in plastic because the manufacturer forgot that
human fingers had to unwrap the packets. Biscuits are useless
unless they can be got at; they are worse than useless when they
emerge mangled and broken after the struggle. Yet many
writers forget that, in a similar way, an ordinary human mind,
lazy and easily tired, has to open that glossy packet of words and
get the information out in recognizable shape.

The aim in most scientific and engineering writing must be to
transfer ideas and information to other people; everything else
is a preparation to this end. This principle is the basis of effective

communication. The ideas and information must be directed towards the receiver, the person who needs to know or understand. If ideas are to get across, if there is to be any communication at all, the attention of the writer must be firmly fixed on the person he or she is communicating with. The means is language, but it is not the end.

The consequences of this are that writers must write in ways that will suit their readers, not in ways that will suit themselves. They must use the sort of language the readers can understand, must choose a level of difficulty appropriate to the readers, and must give the readers the amount of material they need, neither too much nor too little. Writers must organize their thinking so that the logical progress of their ideas starts from what the readers are familiar with, and goes forward in a way that follows the readers' interests and knowledge.

To be effective communicators, writers must also recognize that they are involved in human interactions. If these interactions are to be successful, the writers must devise strategies that take account of all the factors that impinge on the total context. They must use their knowledge of their audiences' needs to adjust their tactics to increase the efficiency of communication. We hope to bring into consciousness the factors which operate in the writing situation, so that the same sense of tactics as we all employ so skilfully in day-to-day interactions can be used in the demanding interaction of written communication.

Models of communication

To rethink the tactics and techniques used to communicate technical and scientific information, we need to step back and take an overall look at the shape of the problem. Making a model, or a simplified analogy to help understand a complex process, is useful in thinking about communication. Models sometimes look trivial in the way they compress massive complexity into neat patterns, but simplification can remind us of obvious, and therefore often forgotten, points. A model also gets back to first principles, offers a fresh look at the structure of a situation, and provides a map of the area we are discussing.

There are many different models of the communication process.[6] We use one here that draws on the familiar conventions of radio transmission. It represents a way in which information, in the most general sense, is regularly transmitted in the real world. Language works in a similar way to a radio transmission system. The information is encoded, transmitted, received, and decoded. In an ideal system, the decoded information would match the original exactly. In the real world, encoding and decoding are liable to distortion, the medium is not entirely transparent, there is noise or interference, and feedback is needed. Here is a diagram of the process of communication (reproduced by permission of The University of Illinois Press).[7]

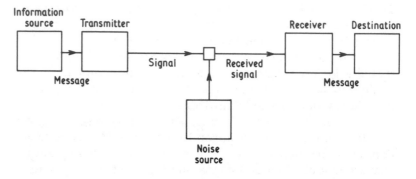

Notice that this model is generalized, and applies both to communication in language and to radio communication. At the centre of communication is the medium, which links the transmitter and the receiver. They must both be 'tuned-in' to the same medium. A radio transmitter must transmit on a wavelength the receiver can receive; the BBC cannot suddenly decide to transmit on say 4000 metres, because there are few receivers that could receive the signal. The BBC has to choose its medium in relation to the receivers of its message. Exactly the same requirement applies to communication using language. A writer cannot say 'I write only in words over three syllables. If readers do not understand me, that is not my problem'. A writer's first job is to choose the medium according to the audience. He or she must ask: 'What sort of information, of what complexity, and in what language can the reader easily receive?'.

Feedback is an important element in radio communication. Similarly there is a type of feedback in communication in language. The lecturer starts by asking, 'Can you hear me at the back of the hall?'. In everyday conversation, the person who is listening gives continual feedback. He or she nods, smiles, says, 'yes' and 'you don't say' and 'really?'. All this establishes that communication, and not just transmission, is taking place. Anyone talking to a person whose face remained completely still and passive would very soon trail off in confusion. In talking, there is always feedback to confirm that the message is being heard and understood.

In written communication, feedback is less obvious, but is still there. Obvious feedback may occur when a paper comes back from an editor or departmental head with a note, 're-write this'. But there is also what we may call 'prior' feedback, which is the knowledge a writer has of whom he or she is writing for. We set out to write in different styles in a letter to a friend and in a report; this prior knowledge of the reader is a type of feedback. Without this sensitivity to feedback, we may transmit but fail to communicate.

Any interference with the signal can be thought of as 'noise'. The more difficult a message is, the more disturbing noise is. A native English speaker can, for instance, understand English spoken against very high levels of background noise. The man on the factory floor shouting above the noise of machinery is understood; but an Englishman, even with a good command of French, can find it impossible to understand a French policeman in a busy Paris street. Similarly, in technical communication, the more demanding the message, the less noise there must be. There are many kinds of interference in written communication which can be described as noise. One example is irrelevant associations; the scientist who wrote, 'with the advent of third-generation devices' was allowing noise to interfere with the message. Readers briefly wonder if they are reading about the immaculate conception. There is also logical noise; examples are confused arguments, or red herrings. Interference is caused too by pomposity, or by subconscious distaste. If the reader feels that the writer is trying to sound clever, then reception of the message may be disturbed.

Noise and redundancy affect communication

Noise is a general category in which we can include many of the barriers to communication. All such barriers interfere with the transmission of the signal, and introduce irrelevances which mask the real message. The encoder always has difficult choices to make from the resources of language available, and these choices must be made with an eye on the effect of noise on the decoder. For the decoder, there are other problems of noise, such as competing stimuli which interrupt reception of the message. All sorts of stresses, both physical and mental, can impair the decoder's efficiency. Mechanical noise, lack of ventilation, tiredness, and factors such as health and general state of mind, all affect the way the message is decoded.

Writers are not helpless when faced with these problems of noise. If they are aware of the complexity of the factors affecting the decoding process, they can adjust the encoding to allow for distraction. By encoding the message comfortably, in a way which does not continually stretch the resources of stamina and attention in readers, they can allow for distractions. By adjusting the rate at which they unload the information, they can allow for tiredness. By careful sign-posting, and by repetition of key points, they can reinforce the message in a way which makes the readers' task less demanding and allows for inattention. Few readers thank a writer who demands maximum concentration without break for long periods; such a writer does not respect their comfort and convenience. Disregard of these factors increases the deterioration of the signal from noise.

Redundancy occurs in most forms of communication. Unnecessary repetition is obviously inefficient, but redundancy is not always bad. Language has a great deal of redundancy built into it in various ways. For instance, in the clause 'they were away', the fact that there are two or more people is signalled both in the plural pronoun 'they' and again in the plural verb 'were'. Such redundancy is useful. It allows both for moments of inattention, and for moments when noise obscures the signal. Because our perception of the message varies in sharpness and clarity, we need some saving redundancy if we are to be able to reconstruct the whole message in our minds.

Redundancy also helps to lower the unloading rate. The speed at which information can be received and processed by readers varies greatly. Individual capacity varies, and it is greatly affected by tiredness and inattention. The familiarity of the message also affects the reader's capacity to receive information; new information or unfamiliar concepts need presenting more slowly than well-known ideas. Few writers seem to realize how easily the reader's capacity for information can be exceeded. Because the *writer* is comfortably familiar with the information, he or she assumes the same easy competence on the part of the reader. But some readers are like a car with a slow-filling petrol tank; if the information is pumped in too quickly, some overflows and runs to waste. Precious facts and ideas are lost. By using redundancy to adjust the rate at which information is unloaded, the writer can do a great deal to improve the efficiency of communication.

A final point emerges from this simple model of communication. There are four places where the message is transferred from one medium to another:

Communication is never perfect

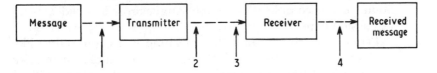

The message is transferred from facts to language, from language to written words, from written words to language in another mind, and out of that language into stored information. Just what the efficiency of transfer is at these stages no-one knows, and it would be very difficult to devise an experiment to find out. None-the-less, in a real world, such transfers are never 100% efficient. If we allow them to be as good as 90%, losses at the four stages still reduce the overall efficiency to less than 65%. By a crude 'guestimate', only a little over half the original message arrives in the reader's mind, and probably much less. Just reflect for a moment on the proportion of the total information you retain after reading a book, or listening to a lecture. Information transfer is often a very inefficient process. Its efficiency levels are around those of steam-engines.

What we are trying to do in this book is to raise the overall efficiency of the communication process. To do this we need to identify the various places where information leaks out, the places where communication is thwarted. Analysing what goes wrong helps to smooth out the flow of ideas and information. We have discussed some of the basic principles to be learnt from a model of the communication process. The model we have used is a simple one, and much of what we have said about it may seem common sense; but the fact remains that a lot of technical communication is unnecessarily inefficient. By looking at first principles, some at least of the problems can be diagnosed, and we have a firm base from which to suggest practical solutions.

Technical information is encoded mainly in words. Even if some information is presented in tables, graphs and equations, the verbal element is still important. We have already seen that one reason why reports and papers are often not well written is that many scientists and engineers undervalue verbal ability.

Language as code

In discussing our model of communication, we talked of using language as a way of *encoding* information for transmission to other minds. But language is not a simple code such as Morse code, nor can it encode messages in the way radio waves can. Some of the complexities of the language code need a brief discussion here.

People sometimes think that meaning is a commodity, like coal, that can be transported. Words are thought of as being like wagons; load them up, send them off, and the goods will be automatically delivered. In fact, words have a range of meanings, and are far from watertight conveyers of ideas. Most words carry overtones. To one person 'socialism' can mean generous community of ownership, a fair economic system and security. To another it can mean danger of revolution, laziness, living off the state. Words also change in meaning. For instance, the proverb 'the exception proves the rule' is nearly always misused today. 'Prove' used to mean simply 'tests', as in 'prove a gun barrel' or 'proof spirit'. Obviously, too, the context alters the meaning of a word. The words 'what a beautiful specimen', mean different things if used about a butterfly or a criminal. Words are complicated things; they can have a variety of meanings, and their meanings change in the course of time.

Often words have fairly simple *denotative* meanings, but a large number of *connotative* meanings. These meanings can vary according to both the person using the word and the person receiving the word. Thus the words 'letter' and 'correspondence' denote the same thing – pieces of paper sent through the post – but they connote different things. For many of us, 'correspondence' connotes work that is done in the office: letters are written at home. Scientific and technical writing often prefers words with strong connotations of formality, and sometimes reasonably so. But over-formality is wearying; what, for example, is the impression created by this writer?

> It is a matter for conjecture as to the reason for this eventuality, but it is hypothesized at this early stage that it will be found to be attributable to the limitations of roll-tube culture rather than to the assay system.

The writer was saying 'I think that . . .' but wrapped it up in such a way that the connotations of formality became obtrusive. Insensitivity to the implications of his use of the language code allowed striving to impress to take precedence over the communication of information.

The meaning code includes not only the counters or small change of meaning we call words, but also the order in which words are threaded together. It is not enough merely to know the correct meaning of words, and to use words with the appropriate connotations. They must also be put in an order which results in the intended meaning being decoded. Grammar, or syntax, is a description of the process by which order communicates meaning. Sometimes the code goes wrong: 'For sale, typewriter, by secretary, with wide carriage'.

Recently, linguists (which now means 'people who study language professionally' and not those with the gift of tongues) have liberalized the rules of correctness in language. Many rigid rules were laid down in the 19th century by dry grammarians. Such rules have never been water-tight, and as language has changed, many rules have now dissolved. For instance, our research shows that 'data is' is now acceptable instead of the traditional 'datum is', or 'data are'. Similarly the subjunctive, which many users of the language were never sure about, has almost vanished. It is now acceptable to regularly split infinitives. Prepositions can now acceptably come at the end of a phrase. The time-honoured distinction between 'will' and 'shall' has gone the same way as many other fiercely defended rules of 'correct' usage.[8] At one time, 'bad' grammar was received with horror. Now linguists have replaced the idea of 'bad' with ideas of 'acceptable' and 'unacceptable' usage. How language is used, not grammatical theory, decides what is right or wrong.

We are not advocating abandoning attention to conventions. Our point is that the conventions are constantly changing, and are different in different circumstances. The scientific writer must develop sensitivity to which conventions are current in the context in which he or she wishes to communicate. A code is useful only if it is effective, and it is only effective if it complies with accepted conventions. Carelessness or ineptness in the use of the syntax code can result in impenetrability; communication can break down because of the barrier created by defective encoding of the message. Where the encoding is slack, messages can be created which are funny:

> Constructed of cement underlay and plastic tiles, with a thin veneer of hard polish over them, the cleaners find the floors simple to keep clean.

It is an amusing picture of durable android cleaning-ladies. But such inept handling of the language code interferes with the smooth communication of information by distracting readers and disturbing their confidence in the writer.

If writing is a question of using a code in an intelligent way, why do writers find this difficult? Perhaps because a great deal of emotion surrounds language, writers feel apprehensive when they try to communicate. They are afraid that their readers will be infuriated by lapses into incorrect use of language. But many of the fears scientific writers had when entering the jungle of words from the sunlit plains of numbers are now unfounded. No longer are spotted and be-clawed grammarians lying in wait. Language is a code, albeit a more complex one than most. Using it depends on a knowledge of its resources, and a knowledge of how the receiver will de-code it. 'Correct' use is no more than conventional use.

The efficiency of the communication process depends on the efficiency of both the encoder and the decoder in handling the complex resources of linguistic conventions. Because communication is a social process, depending on both encoder and decoder, there must be a satisfactory common recognition and operation of conventions of vocabulary, structure and punctuation. These conventions include more than simple relations between the code symbol and the object in the real world. Questions of accuracy, tone, and propriety as well as comfort and convenience also bear on the success or otherwise of the use of the code.

Luckily, it is not as difficult as it all sounds. All human beings have an inborn ability to manipulate this code. Every child somewhere between one and five acquires, even if not attentively taught, an amazing skill in the meaningful manipulation of this code. In the slums of South America, children with no education, and little help from harassed parents, acquire a dexterity in expressing subtle shades of friendship or insult. They can manipulate delicate social interactions in a way which is still beyond the conscious skills of linguists to catalogue and explain. We all acquire huge resources of skill in the use of the complex and ingenious code we call language. We are all endlessly adroit in the shaping of our meanings in this common medium. The art we are looking for, and the science we hope this book will nurture, is to be aware of the ways the code can be manipulated to overcome the barriers of misunderstanding and to communicate meaning.

Much of our advice in the following chapters encourages writers to simplify both the layout and the style of technical documentation. Yet we recognize that some writers are afraid to write too simply, because they feel it exposes them to the biting winds of criticism. They feel that a simple style is not 'scientific' enough. They fear their work may be devalued unless it is impressively packaged. In 1978, we did some research designed to find whether a complex style was more impressive than a simple one. We describe this work and its results briefly now because it may settle a doubt which lurks in people's minds when they are advised to write clearly and simply.

A survey designed at the University of Wales Institute of Science and Technology (UWIST) offered two different ways of writing up the same information. The two versions were given neutral names, 'Smith's' and 'Brown's'. Read them through, without pausing too much, and then reflect for a moment on your own impressions of the quality of each writer as a scientist, before reading what other scientists thought of them.

Brown's version

In the first experiment of the series using mice it was discovered that total removal of the adrenal glands effects reduction of aggressiveness and that aggressiveness in adrenalectomized mice is restorable to the level of intact mice by treatment with corticosterone. These results point to the indispensability of the adrenals for the full expression of aggression. Nevertheless, since adrenalectomy is followed by an increase in the release of adrenocorticotrophic hormone (ACTH), and since ACTH has been reported (Brain, 1972), to decrease the aggressiveness of intact mice, it is possible that the effects of adrenalectomy on aggressiveness are a function of the concurrent increased levels of ACTH. However, high levels of ACTH, in addition to causing increases in glucocorticoids (which possibly accounts for the depression of aggression in intact mice by ACTH), also result in decreased androgen levels. In view of the fact that animals with low androgen levels are characterised by decreased aggressiveness the possibility exists that adrenalectomy, rather than affecting aggression directly, has the effect of reducing aggressiveness by producing an ACTH-mediated condition of decreased androgen levels.

Making your writing more impressive

Smith's version

The first experiment in our series with mice showed that total removal of the adrenal glands reduces aggressiveness. Moreover, when treated with corticosterone, mice that had their adrenals taken out became as aggressive as intact animals again. These findings suggest that the adrenals are necessary for animals to show full aggressiveness.

But removal of the adrenals raises the levels of adrenocorticotrophic hormone (ACTH), and Brain[2] found that ACTH lowers the aggressiveness of intact mice. Thus the reduction of aggressiveness after this operation might be due to the higher levels of ACTH which accompany it.

However, high levels of ACTH have two effects. First, the levels of glucocorticoids rise, which might account for Brain's results. Second, the levels of adrogen fall. Since animals with low levels of androgen are less aggressive, it is possible that removal of the adrenals reduces aggressiveness only indirectly: by raising the levels of ACTH it causes androgen levels to drop.

You will not be surprised that 69.5% of the scientists who answered the questionnaire 'preferred' Smith's version. In all, 1580 scientists from industry and the academic world gave their views. Not only did they prefer the easier passage, but also they found it 'more stimulating' and 'more interesting'. But the main interest of the research was to see if fellow scientists would make a judgement about the competence of the writers, and if so what it would be. In answer to the question 'does one author seem to have a better organized mind' three-quarters said, 'yes, Smith'.[9]

These results are important for anyone who has to write to communicate information. If the writing is clear and simple, fellow scientists will not only find your writing pleasanter to read, but they will also think you are a better scientist, have a better organized mind, and are more competent. Readers seem less and less prepared to accept the traditional smokescreen. If they can understand easily, they are *more* likely to be impressed with the quality of the thought behind the words.

It is worth briefly looking back at the two passages to see just what the difference between them is. A majority of the scientists who answered the questionnaire perceived Smith's version as more impressive, more credible, and more worthy of esteem than the Brown version. These readers saw differences in personality between the writers, such as helpfulness, dynamism, and quality of mind. By looking carefully at the passages, we can distinguish between *what is perceived* and *what the linguistic facts are*. In fact, in both passages the information, and the order in which it is presented, are exactly the same. The use of technical terms is the same too – both passages use only five technical words (adrenal, corticosterone, hormone, glucocorticoids, androgen). The difference is in the use of ordinary language, not in the technical language. Smith's version is readable because it is written in short sentences with direct, active constructions. It avoids unfamiliar words, and inflated roundabout phrases. Brown's version is difficult to read, with long sentences, long words, and convoluted constructions. It was these differences in style, not the technical content and organization, which made readers feel that Smith was a more impressive writer.

We think most writers would prefer to read, and probably to write, a simple, direct style. But they are afraid that such a simple style would make their work less impressive. The wish to make a good impression is often in the forefront of a writer's mind, before even the wish to communicate information. Students, junior researchers, young professionals, and anyone with a career to forge in science and technology wants, and needs, to be impressive. Anxious to write like the established leaders in their subject, they adopt a 'traditional' style, thinking that it will be most impressive.

It is quite legitimate to try to appear at your best in writing. The mistake is to think that the long-winded style is most impressive. This research shows quite clearly that a simple and straightforward style, where the quality of the science is not hidden in a jungle of verbiage, is far more impressive for the reader. The conclusion for the writer is clear. Write impressively – that is important – but that means writing simply.

We can conclude this discussion of what communication is, and why it often goes wrong, with the answer that scientific and technical writing often fails because writers do not think enough about their real purposes, about whom they are writing for, and about the nature of the code they are using. In this book, we ask you to take a new look at the job of writing. Remember, first, that you are trying to *communicate* information, not just to make information available on paper. To do this effectively, you must re-think many assumptions about writing.

References   1. Johnston, Professor Edgeworth (1961), A Survey of Chemical Engineering Education and Practice *Transactions of the Institution of Chemical Engineers*, **39**(4), 263.
2. Newton, Sir Isaac, *Optiks* London (1704), quoted by Pyke, Magnus (1960) in: This Scientific Babel *The Listener*, **LXIV** (1641)(8th September), 380.
3. Gardner, B.B., *Human Relations in Industry*, Irwin, R.D., Chicago (1945) 131, quoted by Bram, V.A., in: *The Efficiency of Forms and Styles of Information Exchange in Industrial and Research Organisations.* Unpublished doctoral thesis, UWIST (September 1976), 45.
4. From interviews reported by Bram, V.A., see ref. [3], 41.
5. Pyke, Magnus (1960) This Scientific Babel. *The Listener*, **LXIV** (1641), 380.
6. The model is taken from a schematic diagram of a general communication system in Shannon, Claude and Weaver, Warren (1949), *The Mathematical Theory of Communication*, Illinois University Press, 34.
7. For further discussion see Turk, C.C.R. (1980), Attitudes to English Usage, *The Communicator of Scientific and Technical Information*, **42**, 8–12.
8. For a more detailed account of this work see Bardell, Ewa (1978) Does Style Influence Credibility and Esteem? *The Communicator of Scientific and Technical Information*, **35** 4–7; also Turk, C.C.R. (1978) Do You Write Impressively? *Bulletin of the British Ecological Society*, **ix**(3) 5–10; Also Wales, LaRae H. (1979) *Technical Writing Style: Attitudes Towards Scientists and Their Writing*, University of Vermont Agricultural Experiment Station. The three separate studies used the same questionnaire and totalled 1580 replies; the figures quoted in the text are an average of all three.

Thinking about 2
aim and audience

In our opening chapter, we made the fundamental point about effective writing that if the message is to be communicated effectively, it must be much more than just scientifically accurate and grammatically correct. It must also be presented in a manner that commands attention, is quickly informative, and is easily digested by the reader. We must look beyond the grammar to the *tactics* of handling language.

To command attention, a writer must have a clear idea of why he or she is writing – that is, why readers should want to attend to what he or she has to say. As you plan and prepare to write, your first question must be: what am I trying to achieve?

Identifying aim

Note that this is not the same question as: what is my subject? Failure to recognize this important distinction undermines many attempts at communication. If you focus on the *subject* rather than the *aim* of writing, you are likely to be tempted simply to re-present information in the form and order in which you first learnt it or had it presented to you. It is rare for your readers' needs and interests to be exactly the same as yours. So if you want to produce the best possible response, you must reshape the information to make it relevant, comfortable and readily usable by your readers.

So, what is the 'aim' of writing? Your objective will rarely be just to display your intellectual wares. Your task may be:

- to describe;
- to explain;
- to instruct;
- to specify;

- to evaluate and recommend;
- to provoke debate but not seem to lead;
- to persuade;
- to concede and apologize;
- to protest;
- to reject.

Which information you include in a document and how you arrange it is dictated largely by your intention in writing it. Do you want your readers simply to *read and understand* your text, but not necessarily to *remember* what you have presented? If so, it will not be necessary to make special efforts to provide key words and phrases to help them memorize the information you are presenting. It will not be necessary to emphasize groups of points by devices of layout, by reiteration or by creating helpful summarizing paragraphs or tables that will lodge easily in their memories – by creating for your readers a powerful 'learning frame'. But if you *are* trying to teach a skill or method, you will have to use these tactics: it will not be enough just to present your material in a way that allows readers to move quickly through it, gaining just an outline understanding of what you are thinking, doing or proposing.

Consider, for example, how you might approach some of the different writing tasks we have mentioned, if your subject was a familiar fire extinguisher or an electric fire. Think what would be essential if you had to:

- describe how it is built;
- explain how it works;
- tell a group how to use it;
- teach a group how to make one.

Would you use the same information in the same way in all these tasks? Clearly not. Each task would start with different information; a description would start with general appearance, an explanation with aim and purpose. Telling someone how to use it would begin with an action, and teaching a group to make one might start by listing raw materials. Thus:

How it is built

A fire extinguisher is a metal cylinder about two feet high, and nine inches across, painted red, with an outlet at the top.

How it works

A fire extinguisher is used to spray water or chemicals under pressure on to a fire to control it . . .

How to use it

Pick up the fire extinguisher, point the nozzle away from yourself and towards the fire, and hit the knob smartly with your fist . . .

How to make it

Take a two-foot length of thick-wall steel tubing . . .

Although each of these pieces of information may appear at some point in each type of writing task, both the *order* and the amount of detail will vary.

Documents in which you have to *evaluate and recommend* are always difficult to write, for in such documents it is not always the technical arguments that prove most powerful. Particular care is needed when you are evaluating the capacity or the potential of equipment, materials or processes. It is not always possible to rely on facts speaking for themselves. A technical argument can be logically impeccable but distasteful to your readers. If you suggest that the productivity figures you are presenting lead inescapably to a particular operational conclusion, you must nevertheless be ready for the possibility that your readers may – irrationally, it seems to you – come to a totally different conclusion. *Appraisal* of facts may be objective and logical; but *decision-taking* is a subjective matter. We all make decisions that take into account external 'political' pressures. We can all give subconscious priority to intuitive feelings that things will not quite work out according to a neat technical plan.

Identify your reader's aim

It is easy for writers to assume that readers are mirror-images of themselves, with matching interests and needs; but only in highly specialized writing is that often true. If you are writing for a high-level research journal, you can reasonably assume that other high-level researchers are much like you. But in most professional contexts, your readers will want to use the information to meet needs different from yours. In particular, in reports within industrial organizations, the amount of detail needed will vary considerably as information rises through the management hierarchy. In general, the higher the managerial level of your readers, the more their interests move from the technical *how* and *why* to the more commercial *to what purpose* and *at what cost*.

It is often helpful to sit and consider just what your reader will do after reading your paper: file it, reach for the 'phone, write a memorandum, sigh deeply, build some apparatus, write a cheque, arrange a meeting, sign an order, delegate someone to talk to you, re-use the information in an examination, or apologize to you? Such speculation is not an invasion of privacy! It is a necessary part of bringing exactly into focus the aim of the document. Many documents fail because writers have not thought *enough* or *clearly* about their aims. Many writers are content with vague ideas about the use of the document.

We are not saying that writers never consider their aims – just that they rarely consider them enough. Tactics must be based not on a half-conscious assumption, but on a detailed examination of the aims, which brings those aims fully into consciousness. We know of no better way of starting this process than visualising what, specifically and physically, your reader will do with the document.

When you have an important paper to write, try to write yourself a short job specification – a few sentences outlining your objectives, audience, constraints, and possible procedures. This 'target statement' will help you cross the mental barrier between a lazy, half-formed idea, and a clear idea. As so often, the act of writing down an idea transforms it. Try writing a target statement for the next piece of writing you undertake. Our target statement for this book might read: 'to make the next document our readers write more effective and helpful for their readers'. A report on the choice of new diesel generators might have a target statement:

> To persuade the works committee to order Swedish generators . . .

or

> To get an investigating committee set up . . .

It may seem easy to compose target statements in theory, but it is often difficult in practice. Writers tend to find themselves thinking of their aim as:

> Tell them about generators . . .

The act of writing down this target makes clear how imprecise it is. If you have written something like that statement, try to refine your aim, in a way that crystallizes the information you have collected into a new, and more effective order.

If you find you cannot write a job specification, give up and go to consult whoever has commissioned the paper from you. In our experience, a great many complaints about inadequate writing should be turned back on the managers who make them; for those managers have often failed to specify clearly what they wanted in the documents they have called for. Writers may have a marvellous command of their subjects and of the English language, but they cannot do justice to themselves or to their employers if they are not clear what they are trying to achieve.

A clear decision on aim is vital, for it governs all subsequent tactics and techniques. And considering the aim brings us immediately to the next main question: whom is the document for?

You must ask five basic questions about your audience:

Who are the audience?

- Are all the readers *alike* or are they a mixed group?
- What do they *know already* about the topic?
- What do they *need* to know?
- What are their *attitudes* to the subject, to the writer, and to the writer's objectives?
- What are the psychological and physical *contexts* within which the new information will be received?

It is essential to consider carefully the readers' backgrounds and experience and to try to decide what they are likely to know. What concepts or procedures will they understand? What terminology will be acceptable? In seeking an answer to these questions, it is usually necessary to find the lowest common denominator in the audience and then to present the story in terms that he or she will understand.

What do they know?

This is not to condemn someone for being slow or dull-witted: it is to recognize that there are varying levels of expertise even within audiences of uniformly high intellectual capacities. If a writer wishes to communicate fully with all members of the audience, acknowledging their varying backgrounds, he or she must find the lowest common denominator in expertise and build the story on that basis.

Young writers often find this worrying; because 'the boss' is second or third on a circulation list of fifteen or twenty, they feel they should write for him or her principally. But that is a mistake; for if they aim consciously at the second or third name on a long circulation list, they are deliberately aiming some of the paper above the heads of the majority of the audience. If they wish to communicate fully and clearly with the whole group, they must not aim at the top of the list. And any boss who complains that a paper is not sufficiently expert, is failing to recognize the true nature of the writing task given to the subordinate.

In reality, a decision on the level at which to pitch an argument or description is not always so easy to arrive at. Sometimes, circulation lists include 95% 'expert' readers and 5% 'inexpert' readers. Should you run the risk of boring such a large majority by taking them all through an account pitched at a level suitable for the 5%? Probably not. In those circumstances, the best tactics are usually to provide helpful low-level material for the inexpert readers in separate sections of your paper, preferably in appendices, and to guide readers carefully by explaining just how you have arranged your paper.

Where an audience is clearly divided into two halves – say engineers in one half, and accountants in the other half – the best solution is to write two separate documents. Thus, a report on diesel generators for the accountants might have details of cost-effectiveness, reliability rates, capital depreciation, and the cost of stocking the spares required; as an appendix, the engineering arguments could be given in more detail. The document for the engineers might concentrate on the engineering arguments, with a summary of the cost arguments. The detailed discussion of costs could be in an appendix. Such a tactic is not as wasteful of effort as it seems. Once the first document is written, it is easy to write the second. Often it is a 'scissors-and-paste job', with extra paragraphs. The writer's extra effort is an economy because it will save time for *several* readers.

Writers should also recognize that acceptable unloading rates are broad bands. Non-expert readers can make an effort to raise their level of attention and comprehension by conscious effort. Expert readers often have some areas of expertise that are hazier than others, and welcome being reminded of what they already 'know'. The writer should try to aim the level of the document where these bands overlap, so that no reader is entirely forsaken. Experts often find the simplistic relaxing; non-experts are prepared to be challenged from time to time. But long stretches of text that are grossly inappropriate will lose all readers.

Many writers seem to have little idea of the way new information meshes into familiar knowledge. It is not simply a question of piling the one on the other. As in a brick wall, there has to be bonding at the joint; existing knowledge in readers' minds needs to be reactivated. Memories need to be stimulated to dredge up information that is there, but may be buried deep by the many other cares and problems that arrive every day. Many of the documents that we see, fail because they do not do this 'bonding'.

What do they need to know?

What the audience *already knows* affects decisions about what must be included. What the audience *needs to know* – what each reader wants from the paper – is equally important.

Think about each reader's objective in reading the paper. Different individuals or groups within a single readership usually require different amounts and ranges of information. Theoretically, as we have said, this should lead to the preparation of separate documents for each of these individuals or groups; but life is too short for such perfectionist behaviour and it is normal to have to make one report or paper serve a range of readers. In such circumstances, it is essential to provide (and signal) various ways through your text. Use all possible devices of organization and layout (discussed in Chapter 4) to help readers find and read rapidly the parts of the document essential to their purposes – to their efficient functioning in *their* roles.

Readers' attitudes

The experience of readers, with which the new information must be made compatible, consists of more than straightforward technical knowledge. Knowledge is compounded with biases built up throughout professional life. Though your readers know that one material has slightly better properties for a job than another, they may prefer the second because it is easier to handle or because it has always been good enough for the job in the past. Though they know a particular mathematical technique is accurate and efficient, they may find it difficult and boring and consequently prefer another way of working. Though they know that the preparation of work plans or the presentation of information can be helped greatly by the use of flow-charts, they may dislike the modes of thought and expression required to produce these charts successfully.

It is necessary, therefore, to ask not only what the readers know, but also what their attitudes will be towards the topic and the presentation technique. Will they be hostile or enthusiastic, interested or indifferent, amenable or sceptical? What are their present beliefs and policies? Are their present beliefs built on reason or emotion? Will the new proposals you wish to put forward seem to confront and condemn previous decisions and practices? Will all members of the audience have the same attitudes or will there be a variety? The shrewd communicator must identify the positions that readers are likely to adopt and either meet potential difficulties or make use of potential support.

Consider, for example, the task confronting a town planner we knew, who had to explain a local authority's proposals for building a new estate close to an existing village. He felt that the authority had an excellent case, based on the national need for new housing, the poor agricultural quality of much of the land, the progressive depopulation of the village over the last century, and the need to have a large enough population in the village to justify expenditure on new services that the existing villagers were already asking for. But he had to recognize that his audience's rational appraisal of his case was likely to be overwhelmed by their in-grown hostility to any planner as a representative of 'them' – the faceless bureaucrats who capriciously manipulate our lives (villager's definition!). His audience might pay lip-service to plans for the common good; but they were likely to fight fiercely to protect their own interests. He was wise to start from their own complaints and requests for change. He looked at his proposals from *their* frame of reference, and arranged his case in a way that acknowledged their views of his topic and of the group he represented.

Readers who are thinking 'but this applies only to social matters or to sales and marketing activities' should pause for a moment. If you are an engineer, consider your opinion of 'pure scientists'. If you are a research chemist, do you have any preconceptions about mechanical engineers? If you are a scientist or an engineer, are your reactions to proposed changes in your designs or manufacturing procedures in any way influenced by the fact that those changes have been proposed by someone in your personnel or training section? If you are working in industry, do you have any subconscious reaction to 'academics'? All writing, especially report-writing, is part of a human interaction and to write *effectively*, we must analyse not only the technical context of the interaction but also the relations that exist between the participants.

It is irrational, but human, for us to develop biased attitudes not only to topics and to people but also towards types of communication. Some people hate using a telephone as a means of communication. Others always write a memorandum rather than face the discomfort (for them) of a face-to-face interaction. Most of us respond with varying degrees of enthusiasm to the various forms of paper we meet in our daily lives. In some organizations, for example, the 'monthly report' stimulates uncontrollable boredom in both writers and readers. New-project proposals may be received enthusiastically by some readers, but with anxiety by others who see them as yet further sources of disturbance to their comfortable routines.

Writers must remain sensitive to the likely attitudes of their readers, and adjust their messages so that they do not run on to the rocks of the readers' disapproval. We would all like to live in an ideal world where everyone was tolerant and understanding; but none of us does. Personal bias, attitudes developed through long careers, or simple differences of point of view (it always looks different from where the other person stands) are inevitable. As writers, we cannot condemn or remove these responses. It is vital, though, for us to develop sensitivity to the attitudes prevailing in our working contexts and to choose content, style, and format for our writing accordingly.

In the final stage of audience analysis – considering the psychological and physical contexts in which each document is to be received – we must ask: what will be the intellectual span of attention of the audience? What will be their capacity to absorb the information and, therefore, what will be an appropriate 'unloading rate'? Some writers fail to consider this point and unload their information at such a rate that after a few moments, readers feel that they must stop and rest while they assimilate the information. Other texts spread their information so thinly that readers become bored and irritated, and wonder if it is worth reading on. Consider this example:

Psychological and physical contexts

In recent years, since the Second World War, a proliferation of the sizes and types of aluminium conductor utilized in overhead electric power lines has occurred. An attempt is made in this article to provide a guide to the range now available to the designer of lines. For super-tension transmission lines, increasing voltage, heavier currents, and longer lines have introduced demands for conductors having greater diameter, larger cross-sectional area, and increased strength, the emphasis on one or other of these factors being variable in accordance with the function for which each particular line is erected.

The production of phase conductors having a high degree of capacitance and a lower level of reactance can be achieved by the utilisation of bundles of two, three and four conductors, which practice usually reduces radio influence and corona loss to levels which are acceptable almost regardless of the route of the line. It is regrettable, however, that special problems are presented by conductors in bundle form in climates of an extreme nature, such as at elevated altitudes or where ice loads or heavy winds are prevalent; and in all environments considerable accentuation of the mechanical problems presented by bundles occurs when the subconductors in the bundle are three or four in number rather than two. Thus, in spite of new developments in respect of bundling, a trend towards large diameter conductors continues to be evident.

The information here is unloaded too slowly. It is not just the verbose style which irritates readers; it is the length of time they have to wait between the new items of information. Their patience becomes exhausted, and their concentration collapses. They gain too little reward in the way of interesting new knowledge, for too much effort. If the same information is condensed, so that readers receive it at a brisker and more invigorating pace, they are more likely to digest it successfully:

> This article is a guide to the sizes and types of aluminium conductor available to the designer of overhead lines. In recent years, the choice has widened. Now that we are concerned with supertension transmission lines, increasing voltages, heavier currents, and longer lines, we need conductors with greater diameter, greater cross-sectional area, and greater strength. Which of these factors is most important depends on the function of the line being erected.
>
> Bundles of two, three and four strandings can be used to make phase conductors with higher capacitance and lower reactance than single conductors, and with acceptable levels of radio influence and corona loss. But bundle conductors set special problems in extreme climates (for example, where there is ice or high wind), and the mechanical problems

presented by bundles are always worse where there are three or four sub-conductors in the bundle rather than two. So large-diameter conductors are still preferred to bundles.

Notice that the argument we are making here is not that the second version is less verbose, and uses less space – although these are both valid points. It is that the unloading rate of the first version is badly judged. Of course, it is possible to unload information at too high a rate, and the same sense of despair will afflict readers. Their minds will clog with indigestible information, and their concentration will wander in search of relief and relaxation from the pressure.

The intellectual span of attention is related not only to the expertise and intellectual qualities of the readers but also to the context in which the document is to be handled and to the physical limits of attention in the audience. Where will this document be read – in a peaceful library, in a noisy laboratory, or in a cramped corner beside a machine for which it gives repair information? Will time be available for careful study? Is it a committee paper to be presented towards the end of a densely packed afternoon? Will the readers be well motivated towards reading the text? Will they be looking forward to it or will they approach it reluctantly? Do you want them simply to understand a general principle or is it important for them to *remember* the salient facts? All these are questions that must be answered before you can begin to select from the available information just those items that will help to achieve your identified aim for this audience.

Selecting information

Failure to select information appropriately is a common weakness in scientific and technical writing. Consider how often, in your experience, writers have blurred their messages to you by giving too much that was irrelevant or superfluous. As you plan your papers, you must *select* from the available material. Discriminate between what is really relevant and what is only mildly interesting. Ask yourself: how much of what *I* know do *they* need? What will be useful and manageable in *their* context? The emphasis throughout the selection process must be on the needs, interests and convenience of *the readers*. How much time will they have, and therefore how much detail should be given? Which details should have priority if some must be omitted? Which details would be best presented by graphs, diagrams or

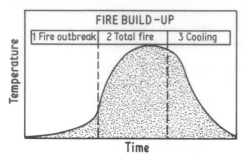

Fig. 1. Characteristic progress of a fire: 1. heating up to out-break of flame; 2. ignition of flame and rapid development of total fire; 3. cooling to smouldering ash.

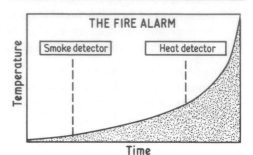

Fig. 2. Alarm set-off points for a smoke detector and a heat detector for a characteristic office fire.

- All modern systems connected to a control board through a cable network.
- Fire starts → triggers detector → alarm indicated at control board and (if desired) automatically relayed to local fire service.
- Smoke detector: reacts to combustion particles formed as fire starts, often before flame can be seen.
- Heat detector: reacts to rise in temperature; sets off alarm when temperature near detector reaches predetermined level, commonly 70°C.
- Flame detector: reacts to varying infra-red light from an open flame; sets off alarm when hit by varying infra-red light.
- At control board: both optical and acoustic signals can be given
  - : lay-out of board can show quickly where alarm has been set off
  - : separate fault signal can be set off if fault occurs in cable network
  - : mechanism to monitor mains power supply continuously can be installed.
- Smoke detectors may be triggered by activities that produce much smoke, for example, lab. work, operation of motor trucks in enclosed space or welding. Other detectors therefore desirable in such areas.
- Desirable to install a system that operates even in event of mains supply failure; require mains supply *and* battery supply connected in parallel so that system will operate even if mains power supply fails.
- Development of a fire: early stages – incomplete combustion releases certain particles and gases before open flame and heavy smoke develop and before temperature rises significantly. Smoke detector triggered by these particles and gases.
- Production of flames visible to an infra-red detector or of temperature rise detectable by ceiling-mounted heat detector set at 70°C requires substantial progress of fire.
- Smoke-, heat-, and flame-detectors can all be linked into same fire protection system. Together they can cover varying demands in any building. Installation of any one type does not preclude subsequent installation of other type.

Fig. 2.1 Fire detection systems. Notes for preparing: (a) an internal recommendation, (b) a sales leaflet (reproduced by permission of the Council of Engineering Institutions).

other illustrations? The information given in note form in Fig. 2.1 relates to fire-detection systems. Consider two possible writing tasks based on this information:

First task

The Works Manager of an engineering company has asked for advice on the installation of a fire-detection system in the main office building, which houses management offices, display showrooms and conference rooms. He has heard that three types of detectors are available: flame detectors, heat detectors and smoke detectors. He has asked you to recommend which type he should evaluate in detail and to mention any specific points he should look for.

Second task

You are a representative of a company that makes and sells fire-detection equipment. You have been asked to prepare a leaflet to explain to non-technical audiences how detectors work and why customers should choose carefully the type of detector best suited to their premises.

For the Works Manager, you would be well advised to start your memorandum with a clear recommendation of a type of detector. This should be followed by a *brief* explanation supporting your recommendation, plus some notes about points he needs to watch in the electricity supplies and alarm signalling. Almost certainly, the illustrations would be unnecessary.

For the leaflet, a preliminary discussion of how fires develop might be best for non-technical readers. It would be helpful to support the prose discussion with the illustrations. This would lead to a more detailed evaluation of the three types of detector, to show the particular advantages of each in different premises. Finally, points about electricity supply and alarm signalling would help general readers see what difficulties there might be in installing a system in their premises.

Arrangement of information

Once information has been selected and sorted, it must be arranged. As receivers of information, we all frequently have to wade through pages of historical introduction or other irrelevant material in search of information that is new and interesting. This is an obstacle to enthusiasm, if not to understanding. We have suggested that a writer's objective must be to make it convenient for receivers to digest the information, and the tactics of preparation we have discussed so far have been directed towards this end. But it is essential to do more than make information convenient to receive. It must command the readers' attention; it must be presented in a way that looks attractive and useful. So, which points will strike the greatest response from the readers? These points must be highlighted by careful ordering and emphasis.

What is the best order for a report, paper or other technical document? Of course, it must be logical; but that means simply that the paper must have connection and sequence, and a variety of orders is possible under this heading. Too many writers interpret the term *logical* to mean chronological, and it has become habitual to begin reports and papers with careful reviews of previous work. Usually, this is tactically weak. Most readers of reports and papers are reading the documents because they are interested in, and know something about, the subject. Therefore, to rehearse to them the findings of previous work is simply to bore them with unnecessary reminders. The interesting thing for them is the new information – the new findings and conclusions. So it is usually best to start with those pieces of information. To give a long chronological account of work or procedures is normally appropriate *only* when the essential point of the paper is the chronological sequence.

Readers usually find papers much more attractive if information is in order of importance *from their point of view*. It is most effective to start with the new, interesting and arresting information, preferably in outline form in a summary. The summary may be detached as a separate unit with a heading or it may be simply a summarizing opening paragraph. But, however it is presented, it should serve the same purpose: giving the reader a quick, clear 'potted' version of the essence of the story that is to come. Detailed advice on the writing of summaries follows in Chapter 9.

Of course, other arrangements of information are sometimes valuable. It may help if your paper follows the order of a manufacturing or fault-finding sequence. Sometimes it may be useful to group topics in relation to particular physical sites or groups of people. Descriptive papers may be organized to guide readers 'from the outside in' – reflecting the real order of perception as a person approaches an object for the first time. Alternatively, it may be better for some readers if the document is organized to reflect the hierarchy of components – starting with the 'heart' of the machine or process and gradually explaining how ancillary elements are related. We discuss this further in Chapter 4.

There is no one *correct* way of organizing engineering and scientific information. Over and over again in our discussion of effective writing we shall come back to this basic point: the best choice of tactics depends on what you are trying to achieve, and for whom you are writing. We have emphasized the need to *plan* and *prepare* to write; in our experience many weaknesses in scientific and technical writing stem from writers' failure to 'think through' the task from beginning to end *before* they start to put pen to paper.

3 Starting to write: a practical approach

The next task the writer faces is turning this preparatory work into an actual document. You are not alone if you tend to delay your start on writing. The vast majority of writers find getting the words flowing difficult; it may comfort you to know that we found it difficult to get started on this book about writing. The solution to the problem of procrastination is not to worry about your hesitation. Hesitation is normal and nearly universal.

Writers create the problem themselves by facing the task in the wrong way. They sit down, take out a sheet of clean, white paper, and only then do they start to think. Their position reminds us of a man who has been left to make his own supper for the first time. He first of all gets out a clean plate, and puts it on the table in front of him; then he sits and stares at it, and wonders why the meal does not suddenly appear by inspiration. Such behaviour is absurd, of course, but it approximates very closely to the behaviour of the writer, panicking over an empty sheet of paper. The paper is like a plate, merely a receptacle for what has been carefully prepared *before*. Writing is a process of dishing up information. It is the last thing you do, and in itself is perhaps one of the easiest of the tasks.

Because the writer's problem in getting started is a psychological one, we suggest psychological solutions. We have a 'seven-point' plan. We have already taken you through the first two stages of this plan. First, analyse your aim; preferably write it down. Already the act of formulating words has started the flow of language. Already you have some phrases which can be worked into the final text. Second, consider your audience. Thinking about their needs will help you to orientate your information in a way which is reassuringly planned and decisive.

Probably all of us were told in school that we should plan our writing. But few of us do. The common excuse for not making a plan is that it absorbs time; why not get straight on with the job? But when no plan is prepared, more time is wasted coping with mental blockages than would have been used in planning. Even if you feel you have a clear picture in your mind of the shape of the document, a plan is worthwhile.

Do not expect the plan to come out in perfect order at the first attempt. Remember you will rarely be working from scratch. You will almost always have a preliminary structure provided by the brief for the job, the laboratory log-book containing observations and results, some details obtained from sources in a library, a computer print-out, some working drawings, or a set of instructions.

To make the plan, one method we find helpful is to take a large sheet of paper and write the major headings spaced out down the page. Then go systematically through your notes, using some system of numbering or cross-referencing to note each point down in turn on this sheet. Thus, the first point in your notes might be best placed in the fourth section, the next point might be for the conclusion, the next for the introduction, and so on. In this way you will gradually fill the blank sheet with key words and phrases to remind you of what needs to go into each section.

In practice, any system of shorthand and sorting will do. Highly disciplined writers use separate index-cards for gathering notes for each chapter or section. Others finish up with several sheets of paper, with headings, notes, quotations and references scribbled in all directions. They then sort them by allocating numbers to the points in the sequence they want. Usually there are several false starts and many transfers and additions while the sequencing is going on. But eventually some sort of order begins to emerge.

Everyone gets stuck with pen poised and a thought half-formed at some stage or other. But do not let that block the planning and preparation stages of your work. If one train of thought sticks or collapses, leave it for the time being and follow up another. And if a thought occurs to you that does not belong to the section you are thinking through at the moment, do not ignore it as inconvenient – make a note of it, anywhere on your paper, so that it does not get lost.

In the end, you will have a sheet of paper that looks as if a spider has been at work. It would be no use to anyone but you, but for you it has done two jobs. First, it has set out your considered decision about the ordering of the individual points as well as the main sections, and it has done this in a way which makes sure none of them is forgotten or overlooked. Second, by going through the notes again you have reminded yourself about the details of the work. You are ready to start writing, with all the details fresh.

If you do not make a plan, and go straight into writing a draft, you may often find that your progress is blocked by nagging worries about whether a particular point should be made at a given stage or saved until later. If you decide to save it, will it be forgotten when the time comes? Will you even remember the phrasing which came to mind when you first considered it? While these worries are in your mind, you are distracted from getting on with the writing. By planning, you achieve confidence in the order. The tactic is to divide and conquer. In writing, no one decision is overwhelmingly difficult; but trying to make several at once soon leaves the mind exhausted and confused, and the writing grinds to a halt.

Stage four –
discuss a
synopsis

You are not unusual if you find it hard to impose order and exact expression on your ideas. Most of us do. And given ten writers, it is likely that they will produce ten different flows of thought. All of these could be equally good; but it is likely that one or two would be tactically more effective than the others. So, if you have the time and the opportunity, it is useful to make a fair copy of your plan, expanding cryptic notes and key words into a form comprehensible to others. This synopsis can then be discussed with colleagues and friends (if they will listen); their ideas and advice can be very helpful.

It is not an admission of weakness to ask for help in planning and preparing the presentation of material to other people. And it is not an affront to your professional integrity to have someone say that he or she cannot grasp what you mean by a set of notes or by a trial page of text. As we write, our minds get set on particular lines of thought, and we unconsciously ignore side-issues or mentally supply steps in an argument. To someone else, the gaps in our thought are obvious at once. Someone else sees implications other than those that stuck in our minds. Points that seemed implicit from our standpoint are often not at all obvious when viewed from someone else's frame of reference.

One tactic we recommend at this stage is that you contact the person who commissioned the document, the manager (or client, editor, or symposium organizer) who is most directly concerned, and ask if he or she can spare ten minutes to discuss the synopsis with you. This tactic has advantages for both of you. The manager can see that the work is progressing; there is often a silent period between the completion of the research and the arrival of the document, when much may be happening in the writer's mind but there is no external evidence of activity. A synopsis is reassuring evidence of progress. The manager will find it impressive to see such indisputable signs of organization and method in the writer.

A second advantage to the manager is also an advantage to you. He or she can see what is going to be produced, and check that it is in line with the sort of document required – that it is angled in the desired way, and that it will answer all relevant questions. He or she can correct any wrong turnings (and so refine and clarify the specification, which may have been vague in the original briefing). The writer gains confidence; and in writing as in so many other things, confidence is a great help to good performance. Knowing that the final document will be acceptable, the writer is more likely to write with speed and assurance.

Now, and only now, the time has come to start drafting the text. Notice that already you are two-thirds of the way through the work; writing is now a question of 'dishing-up', since the most important decisions about content and order have already been taken. Time spent in preparation of your synopsis will now be amply repaid as you come to clothe the outline with words. For most of us, uncertainty about which words to use stems mainly from uncertainty about what we want to say. Usually, if we have the underlying framework of our ideas straight, the writing of the first full prose draft can go ahead much more confidently and rapidly than if we are still trying to work out what sequence of statements we should make.

Stage five – draft the text

Aim to get the most rapid possible flow of ideas on to the paper at each preliminary sitting. Your mind can work at a vastly greater speed than your hand. So do not try to write a full text in 'good English'; do not stop to formulate delicate nuances of expression or to debate whether a given sequence of statements would be best punctuated with colons, commas or full stops. First, get down a flow of words.

Note that we talked of 'each preliminary sitting'. Sometimes, pressure is great and it is necessary to try to complete a report or paper at a single sitting. But, normally, productivity falls as time progresses and you will use your time more profitably if you plan to work for several separated blocks of one or two hours, not straight through one or two days. It is best to switch from writing to a different task and then back again, if possible; but even to change from one writing task to another is helpful in clearing blocked lines of thought and helping you forward with new impetus.

Remember that there is a further revision to come. Leaving blanks – with hasty notes about a point you want to look up later – prevents your mind being diverted. Ignore problems of spelling, punctuation, and grammar; do not worry too much about 'good style' at this stage. Few writers produce perfect, incisive phrasing first time. The first aim is to get words on paper. If you are dissatisfied with a particular formulation, and think of a better way, carry on and write it down. In revision these two attempts can be pondered over, and the better one chosen; perhaps you will ultimately combine the two sets of phrases into something better than either. The main thing is not to lose impetus.

A final point about writing a draft: do not feel you must always start at the beginning. Worries over the opening paragraph cause more delays than anything else. The best place to start writing is the section where you have the most secure grasp of the content, and feel most confident. Start the next section on a fresh sheet of paper. Do not necessarily follow the sequence of the final document, but follow the sequence of your confidence. It is best to write the conclusion next to last, and the introduction or opening section last of all. All that remains when the whole document is drafted is to shuffle the pages into the final order, as decided in your planning stage, and the main part of the task is over.

Many people resist writing drafts because they feel it is a waste of time. But unless the document is little more than an extended memo, drafting makes the task easier for the writer, because the process has been divided up. Decisions about selection and order have already been taken before drafting starts. Decisions about the exact choices of words have been pushed forward in time. The effect is like replacing a high jump by a series of small hurdles. Divided up in this way, the components of the writing process can be dealt with in the course of the normal day's work.

Try to leave the draft for a few days, or at least overnight. Then, when you look at it again, you will have forgotten the precise line of thought that was in your mind on the day you wrote it – what you *meant* to say! You will be obliged to look more closely at what the words on the page actually *do say*. We recognize that pressures of work frequently do not allow this approach. Often, it is not possible to leave a draft even overnight before having it finally copied and issued. In those circumstances, before you issue your text, it is essential to make a conscious effort to step back from your work and review it. Such self-editing is never easy. When you have just finished writing, your mind is still full of the implications you meant to put into the text.

Stage six – forget it!

A considerable conscious effort is required to ask: if I were reading this for the first time, what would the words on the page really say? Unfortunately, we know of no secret technique for doing this. All we can recommend is that you deliberately build into your working habits the self-discipline of conscious re-appraisal of each major piece of writing. If you do, you will be well on the way to producing effective writing.

Revising, like other writing tasks, is best done in stages. First read through the draft without stopping. This enables you to perceive the overall flow of ideas and information. We suggest that at this stage you simply draw a line in the margin against passages which need more careful attention later. You can also circle words with doubtful spelling, constructions which need tidying up, and facts which need checking. If you go any further than such simple marks at this stage, you will blunt your judgement of the effective flow of thought.

Stage seven – revise and edit

Next, work through the difficulties you noted at the first reading. Again, it is usually best to do this in stages. Spend some time reflecting on the passages which need restructuring; then work through the facts which need checking, perhaps in the library, or with your laboratory note-book beside you. Finally, turn your attention to the style and to the mechanics of language.

You will find the 'scissors and paste' technique useful at this stage. Where a set of points needs restructuring, try cutting them up into separate strips of paper. You can then make trial assemblies of them on your desk. When you are satisfied, paste, Sellotape, paper-clips, or staples can be used to fix them on to a sheet of paper in the best order. Much of the draft of our book was a rag-bag of strips and fragments, peppered with staples. It looks untidy, but it works. When the reassembled text is re-typed, it will need reading through again, because there are often gaps when a text is pulled apart and reassembled in this way. But overall you will probably be surprised how much more logically it reads after such close and detailed attention.

Editing for style is a skill which grows with practice. Chapter 7 of this book, 'Style for Readability', discusses what to look for. In summary, look out for long, rambling sentences, pompous words and phrases, and roundabout constructions which can be made terser. Even experienced writers often write in a round-about way in the first draft. When the mind is thinking round an issue, it often makes a series of false starts. We all know that a clumsily started sentence can usually be 'saved' by a series of tortuously phrased afterthoughts. Editing should remove these unnecessarily long structures, and find more direct expressions. Picking out active verbs usually makes the rest of the sentence fall into a natural order. Most writers can find ways of shortening their texts considerably. As an example, our first draft of part of Chapter 1, as it came off the typewriter, read:

> The tradition of verbose writing is a modern one. It has been laughed at often enough, but how many can honestly say that the style is never used, deliberately or not, by the technical writers they have read. The point is that Newton didn't feel the need to elaborate, decorate and obfuscate his meaning with inflated style. It was exciting enough in itself. The clear, simple language of great thinking was enough. Why do so many modern scientists, engineers and technologists feel the need to wrap up their meanings?

A fortnight later, we read it through, and revised it:

> The "tradition" of verbose writing is a modern one. It
> has been pilloried ~~laughed at~~ often enough, but ~~how many can
> honestly say that the style is never used, deliberately
> or not, by the~~ /many ~~technical~~ writers still turn to it. ~~they have read? The
> point is that~~ Newton did not feel the need to ~~elaborate,
> decorate and~~ obfuscate his meaning with inflated style.
> ~~It was~~ (exciting enough) ~~in itself.~~ The ~~clear,~~ clear simple
> language of ~~great~~ thinking was ~~enough.~~ without decoration. Too Why do so/many
> modern scientists /and engineers ~~and technologists feel the~~ Seeing to
> need to wrap up their meanings/.

Of course, no one set of writing procedures suits everyone; we do not suggest that the writing plan we have outlined here is the only way to write. But we do recommend the principle of the division of labour that the plan offers. Breaking down the various decisions involved in writing into separate stages reduces panic by making the job less awesome. It also makes writing a routine. No longer are moods of inspiration needed, no longer is writing only possible when you are exceptionally awake and fresh. The various stages can be worked through even when you are tired, or simply not feeling like concentrated creative thought. All professional writers learn this early in their careers. You probably use writing as an adjunct to professionalism in other spheres; but learning the divide-and-conquer techniques of the professional writer is still a valuable career asset.

The complete text

4 Organization and layout of information

It follows from what we have said in earlier chapters that it is not possible to set out here just one ideal way of organizing and laying out reports or papers. The tactics of arrangement and physical layout must be varied according to the task involved and the needs of the audience. If, in this chapter, we tried to discuss the specific tactics of layout to be used in every type of report, paper, or other document, it would require almost a book by itself. So we propose here to discuss the best tactics for organizing and laying out detailed technical reports and papers, such as progress reports, project reports, and research papers. At the end of the chapter, we discuss briefly how the principles we set out here relate to the other tasks that confront you.

The initial impact The first thing to realize is that your papers begin to produce a response from the readers – begin to work for or against you – as soon as they land on those readers' desks. Indeed, it is possible to argue that reports and papers begin to work for or against their writers even before that. Readers' over-all responses to papers are influenced by the ease with which they can identify the papers they want and retrieve them from libraries or information storage systems.

We begin by emphasizing that there are at least *two* broad groups of readers to consider; those who have asked for the paper, and those who have not been expecting the paper or report that has arrived.

The first group, who have asked for the report or paper to be sent to them, want to know immediately 'Is this the right paper?'; 'Does it have the information that I wanted?'; 'Should I read it now or later?'.

The second group, who have not been expecting the paper, have at least four questions that run through their minds:

- What's this all about?
- Is it of relevance to me?
- Does it contain significant new information?
- Should I allocate time for reading it now?

Both groups are looking for *information* to help focus quickly on the orientation and content of the document. They want a prominent, succinct and apt title. They want to find quickly a terse but reliable summing up of the essence of the work, showing the points that touch their interests or needs – the reasons why the paper has come to them. They want a clear summary of the conclusions drawn from the work and of the recommendations consequent upon those conclusions. If your paper is to get off to a good start, give your readers the information they want in the quickest and most accessible way.

Do you need to take all this trouble, especially when managers have asked you to write the paper, and your readers are being paid to read it? The answer is 'yes'; because no matter whether they are being paid to read your paper or not, your readers are unlikely to seize it with excitement and enthusiasm. All of us complain that we have too much to do, especially that we have too much paper to read. Any new document that arrives must compete for attention.

Consider our own response to most papers we receive. Do we settle down to careful reading at once? Usually not. We pick up the paper and weigh (sometimes literally!) and consider it. We look at its size and organization. We glance at its cover and 'headlines' and riffle quickly through to get a sense of its organization and density. We debate the attractiveness of reading the paper and – of great importance – we estimate the resources of time and effort that will be needed to deal with it. As we do this, an attitude to the paper begins to form – we begin to respond to it. Our response-to-papers meter begins to register on a scale such as:

- Is that really so, how interesting!
- Looks very interesting.
- Interesting.
- Could just be interesting.
- I wonder if this is worth reading.
- Looks damned heavy going.
- Have I really got to read all this?

The front page   The very appearance of a report or paper should begin the campaign to win the attention of both groups of readers. Does it look heavy, dauntingly thick and covered with dense black type? Does the design of the front page draw the reader's attention immediately to the answers to the questions that have crossed his or her mind? As you look at the example of the front page shown in Fig. 4.1, consider whether your eye is drawn immediately to the answers to the questions mentioned earlier: is this the right report, what's it about, why is it of relevance to me?

Most readers who see the front page in Fig. 4.1 (which is a genuine front page, with only names and numbers changed) complain that their eyes are drawn immediately to information of secondary importance. Some readers see first the section about confidentiality. Others notice first the heavy black prominence of the company's name in the top left-hand corner. Yet others see first the large section devoted to the distribution list. Most have to *search* for the title, which gives the main answer to the question: what is this paper about?

Of course, a note on confidentiality, or the company's name, or the circulation list has every right to appear on the front page of a report. But in Fig. 4.1, those items are too prominent. Our point is that the secondary material has been given a prominence that it does not deserve – a prominence that *should* have been given to the title and the information of principal importance and use to the reader.

Factors that   We have mentioned three factors that are important in achieving
give emphasis   prominence for items of information on a page: position on the page, size of the area allocated to the information, and size of the type faces used in the printing of the information. These three factors can be used alone or in various combinations to draw readers' eyes to those things that you wish to highlight.

To give the title of a paper maximum prominence, it is best to place it as near as possible to the position that breaks the page into ideal proportions – the 'golden section'. As *The Penguin Encyclopaedia* states,[1] the golden section is not easy to define exactly:

> An ideal proportion used by architects and artists which cannot be resolved mathematically; expressed by a line divided so that the smaller part is to the greater as the greater

PARK PLACE CHEMICAL CORPORATION
TECHNICAL SERVICES DEPARTMENT
CARDIFF

Job. No. 422101561
Report No. 2
Date: 9th August 1988

PROGRESS REPORT

CONFIDENTIAL

This report contains confidential information which is the property of Park Place Chemical Corporation. The recipient is held accountable for the filing, safe custody and further distribution to other Park Place Chemicals staff of the report, and for its destruction when no longer needed.

DISTRIBUTION

Information Centre, Cardiff (2)
Information Centre, Newport (2)
Information Centre, London (2)
A Black, Information Centre
B White, Cardiff
C Brown, Cardiff
D Grey, Cardiff
E Green, Newport
F Pink, Newport
G Blue, Newport

TITLE: Improving Chlorine Flow Control

AUTHOR(S): B White, Cardiff TSD

Fig. 4.1 Confusing front page layout.

is to the whole; very roughly, 8:13. In classical times and during the Renaissance it was supposed to provide a key to the harmony of the universe, and architects and artists sought to compose their works in accordance with it.

In Western civilization, readers expect to find titles 'balanced' comfortably on the page, and this means that their eyes are inclined to go first to a position about one third of the way down from the top of the page and in the centre. This is one of the reasons why the confidentiality section in Fig. 4.1 draws too much attention.

It helps if the title is in larger type than the rest of the information surrounding it on the front page; and if possible, it should be separated from all other information by ample areas of white space, which will make it stand out. Another device for giving emphasis is the use of underlining and ruling. But combination of several devices is usually overwhelming. Titles that are in large type and are clearly spaced do not need underlining as well. The effect of the extra horizontal lines in Fig. 4.1 is to make the apparatus of layout overwhelm the information.

Notice that we have not said that the title should be alone on the front page of a document. Most of the items of information that appear on the front page in Fig. 4.1 *are* of relevance to the readers. Readers need to know a job number and a report number – where this paper fits into a sequence of information. They need to know the date on which the paper was written, to know what currency it has. They will be helped by having a distribution list readily accessible on the front page, because it tells them who else has received the information and is therefore 'in the know'.

Though all persons reading internal documents should be well aware of the name of the organization for which they work, it is reasonable that the organization's name should appear on every document that is circulated. A recognizable house style helps to build a sense of identity and 'belonging'. It is certainly important that readers should know which department, section or group the paper emerges from. Likewise, it is vital to know who has written and who has approved the circulation of the paper. And if a paper must be kept confidential, that is one of the first things readers must be told.

All these *are* relevant pieces of information and should, if possible, appear on the front page of the document; but they

PARK PLACE CHEMICAL CORPORATION
TECHNICAL SERVICES DEPARTMENT
CARDIFF

Job.No. 422101561
Report No. 2

IMPROVING CHLORINE FLOW CONTROL

Progress Report

by

B. White, Cardiff TSD .

9th August 1988

Fig. 4.2 Clear front page layout.

PARK PLACE CHEMICAL CORPORATION   Job.No. 422101561
TECHNICAL SERVICES DEPARTMENT   Report No. 2
CARDIFF

IMPROVING CHLORINE FLOW CONTROL

Progress Report

by

B.White, Cardiff TSD
9th August 1988

SUMMARY

The glass rotameter measuring the chlorine vapour
flow rate to the chlorinator is unsatisfactory. It is
slow and in some circumstances could be unsafe. The
existing rotameter and chlorine line in Building 3
should be dismantled and scrapped. A new chlorine
line, measuring unit (Measurit Superkwik) and
recorder/controller unit should be purchased. The
cost of these items, with the cost of the
necessary valve changes, would be £14,700

Distribution

Information Centre, Cardiff (2)   C Brown, Cardiff
Information Centre, Newport (2)   D Grey, Cardiff
Information Centre, London (2)   E Green, Newport
A Black, Information Centre   F Pink, Newport
B White, Cardiff   G Blue, Newport

Fig. 4.3 Clear front page with summary.

should be kept in subordinate positions so that the principal emphasis is always thrown on the title of the paper. This can be done without producing the cluttered effect demonstrated in Fig. 4.1. Figure 4.2 shows a revised version. Figure 4.3 shows that, by including the summary, it is often possible to give readers even more information on the front page without the cluttering effect shown in Fig. 4.1.

We want to make two further points about titles, both designed to help make a sharp impact on readers: titles should be short, preferably on one line only; and they should specify exactly what the paper is talking about, not simply name a whole subject.

Wording of titles

A title such as the following will not make a sharp impression on a reader's mind:

Construction and instrumentation of an experimental concrete road on the trunk road D7 Upbridge bypass to determine the effect of omitting expansion joints.

There is too much information to take in 'at a glance'. If all the information is essential, at least it should be broken into two or three manageable pieces. Here is a possible revision:

Effect of omitting expansion joints in concrete roads
Construction and Instrumentation
of an experiment on the D7

Your readers will find it helpful, too, if your title signals *exactly* what is to come in the paper. For example, a heading such as **non-metallic inclusions in steel** is not particularly helpful to readers, since it seems to offer all there is to know about non-metallic inclusions in steel. Is the paper about how to measure these inclusions, or about the influence of these inclusions on the workability or strength of the steel? A much better title would be **Measuring non-metallic inclusions in steel**, or **The influence of non-metallic inclusions on phase-change in steel**.

Titles have two jobs to do. First, they have to inform readers about what is in the document. Second, they have to distinguish one document from another. If readers are flicking through piles of documents in their in-trays or in the reference section of a library, they want a brief title which can be taken in at a single glance, and which will distinguish one document from all the others.

If you had a pile of documents on your desk, most of which were short stories with arresting titles, the single word 'report' on one document would focus your attention sharply. But for managers in a steel plant, a title like 'Report on steel-making problems' would be useless. Almost every document on their desks would be in that category. A more useful title might be:

Rapid measurement of carbon content in steel

Many writers think of titles as doing only the first of these jobs, and therefore write long titles. But a long title dazzles the eye as it glances at a document.

A useful technique for testing the words in a title to see which are doing work, is to decide which of the words would be used in a keyword index. A keyword index picks out every important word, and indexes the document separately under each. Go through your title, underlining words that could be used in a keyword index; all those not underlined are doing less work, and may be redundant. They divert and distract the scanning eye, without helping the mind to recognize the uniqueness of this document. The following title has redundant words in it:

An investigation into the suitability of CSPFA as a base material

Clearly, most reports are about investigations, and few of the investigations were consciously looking for something *un*suitable. By using these words, the writer has lost the opportunity to use other, more informative, words. A report would never be recorded in a keyword file under words like 'investigation' or 'suitability'. Choose titles which avoid redundant words.

Positioning
the summary   So far, we have been discussing what we call the orientation section of the report – the section that influences the readers' initial attitude to and interest in the paper. We have said that the summary plays an important part in this section. Indeed, we think summaries are such important parts of reports and papers that we have given them a separate chapter – Chapter 9. At this point in our discussion of how to organize information effectively, we wish simply to emphasize that most reports and papers need a summary on the title page or on the page immediately following. And since the main aim of the summary

is to emphasize what is new and interesting to potential readers, the principal emphasis in the summary should be on findings, conclusions and recommendations.

Of course, if your report is to be only one or two pages long, a separate title page and summary will seem over-elaborate. But even in those circumstances, get your paper off to a good start by ensuring that the heading of your first page is comfortably spaced and incorporates a sharp, focusing title. If you decide against having a separate summary, at least bring your attention-catching information forward into a summarizing opening paragraph.

After the orientation section – the title page and summary – comes the body of the report, in which you present the full 'story' for readers who want complete details.

The body of the report

We suggest that the following arrangement will be effective for most reports:

Table of contents
List of symbols, abbreviations, definitions
Introductory material
Report of the work done
Results/findings
Discussion/analysis/argument, leading to conclusions
Conclusions
Recommendations
Acknowledgements
References
Appendix for tables, figures and graphs
Other appendices

These headings represent a full format; not all reports will require all these sections and a selection must be made for the particular reporting task on hand. Never write a section under each heading just because the headings are there. We have seen a report, written according to a rigid 'house' format, which duly went through every section. In the introduction it said that the test equipment available was inadequate, and the tests had to be abandoned without results. This fact was repeated under 'report of work done'. The 'results/findings' section contained a re-phrasing of the same information, as did the 'discussion of results' section. Finally, the conclusions laboriously repeated that no results were obtained because the test equipment was not up to the job. Such absurdities arise when writers slavishly follow rigid formats. Every reporting task needs its own format; the writer must be prepared (and free) to delete, or reverse, the order of sections to produce the most effective reporting of his or her particular information.

Table of contents   It is sensible to begin by providing your readers with a detailed table of contents which will show the pattern of ideas through which you are about to lead them. The table of contents is not provided simply to enable people to find a page on which they will be able to read about a topic. Just as most of us like to have some idea of the route we are to follow when we set off on a journey, so most of us like to know the general pattern of ideas through which we are to be led in a paper or a talk. A well-designed table of contents, showing main headings and all sub-headings, and showing the relationship of those parts by indentation and a clear numbering system, provides readers with this overview of the document they are about to read.

An unhelpful table of contents is shown in Fig. 4.4. Standard titles like 'results' are uninformative; such a list of headings could be used for almost any report ever written. Certainly it does neither the job of giving readers an over-view or map of the territory they are about to enter, nor the job of helping them find

CONTENTS	PAGE NO.
1. INTRODUCTION	1
2. METHOD	3
3. REQUIREMENTS	10
4. RECOMMENDATIONS	16
5. REFERENCES	16
6. APPENDICES	17

Fig. 4.4   Uninformative contents page.

CONTENTS

1.	INTRODUCTION		1
2.	METHOD OF TREATMENT		
	2.1	General	3
	2.2	Survey of Reducing Agents	4
	2.3	Survey of Precipitating Agents	6
	2.4	Chemical Treatment Procedure	7
3.	PLANT REQUIREMENTS AND USAGE		
	3.1	Pre-Treatment Storage Tank	10
	3.2	Treatment Tanks	10
	3.3	NO_2 Handling Equipment	12
	3.4	Hydrochloric Acid Handling Equipment	13
	3.5	Storage of Cuprous Sulphide Quintahydrate	14
	3.6	Tanks for Calcium Hydroxide Liquor	14
	3.7	Vent Fan and Scrubber	15
4.	FURTHER ACTION		16
5.	REFERENCES		16
	APPENDIX 1	Suppliers of Raw Materials	17
	APPENDIX 2	Specifications for Treatment Tanks	20
	APPENDIX 3	Specifications for the Vent Fan and Scrubber	22

Fig. 4.5 Informative contents page.

any particular section they are interested in. The table of contents shown in Fig. 4.5 is more helpful. Notice that subheadings, as well as main headings, are included. Notice too that most headings are full and informative, and only two are single standard words. Finally, notice that a decimal numbering system, indentation, and varying weight of type all contribute to the ease with which we can see the sense, shape and content of the document.

Some writers worry about how long a document must be to need a contents list. Other writers always put one in, even if the document is only two pages. Clearly, adding 50% to the length and bulk of the document in this way is unnecessary. As always, consider how the reader will use a contents list, and use this to decide if it is needed. In a short document, it is probably just as quick to flick over two or three pages looking at the headings as it is to glance over a contents page. If the document has only a few obvious sections, then a contents page is probably unnecessary, even if the document is five or six pages long. But in a short document, with a number of disparate sections, some of which will be isolated and picked out by readers not interested in the rest of the text, a contents page is needed.

List of symbols, abbreviations and definitions

Next, it will help your readers if you provide a list of new symbols, abbreviations, and definitions used in the report. Of course, there may not be any new symbols to list at this point. Also, we must emphasize that your main obligation is to explain each new term, symbol or abbreviation at the first point in the text at which you introduce it. But it is often helpful to your readers, if a new term is used infrequently, to list it in a glossary. And that glossary is best placed at the *beginning* of the report, not at the end, so that readers know where they can remind themselves of definitions that they have forgotten since they first read them in the text.

Introductory material

Once readers have been shown the pattern of ideas they are to be led through, it is useful to set out the background to the report in full. Readers who want a fully detailed account of your work find it helpful if you state in full the problem you were aiming to solve or the aspect you were setting out to investigate. Why was the work undertaken? What scope was given? What limitations of time, personnel and materials were imposed? It may help readers if you give an outline of previous relevant work at this point – a survey of the history of related work and a theoretical analysis of problems related to your topic. Anything that fills in the background up to the point at which the work began is relevant to the introductory section.

Beware of introducing into this section any material that you now know as a result of having done the work that you are about to describe. A common source of distraction in introductions to reports is failure to distinguish what had been done *before* the work to be reported was started, and the inclusion of information that the writer could have known only after he had completed the work. Consider the following example:

Introduction

This report relates to work on the active rudders on HMS Park Place during 1987. The work was undertaken because of problems in the past of ships losing propellers and breaking drive shafts. In the past this loss has been prevented by securing the active rudders to prevent rotation, but this was not satisfactory due to the time and effort required. To try and prevent further loss, a new design was instigated and at the same time, measurements were to be made of the various forces present when operating normally. These measurements were made on one of the modified shaft/propeller combinations and whereas the stresses measured would not be the same as the original shafts, the forces acting on the various components would be representative of the original system.

The report is divided into three main sections:

Design and manufacture of instrumentation.
Measurement and recording of signals whilst at sea.
Analysis of data.

The difficulty for the reader here is to guess when 'a new design was instigated' (line 7). Was it 'in the past'? It seems so from the way this introduction is written. But when the reader reaches the end of the section, it becomes plain that the writer meant, 'So we decided (or were commissioned) to instigate a new design and at the same time to measure . . .'

In the next example, the writer includes in the introduction the findings of the work he is about to report:

Introduction

Corrosion affects the materials used in constructing chemical plants, the main areas of attack being crevices, welds, and bimetallic contacts. Undue stress and vibrations must be avoided. Many expensive materials can be profitably used as thin linings supported by cheaper, more corrosive, stronger materials. This technique decreases corrosion in plants which handle chlorides. The change can be hampered by cost, but as the technique improves, the cost will decrease. Linings of tantalum, zirconium and titanium are the most satisfactory.

The work to be reported in the paper was an exploration of which materials would be best for use as thin linings. Did the writer know before he started that linings of tantalum, zirconium and titanium would be most satisfactory? No, that is the conclusion he came to as a result of doing his work; but that became plain to the reader only after reading the whole report. The ten-line 'introduction' above is more of a summary than an introduction.

You will help yourself get the right perspective on writing an introduction if you consider that you are trying to say to your readers, 'this is the position as we saw it before we began our work'. That leads naturally into the body of the report in which you say, in effect, 'so this is what we did and this is what we discovered'. Here is an example of a better introduction:

Introduction

Development Department is interested in the possibility of using resin cloth for electrical insulation. As overheating of electrical equipment could cause heating of the resin cloth, which could lead to the evolution of flammable gases from the resin, they asked us to investigate the pyrolysis products of the resin.

We decided that it was necessary to approach this task in two stages:
1. to establish a reliable analytical procedure;
2. to identify and measure the products from pyrolysis of resin cloths A and B.

We could find no helpful literature on the thermal decomposition of resin cloths or on directly suitable analytical procedures. We therefore decided to attempt to modify the 'Rapid Combustion' method of Belcher and Ingram,[1] which we have used previously in other analyses.

This report describes our experiments to establish a reliable analytical procedure. A later report will give details of the pyrolysis products from resin cloths A and B.

Account of the work done   The account of the work you did will probably be the longest section in your report. It is difficult for us to discuss in general terms what should go in this section. The precise data that the reader will find helpful will vary according to such factors as whether you are describing a design, a survey procedure, a test method, or an experimental procedure. But here is a helpful check-list of what readers in an industrial setting will want to know in various types of papers.[2]

What readers will want to know

1. About new products: the potential uses, the risks, the commercial requirements, the technical requirements, if any

more work needs to be done on problems, manpower requirements, financial requirements, material requirements, the probable life of the product or project, the relative importance of the product or project compared with other products or projects, and proposed schedules for development.

2. About technical problems: just what the problem is, how big and important it is, whether it has arisen before and what has been done and by whom, whether the problem is temporary or permanent, whether the solution being put forward in the report is the only solution and if not, what others were considered and why they were rejected, what should be done now, who and what will be involved in the recommendations, and whether any redesign will be called for.

3. About surveys of materials or processes: the properties, characteristics, and capabilities of the material, its limitations, whether its properties vary in varying conditions, where the material could be used and how, whether the materials are readily available or are to be made by the company, the costs of the materials or processes, the costs of plant required, if any, to handle the materials or processes, the materials and/or processes which the new materials or processes would compete with, how the new materials and processes would fit in with present company plans, processes, and future programme.

The way in which you arrange a description or explanation of your work will inevitably be related to your decisions about the aim and audience for your paper. As we suggested at the end of Chapter 2, there are many ways of organizing even an apparently simple description, depending on your readers' orientation or interests. For some readers, a description may be best arranged to guide them 'from the outside in' – reflecting the real order of perception as a person approaches an object for the first time; but for other readers, who have some understanding of the object you are describing, it may be better to write in a way that reflects the hierarchy of components – starting with the 'heart' of the machine or process, and gradually explaining how ancillary elements are related or how your work involved modifying customary structures or procedures.

If you have information to present about activities at three sites, A, B and C, and if you want to describe the ways in which you experimented with variations in manpower, machinery and materials, you have at least two patterns of organization available:

Arrangement 1

Site A	— manpower
	— machinery
	— materials
Site B	— manpower
	— machinery
	— materials
Site C	— manpower
	— machinery
	— materials

Arrangement 2

Manpower	— site A
	— site B
	— site C
Machinery	— site A
	— site B
	— site C
Materials	— site A
	— site B
	— site C

We discuss the writing of descriptions further in Chapter 12. But we want to emphasize again here that your choice must be dictated by your readers' principal interests and by the particular impact you wish to make with your account.

Order of arrangement   In our discussions so far, we have been advocating that you arrange your reports and papers in order of importance *from the readers' point of view*. We have been advocating a *descending* order of importance, presenting the new, most important information in outline at the beginning of the paper, and giving the supporting evidence or detail afterwards. This is not simply to help focus and orientation. It is also because readers find it easier to assimilate detailed information if they have first been given a general framework into which to fit the detail.

Imagine a man who is called for jury duty, and finds himself watching a grave be-wigged figure rise to open the case: 'My Lord, the accused is a man of previous good character; he is married, My Lord, and has been married for eighteen years. He has three children, My Lord, lives in a detached house in a good part of town, and has worked for his present employer in the same capacity for over twenty years . . .' As the barrister drones on, ask yourself, is the defendant guilty or not?

The question is unanswerable, because much depends on whether he is accused of speeding or of murdering his wife. What the evidence is *for* determines our view of its importance. Unless we know what case we are trying, we cannot assess each item of information as we receive it. If it does not fit into a pattern or framework, it is rapidly lost in a confusion of formless detail. Yet such confusion is often caused by writers who give detailed evidence before stating their objectives and conclusions. Readers do not know what the evidence is for, or where it is leading, and so are unable to make it do any work in their minds.

Pyramids of evidence

Evidence, in a document which is explaining, proving, or arguing a case, must be marshalled to support that case. And it will be of use to the reader only if he or she is clearly told what that case is.

Too often writers let the evidence swamp the case. We must emphasize again that there is a difference between the order of discovery and the order of announcement. And that the thoroughness necessary to make and check discoveries is opposite to the parsimony needed to explain them without confusion.

We are aware that there are some types of writing that can make use of *ascending* order – starting with minor matters and gradually building to a striking climax. In theory, this technique can be psychologically effective: it makes use of the readers' curiosity and encourages them to read on to learn the final outcome. It is the detective story style, with clues dropped here and there to intrigue us and a final dramatic revelation of where responsibility and innocence really lie. But we think it is rarely appropriate for professional reports and papers to use this 'intriguing' technique. Perhaps if you have a particularly delicate topic to broach, it may be appropriate to approach it obliquely: but most readers of reports and papers are looking for a more open and rigorous approach. They will be at least suspicious and at worst hostile to your apparent reluctance to 'come to the point'.

Most reports and papers, then, will be best organized in a

pyramid structure, in order of importance, with a summary at the top and a gradual expansion into greater detail within the body of the paper. The base of the pyramid will be your appendices, containing the most detailed information. This arrangement has the advantage of making readily accessible the information wanted by the majority of readers. Readers can stop reading when they have obtained as much detail as they need. Perhaps only a few will read right through to the appendices. Your readership will probably be an inverted pyramid:

Title and summary focus and orientation

Body of report

Most detailed information

Most readers

Few readers

However, *within* your order of importance, it is possible to arrange sections of the account in many ways, to reflect, for example:

- spatial or topographical arrangements;
- experimental or manufacturing sequences;
- fault-finding or operating sequences;
- order of discovery;
- existing patterns of information in libraries or other stores.

Each one of these ways of organizing a paper is 'logical' in its own terms. But the internal logic of such organizational structures is of little interest to readers. The logic which matters to them as they read is the logic of their understanding. This starts from the familiar (which may be the old process, or the desired end-product, or a familiar part of the machine which will be retained intact in modification), and moves onwards to the unfamiliar. Just what is familiar or unfamiliar depends on what the reader already knows, not what the *writer* knows. Many writers hand information over to their readers like a dinner-table guest passing a knife with the sharp end pointing outwards. Polite people turn it round, offering the comfortable handle first. So with information. In most cases it has to be turned round, so that the reader can grasp it comfortably.

The amount of detail in your account must also vary according to your purpose in writing and according to your audience. Are you aiming to assemble and write about all available information for permanent record or are you aiming simply to describe how and why you came to a particular set of conclusions? In our experience, junior staff frequently misjudge what their supervisors want from them. A major complaint from managers in business and industry is that new recruits still think they are writing school and university essays, emphasizing *how much* they know about a topic. Report-writing in business and industry is mainly a *management* activity, and not part of the academic activity of generating and making available new knowledge for anyone who may be interested. Report-writing in business and industry should focus more sharply on what needs to be said in order *to get something done*, and details in reports and papers should be sorted and selected with that objective uppermost in mind.

Note, however, that it would be simplistic to set up too sharp a contrast between 'writing to get something done' and 'writing for the record'. A good paper will often need to contain both types of writing. Indeed, you may find that you have to write at three levels: in outline in your summary; in greater detail as you present evidence supporting a particular conclusion in the body of your report; and in very great detail in your appendices. It may be desirable to record in your appendices your false starts, negative findings and test details, for the benefit of just a few readers who might otherwise waste time and money in the future by re-exploring ground you have covered already.

We mentioned in Chapter 2 that it is important to provide a clear signalling system within your report to help readers find the details they want – to find their way around. To do this, make liberal use of headings and sub-headings that act as sign-posts signalling routes and announcing the content of sections. You may feel that this uses more paper. But the disadvantage of increasing the amount of paper must be weighed against the advantage of making it possible for your reader to get a sense of rapid, comfortable progress through the story. Normally, this sense of comfortable progress will be helped by the division of the work into logically related, manageable sections, and by the liberal use of headings and sub-headings. Our advice on the use of headings and numbering is given in Chapter 5.

Results and findings

The results section in the body of your report should rarely by bulky. Bring forward into the results section just the main facts and figures that are necessary to support and explain the argument you are presenting. Do not 'clog up' the centre of the report with a mass of data that it is not essential for readers to consider as they follow the description or argument.

We are not saying that you should not present all your findings, negative and otherwise: we are suggesting that these findings *in detail* should be presented in appendices to the main report. In the main text, give the reader just the pieces of information that are necessary to make the argument logically acceptable and technically persuasive.

It is too easy to swamp a clear argument, which requires underpinning with carefully selected facts, with a mountain of detailed evidence. Readers should not be expected to repeat all the sifting the writer did in arriving at his or her conclusions. Our experience is that the urge to be complete often leads writers to ignore the readers' need to have a *manageable* argument to grasp. *Less* evidence is usually needed if the reader is to *understand* the point. To record and discuss every result is overkill, and some detail should be left either in the appendix, or in your filing cabinet.

Discussion and analysis

After the statement of your findings, it will be natural for you to discuss the conclusions to which these lead. What is implied by the data that has emerged from your experiments, surveys or evaluations of material? In your discussion, you will state the inferences you draw from your observations. Drawing inferences means talking about results, not simply repeating them. Many report writers let themselves down badly at this point by failing to state implications, to recognize trends and changes, to draw attention to comparisons and contrasts, and to sum up differences. Repetition of readings should rarely be necessary: a discussion will normally require speculation about causes and effects, and analysis of implications for the future.

A discussion of what the facts imply must include a statement of the conclusions drawn from the premises laid down. For this reason it is not essential in all reports to follow the discussion section by another section re-stating your conclusions. A well-written report will have included the conclusions and recommendations at the front in its summary; it will have mentioned its conclusions again in the course of its discussion; so it is not essential to state the conclusions a third time after the discussion section. However, in a long and detailed report, it may be desirable to have a full statement of conclusions in a separate section after the discussion within the body of the report, and to give a summary of the conclusions at the beginning.

In English, the word *conclusion* can signal two meanings: it can mean 'concluding remarks', with *concluding* meaning simply last or final; or it can mean 'a logical outcome', what is implied by or inferred from previous pieces of argument. In reports, you can legitimately use the heading *Conclusions* in either of the ways defined above. But we suggest that your 'concluding remarks' are best placed in your discussion section, leaving you free to imply by your use of the heading *Conclusions* that you are presenting a section that repeats succinctly the logical outcome from all that has gone before.

Conclusions

A text that is laid out as a report invites the reader to expect an argument, moving from a statement of a problem, through evidence and discussion, to a statement of implications or inferences. It is therefore unsatisfying to find under the heading *Conclusions* such paragraphs as these extracts from two different reports:

Conclusions

Apart from the lack of rough weather trials, the test programme went very smoothly and the results appear to be as expected. The only problem which has become apparent is the armoured cable outer which has broken, necessitating the removal of both units, which will make any further test impossible until the ship is in dry-dock.

Conclusions

Accidents in fog totalled 192 in the three-year period 1985–1987, making up four per cent of the total: 129 of these occurred during daylight hours. Accidents were on average more serious, with more casualties per accident, than those occurring in other weather conditions. About forty five per cent of fog accidents and twenty two per cent of non-fog accidents occurred on about one-seventh (160 km) of the motorway network.

The first extract gives findings, not conclusions. The second extract again gives no conclusions: it simply reiterates facts. In contrast, the following extract from another report genuinely focuses readers' attention on a succinct statement of principal conclusions:

Conclusions

1. If an oil-cooling system is caught at the 'incipient failure' stage but does not show gross contamination, the oil should be changed without flushing (Section 3.4).
2. Sludge-bound oil coolers should be cleaned by a flushing procedure (described in Section 3.5).
3. Systems that are grossly contaminated after component failure should be stripped and cleaned on site (Section 3.7).
4. Metal-contaminated oil coolers should be returned to the manufacturer for complete stripping and cleaning (Section 3.8).

Recommen-
dations   Recommendations should be clear-cut. There should be no discussion within a recommendation section: discussion should have been completed in the *Discussion* section. If you have a separately headed section for recommendations, those recommendations should be direct and to the point. Once again, the crucial argument is how *readers* will use the recommendations section. Having read through the report, they will already have a fair idea of what is to be recommended. Indeed, most papers will already have dealt with the recommendations one at a time as they arose. Therefore the recommendations section is not something for discursive reading. It acts as a check list; it enables readers to tick-off in their minds the various points; they can mentally sum up the total recommendation. For this reason, the recommendations section is often best presented as a list. For example:

Recommendations

1. Procedures for servicing of oil coolers should be as described in Section 7 (Conclusions).
2. Duties and responsibilities related to these procedures should be allocated at the January service group meeting and the procedures put into effect immediately after that meeting.

Acknowledge-
ments   The recommendations complete the argument or 'story' of your report. After this, it is appropriate to acknowledge any help you

have been given in the course of your work. A minor problem in doing so is to prevent the tone of the section from becoming fawning or trivial. Your objective should be to acknowledge openly any substantial contributions from other individuals or organizations. But, as a rough guide, acknowledgements should normally be restricted to help from outside your own organization. It is not necessary to thank those whose job it was to help you anyway. It is not possible to give a 'rule' for writing acknowledgements, but a rough guide is to restrict thanks to 'outsiders' and outside sources. Thank 'insiders' only if their contribution has been well beyond the normal call of duty.

Consider the purpose of an acknowledgements section. It should not be a place for you to boast about how much work you have done, about your extensive acquaintances, or about the devotion of your friends. Neither, it seems to us, is the acknowledgements section a place for a writer to make providers of information feel generous and altruistic. It is not for flattery; it is to help readers know where information came from, who are the experts in the field and where they can go for help if they want to do their own further investigations.

In the references section, if you have one, give details of any sources of information that you have quoted in your report itself. For instance, these examples show ways of citing a book,[1] an article in a journal,[2] a published report,[3] a paper or chapter in a book,[4] and a paper published in conference proceedings.[5]

References section

References

1. Miles, J. (1987) *Design for Desktop Publishing*, Gordon Fraser Gallery Ltd, London.
2. Youra, S. (1987) Rewriting the engineering curriculum: professionalism and professional communication. *J. Technical Writing and Communication*, **17**(4), 407–16.
3. Deis, J. (1985) Bering Sea Summary Report (September 1984), *US Department of the Interior OCS Information Report*, MMS 84–0076.
4. Charrow, V., Crandall, J.A. and Charrow, R. (1982) Characteristics and functions of legal language. In *Sublanguage*, R. Kittredge and J. Lehrberger (eds), Walter de Gruyter, New York, pp. 175–90.
5. Cherry, L. (1981) *Computer Aids for Writers*, Proceedings of the ACM SIGPLAN SIGOA Symposium on Text Manipula-

tion, Portland, Oregon, 1981, ACM SIGOA Newsletter Vol.2, Nos 1 and 2, Spring/Summer 1981, pp. 62–7, The Association for Computing Machinery Inc., New York.

To insist on exactness about references is not pedantry. References are given to help the reader find an original source that you refer to in your text. References should not be used to add information that *may* be useful: if information may be useful, put it in your text; if you are in doubt, leave it out.

Occasionally, you may be writing a document in which you wish to tell readers of a range of sources that give background information. If that is so, give them a *bibliography* or book list. A reference section has a different function from a bibliography. A reference section tells people where they can find the sources you have referred to; it should be arranged in a numerical sequence that reflects the order in which you referred to the sources in the text. A bibliography is a list of books that your readers may find interesting to go on to read next; it should be arranged alphabetically, like a library catalogue.

Citing references in the text   Within the body of your report, the least obtrusive way to cite references from the readers' point of view, is to use superscript numbers:

> Results of laboratory tests[1,2] have shown that there is no fundamental differences in the drying shrinkage characteristics[3] or creep characteristics[4] of lightweight and normal-weight concretes. Studies by the US Bureau of Reclamation,[5] gave a considerable boost to the use of expanded shales, clays and slates in structural light-weight concrete . . .

Some professional journals and magazines require you to use systems other than the superscript number system. We have selected three of these alternative systems. As you read through, note the effect the referencing conventions have on your comfortable progress through the text, and on your easy understanding of the prime content of each passage:

> . . . This delay is called System Response Time (SRT). It is widely recognised (Miller, 1968; Martin, 1973; Engel and Granda, 1975; Goodman and Spence, 1981) that SRT is an important characteristic in interactive computing. . . . Although some authors (Goodman and Spence, 1981) report on experiments in which . . . . . . the learning task (SCL task)

as described by Johnson (1971, 1978) . . . . . . The use of this task not only provides us with rather straightforward measures of subject performance (e.g. time needed to solve the problem), but also permits. . . .

Notice the disturbing effect on the reader of the parenthetical information about sources. It is difficult to hold in mind the main information that is being presented by the statement and *at the same time* to take in the sources and dates of that information. It is at least momentarily confusing to find that the material enclosed in parentheses is sometimes information related to the statement and sometimes simply reference information. Also, the reader has to adjust to the fact that the citation sometimes consists of name and date, and sometimes just of date.

A second convention is:

> There are approximately 400 molecules of DNA polymerase I (Kornberg, 1969) and 20 molecules of DNA polymerase II (Wickner *et al.*, 1972) per bacterial cell. The number of molecules per cell of DNA polymerase III can be estimated from its molecular weight (140 000; Otto *et al.*, 1973) and its purity is about 10 (Kornberg and Gefter, 1972; Otto *et al.*, 1973).

Notice here not only the clumsiness of the parentheses but also a confusing technique – the use of a single bracket to enclose two types of information: data to be added to the main statement and information about source and date. A third possibility is:

> Of the solution methods available, that involving the use of a Sturm sequence [2, 3] most adequately satisfied the normal engineering requirements. Ref.[3] however, would be unfamiliar to . . .

Note the clumsy opening to a sentence 'Ref. [3] . . .' caused by editorial insistence that all source materials be referred to solely by a number in square brackets. Another objection to showing references as single numbers in brackets is that bracketed numbers are often used to identify equations and formulae in mathematical and chemical discussions, and confusion can arise from using bracketed numbers for two purposes.

We believe the system used for citing references should be designed to give minimum interruption to readers' progress through the text. It should allow them to concentrate on primary

Using superscript numbers

information. The superscript number system achieves this most effectively. It shows that secondary bibliographic information is available, but does not distract readers by making the signal too obtrusive. The readers can then search for the secondary material later.

We recognize that the name of a source is often important *primary* information. The importance to be attached to information brought forward in an argument varies according to the repute of the source. We contend, however, that this is not an objection to the superscript system in itself, but to inept use of that system. If the name of the source contributes to the weight of the statement, it should be included in the wording of that statement.

Not:

> Standard mounting designs have been dismissed[1] as inadequate for this purpose, and a welded rig has proved more satisfactory;[2,3] but it is considered that it will be necessary to use . . . (Version 1)

but:

> Brown[1] has shown that standard mounting designs are inadequate for this purpose. Green[2] and Black[3] have used welded rigs and obtained more satisfactory results, but we think we shall need to use . . . (Version 2).

Much awkward referencing, whether using the superscript system or any other system, stems from attempts to remove all traces of people from engineering and scientific writing. In Chapter 7, we shall discuss in detail the desirability of attempting to do that. For the moment, let us simply point out here that the attempt to write impersonally in Version 1 has led to awkward referencing and to uncertainty about who considers 'that it will be necessary to use . . .'. Version 2 is more informative and is unambiguous.

One of the disadvantages of the more elaborate name-plus-date citation technique is that it tempts writers into a clumsy, so-called impersonal, style:

> It has been suggested (White B. and Grey N., 1980) . . .

A briefer, more direct statement would have been:

> B. White and N. Grey have suggested[1] that . . .

The superscript number system can cause confusion if it is used carelessly in a chemical text that also contains superscript numbers attached to chemical symbols:

> . . . is a function of crystallization.[13] The maximum rate and amount of crystallization occur at about 170°C.[14] It is usual to anneal the film at 180–210°C so as to reduce the tendency to shrink on heating.[15]

The placing of the superscript reference 14 *should* not have caused misunderstanding, but some readers could have been confused momentarily by reading the signal as the element C^{14}. So it would have been better to re-write the sentence 'At about 170°C, the maximum rate and amount of crystallization occur[14].

The superscript number system also sometimes presents problems for typists, especially when the text is prepared in small, close-set type. Nevertheless, on balance we recommend it because in a well-written text it is the clearest yet least disruptive way of signalling to readers that secondary information is available if they need it.

Footnotes

Distinguish between references and footnotes. References are statements that help readers find source material that is referred to in a text. Footnotes are additional comments, details or notes that the writer chooses to place outside the main stream of the account.

Footnotes at the bottom of the page are usually a sign that the writer has not thought out carefully what he or she wanted to say, or what importance to attach to each piece of information. Broadly speaking, if a piece of information is relevant to your readers' understanding of what is being said, that piece of information should be included within the main text, not slipped in at the bottom of the page. The placing of items at the bottom of the page is an irritating distraction to readers, especially when they find that there is *no* additional information in the footnote or that it is information they did not need. After skipping to the bottom of the page, readers have to go back to the main text, find the appropriate place and pick up the threads of the argument as best they can. If the information you are tempted to put at the bottom of the page will be useful to your readers, put it in the main text. If the information is not important enough to be included in the text itself, that information is probably not worth including anywhere.

We are not arguing that all information is of equal importance.

All writers occasionally find it helpful to offer their readers an 'aside' or parenthetical remark. But the most comfortable way to present such remarks is in parentheses, at least preserving the linear sequence for readers. Footnotes almost always introduce a sense of 'choppiness'. They should, therefore, be reserved for special circumstances.

Placing of illustrations

Sometimes, you may feel that you can make your points most clearly by using non-verbal techniques of presentation. If so, place your tables or illustrations as close as possible in the text to the point at which you want readers to refer to them.

This will cause difficulties when you are producing a text simply in typescript. You will not always be able to include your graph, diagram or picture in a convenient place in the text. It may be necessary to collect all your graphs and figures in an appendix or on several separate pages at the end of a section of your report. If you do this, remember to tell your reader where the illustrations are. You can also consider presenting your illustrations on fold-out pages, to minimize the amount of turning to and fro that the reader has to do. Or, if you dislike this lay-out because fold-out pages can get tattered, consider the possibility of using two spiral bindings, as shown in Fig. 4.6.

Beware of the temptation to include graphs and other illustrations in the body of your report simply because you have drawn them during the course of your work. Each time you are thinking about including an illustration, ask yourself whether that particular illustration will most effectively make the point you wish to press home to your reader. Are you being tempted to include the illustration simply to duplicate something that you have already said in words with adequate clarity? It is an irritating distraction for a reader to be encouraged to look at an illustration that provides no information in addition to that already in the prose text.

For example, one often reads statements such as 'the results show that as the temperature rose, the viscosity decreased, until at point X there was no further change. See Fig. 5'. The reader then dutifully looks at Fig. 5 and after a few moments' scrutiny can see that as the temperature rose, the viscosity decreased, until at point X there was no further change. The reader, having gained no additional information from looking at the illustration, has then to go back and find the place in the prose text, pick up the threads of the argument and go ahead. Concentra-

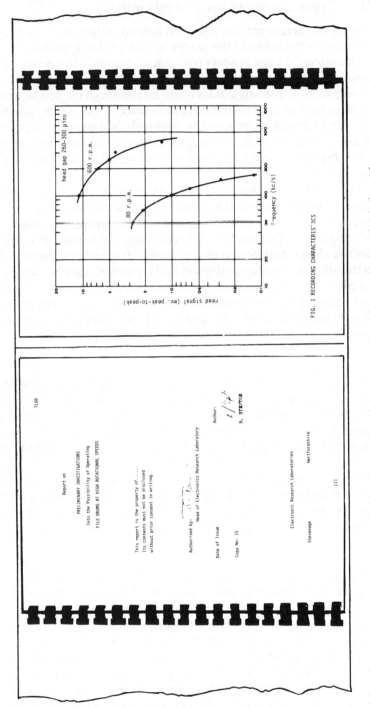

Fig. 4.6 Report with multiple spiral-bindings, allowing text and illustrations to be read side-by-side.

tion on the argument has not been helped, rather hindered, by the writer's direction of the reader to look at the illustration.

Of course, if your readers *can* gain additional information by looking at the illustration, for example by extrapolating beyond given points or readings, then it will be beneficial for you to urge them to look at the illustration; but beware of the temptation to provide illustrations in scientific and technical papers simply to 'make it look scientific', or simply to show that you have been assiduous in drawing graphs and making tables as your work progressed.

Remember, too, that there is a difference between tables and graphs that are designed to make a point in an argument, and tables and graphs that are designed to make available a mass of information so that readers can scrutinize it at leisure. We shall discuss choice and design of non-verbal material in Chapter 10. In this discussion of organization and lay-out of papers, we wish simply to emphasize that, wherever possible, masses of data and supporting illustrations are best placed in an appendix. Give your reader a smooth, uninterrupted passage through the argument or description in the body of your report.

Appendices   Use appendices, then, to clear supporting information out of the way of the readers' concentration on the main theme. Is it necessary to include in the main text the specifications for materials and equipment used? Is it necessary to include in the main text your inspection-test data? Do you need to include in the main text the mathematical calculations by which you derived formulae? Do you need to include start-up procedures? Most material of this sort can reasonably be placed in an appendix where it is available if necessary but where it will not interfere with the progress of readers who do not need it.

Structure for   This discussion has concentrated on structure for reports and
other types of   papers. The same structure, a pyramid starting with an incisive
documents   title, expanding gradually through a summary to the main story, and based on fully detailed appendices, normally works effectively for most other scientific and technical documents. In using the pyramid structure, you make it possible for readers to stop at various points on their way through the report, having accumulated as much as they need on their way up to that point. A well-written journal article makes it possible for readers

to do the same. It provides an effective, orienting title and summary. It then expands into full detail for those who want to know more about a procedure or survey method, or the advantages and disadvantages of various materials and activities. If the journal editor can find room for full details of matters such as specifications or experimental procedures, they are best left at the end for those readers whose interest continues to this level of detail.

Handbooks, instruction sheets, specifications, and most other technical documents benefit from the same structure. A well-written set of instructions preferably starts with a statement of the overall aim of the procedure or an outline of the various steps or stages in the instructions. A well-written handbook for maintenance of equipment preferably starts with an orienting section which at least describes the remainder of the text.

Sales documentation is not the subject of our advice in this book – it calls for special techniques. But if you have to write technical information documents to be used in conjunction with sales literature, remember that new information is what readers are interested in. They will not welcome a laborious repetition of first principles, known to everyone in the industry. Nor will they welcome having to wade through detailed descriptions of the mode of action of a type of machine they know very well. What *they do* want to know is how this particular product differs from familiar and established ones.

Other types of document include requests for capital, and recommendations for the purchase of machinery or services. Here, again, make sure readers know clearly *what* you want, before swamping them with details as to *why* you want it. Recognize that they may not want *full* details of all the alternatives, although they will need to be assured that you have checked all other possibilities before recommending one. However, they do not want to re-do your job, and go through all the possibilities again themselves. For example, if you have eight possibilities to choose from, by all means give brief details of all eight in an appendix. But in the text, dismiss most of them quickly on the basis of their obvious inadequacies, and discuss in detail only two or three. This gives the assurance of a realistic choice, without the confusion of too much detail.

Even documents which group information according to physical location or manufacturing procedures are most effective if the whole document (and probably each section within it) starts with a summarizing sentence or paragraph outlining what is to come. It is a basic tenet of all good communication that one starts by presenting an audience with some orientation material, an outline of the whole, before beginning to discuss the parts. Only in documents that aim at presenting a chronological account is it preferable to depart from an order of importance such as we have described; and even in such documents, it is probably best to start with some orienting information explaining why the historical account is being given.

We would boil down the advice in this Chapter to two main points. First, choose an order for your information which works from main points downwards to details, and not the other way. Second, always be flexible in your choice of organization and lay-out. Resist the temptation to categorise each writing task, and then to squeeze and distort the information into a recognized and stereotyped format. Choose your path through the facts you have to communicate with a careful eye on the readers' convenience. Each task requires an individual structure.

References   1. *The Penguin Encyclopedia*, ed. J. Summerscale (1965), London, p. 265.
2. *Chemical Engineering* (March, 1963), 196.

The use of headings and numbering 5

Usually, it helps if you make generous use of headings and sub-headings. Headings break text into manageable sections, and help by increasing the 'white space' around the blocks of type, especially when the type is single-spaced. They also act as signposts, pointing out what is to be found in each section. Formal headings such as *Problem*, or *Experimental*, or *Discussion* are neither informative nor useful, because they do not focus attention on the essence of the following paragraphs. Better headings, such as *Updating Operation Flow Charts* or *The Influence of Sunlight on Linings*, convey real information about the content of the section.

Formal and informative headings

In word-processed text, there are four ways in which the relative hierarchy of the headings can be shown:

- numbering;
- indenting;
- using capitals and lower case letters;
- bolding (use of heavy type).
  (In typewritten texts, underlining has to take the place of bolding.)

To ensure that readers grasp the relationships at a glance, documents that use all four systems are best.

The usual hierarchy of size and letter forms is:

1. **CAPITALS BOLDED** (OR UNDERLINED)
2. CAPITALS NOT BOLDED (OR UNDERLINED)
3. **Lower Case Bolded** (or underlined)
4. Lower case not bolded (or underlined)

A decimal numbering system helps further, but note the effect of the following layout:

7.   **FIRST LEVEL HEADING**
7.1.   SECOND LEVEL HEADING
7.1.1   **Third Level Heading**
7.2.1.2 Fourth level heading

Because a number like '7.2.1.2' is longer than the single '7' it seems more important. So it is preferable to use indenting as well, in order to complete the visual representation of the hierarchy of sections. Some writers (or their typists or managers) will not use indentation because they believe that progressively increasing left-hand margins wastes paper. We think that nothing is a waste of paper that helps the reader. In any case, if the indentation is only two or three spaces each time, the margins never get very wide. But if managers insist that indenting the text is wasteful, a good compromise is to indent the headings only, leaving all the text on the margin. The use of decimal numbering, differing weights of type, and indentation for the headings shows the reader the 'shape' of the information. Examples of an indented and a 'left-justified' (non-indented) system in a typescript are shown in Fig. 5.1 and 5.2.

Systems of Three systems of numbering are widely used in business,
numbering industrial and research writing:

- the decimal system;
- mixtures of numbers and letters;
- the HMSO system.

The *decimal system* is generally accepted as the clearest numbering system available. In this system, the headed sections and sub-sections only are numbered, not every paragraph. There can be any number of paragraphs in a section or sub-section.

When you have sub-divisions, your first sub-division number and heading should always come immediately after the division number and heading. Numbering to three or four places of decimals is usually a sign that grouping and sub-division of ideas need to be reviewed.

If you wish to set items in a list within your sub-sections, use simple numbers. Remember that the decimal numbering system is for *headings* only. Lists within sections are not headings, and

---

Fig. 5.1   Indented decimal numbering.

2. BASIC FACTORS AFFECTING MIX COSTS

2.1 Water

The water content of concrete is fundamental to all economic considerations. Concrete strength is directly related to the ratio of the weights of water and cement: consequently it may be possible to achieve a specified strength with a lean mix having a low water content. However a mix of this type may have a very low workability and the savings in material costs may be negated by increased plant and labour costs.

2.2 Cement

A specification may well contain a minimum cement content require-ment to ensure the durability of the concrete. In some cases this minimum cement content may be greater than that which would be required when considering compressive strength alone. The estimator must therefore read the specification or bill carefully and make appropriate adjustments to the cost estimate if a minimum cement content is called for. Ready-mixed concrete suppliers must also be informed of any such requirements before being asked to submit quotations.

2.3 Aggregates

2.3.1 Maximum sizes

The maximum size, particle shape and surface texture of aggregates have a major influence on workability and hence on the cement content of the concrete.

Aggregates for concrete are usually processed to comply with BS 882 : 1974[3] and full description of aggregates covering such character-istics as particle shape and surface texture are given in BS 812 : 1965[4].

Coarse aggregates, ie larger than 5mm in size, generally comprise gravels or crushed rock. Gravels are naturally occurring deposits of rounded or irregular particles having generally a smooth surface texture, whereas crushed rock is the product formed by the processing of bedrock formations and is usually angular in shape and of a rough texture.

Fine aggregates, which are smaller than 5mm in size, can be either a natural sand or a crushed rock fine.

2.3.2 Costs

The maximum size, particle shape and surface texture of aggregate affect the mix costs. A concrete mix containing an angular coarse aggregate with rough surface texture will require more water to produce a given workability than a smooth rounded gravel of similar size. The larger the maximum size of a coarse aggregate the less water is necessary but the maximum size selected depends on many factors such as reinforcement spacing and depth of cover.

THE USE OF HEADINGS AND NUMBERING

7.1 Formal and Informative Headings

Usually, it helps if you make generous use of headings and sub-headings. Headings break text into manageable sections, and help by increasing the "white space" around the blocks of type, especially when the type is single-spaced. They also act as signposts, pointing out what is to be found in each section.

Formal headings such as PROBLEM or EXPERIMENTAL or DISCUSSION are not as useful as informative headings that genuinely focus attention on the essence of the following paragraphs.

Emphasise the relative importance of the divisions and sub-divisions by careful use of capital and lower-case letters in your headings, and by moving successive sub-divisions further to the right.

Make your headings stand out from the text by underlining or by using a bold typeface.

7.2 Systems of Numbering

7.2.1 The range of systems available

Three systems of numbering are widely used in business, industrial and research writing in Britain:

1. the decimal system;
2. mixtures of numbers and letters;
3. the HMSO system.

7.2.2 The decimal system

The decimal system is generally accepted as the clearest available. In this system, the headed sections and sub-sections only are numbered, not every paragraph. There can be any number of paragraphs in a section or sub-section.

When you have sub-divisions, your first sub-division, number and heading should always come immediately after the division number and heading: there should be no paragraphs apparently floating unattached.

Numbering to three or four places of decimals is usually a sign that grouping and sub-divisions of ideas need to be reviewed.

If you wish to set items in a list within your sub-sections, use simple numbers (as in 7.2.1 above).

7.2.3 Mixtures of numbers and letters

Systems which mix Roman numerals, Arabic numerals and letters of the alphabet are often confusing:
" ...as in Section IV(g)3(ii) ..."

7.2.4 The HMSO system

Her Majesty's Stationery Office frequently numbers every paragraph of a text in a sequence from beginning to end. Headings are not numbered, but a sub-heading may be included in the first line of a paragraph. This system can be confusing when there is much mathematics in the text.

8 PRODUCTION OF TYPESCRIPT

Typists should take care that the typescript is produced with careful attention to the details of layout. The author's directions should be given a simple sequence of numbers or letters. an example of this is in section 7.2.1 of Fig. 5.1.

A numbering system which *mixes* Roman numerals, Arabic numerals and letters of the alphabet is often confusing: '. . . as in Section IV(g) 3(ii) . . .'

Her Majesty's Stationery Office (HMSO) in the UK frequently numbers every paragraph of the text in a sequence from beginning to end. Headings are not numbered and stand outside the paragraphing system, but a sub-heading may be included in the first line of the paragraph. This system can be confusing when there is much mathematics in the text.

The great virtue of the decimal system is that it constantly reminds readers of which major section they are in. A system which mixes Roman numerals and letters of the alphabet is often puzzling. Readers may arrive at a section labelled simply (g), but recall having read a section (g) a few moments ago; they become confused about how the information has been organized since that time and where they are now.

Fig. 5.2 Non-indented text with idented headings.

6 Algorithms for complex possibilities and procedures

Another aspect of organization which we wish to discuss separately is the need to arrange information physically so that readers can easily find their route through a mass of information that must be made available, but will not all be relevant to all readers. It is often necessary to present information which has complex inter-relations, and to show how those inter-relations can lead to various outcomes. Similarly, it is often necessary to explain that various combinations of conditions can produce a particular state (perhaps a fault), and to explain that various actions must be taken according to which conditions exist.

From reading tax guides or instruction manuals for equipment, we all know that prose accounts of this sort of information can be extraordinarily complex. They often read like conundrums. Though the sentences may be short and simple, the complexity of the relations is confusing, principally because we have to read about all the possible situations. Normally, however, readers are interested in only one set of conditions, and wish to know the outcome from these only. They want the information presented in a way that will help them sort out the possible relationships or conditions and isolate the set relevant to their interests.

In these circumstances, it is not enough just to 'present' the complex information – to make a mass of data available to any reader prepared to work through it. For effective communication, the writer must enable readers to find their way quickly and easily to the decisions they need, which means helping them to ignore information not relevant to them. The writer must make the right information available for use, yet make minimum demands on the readers' time and attention.

Often, the best way to meet these objectives when writing about procedures is to use an algorithm. An algorithm is a carefully planned sequence of statements, questions or instructions arranged in a logical hierarchy and requiring readers to read only the starting item and such subsequent items of information as are relevant to their needs.

The most common forms of algorithms in engineering and scientific work are list-form algorithms, flow-charts (logical trees) and MAP layouts (Maintenance Analysis Procedure – a format evolved by the IBM Corporation). All achieve the same purpose: they enable readers to concentrate on finding a clear path through a complex set of relationships or conditions by ignoring anything that does not apply to their situations. They

```
Before the adapter test can be carried out it is essential
to check that there is a gap of 0.13 to 0.25 mm between the
cardreader lamp and the optic surface at the bottom of the
lampholder screw-hole.

If there is no gap or if the gap is not within the specified
measurements, disconnect the cardreader lamp terminals, screw
the lamp out of the lampholder and inspect the optic surface
beneath the lampholder screw-hole for dirt, dust or damage.
If the optic surface is in good condition (shiny), the lamp can
be reinstalled, ensuring that the gap between the lamp and the
optic surface at the bottom of the lampholder screw-hole is
between 0.13 and 0.25 mm. Use a card strip to check this
gap. If the optic surface is dirty or dusty, clean the surface
with lintfree cloth (and alcohol if necessary) and then
reinstall the lamp, ensuring that the correct gap is present
between the lamp and the optic surface. If the optic surface
is not dirty or dusty but is in unsatisfactory condition for
some other reason, exchange the fibre optic assembly (see
Section 10 for procedure) and then reinstall the lamp, ensuring
that the correct lamp-to-surface gap is present.

When the lamp is reinstalled, reconnect the lamp terminals.
Then press the FAD button to signal that the cardreader is
ready for the adapter test.
```

Fig. 6.1 Prose account of a maintenance procedure.

1. Use a card strip to check the gap between
   the cardreader lamp and the optic surface.
   Is there a gap of 0.13 to 0.25 mm?   YES: Read 8
                                                    NO: Read 2

---

2. Disconnect cardreader lamp terminals.
   Screw lamp out of holder.
   Inspect optic surface beneath the lamp-
   holder screw-hole for dirt, dust or
   damage. Is the optic surface in good
   condition (shiny)   YES: Read 7
                                                    NO: Read 3

---

3. Is the optic surface damaged?   YES: Read 4
                                                    NO: Read 5

---

4. Exchange the fibre optic assembly
   (see Section 10 for procedure), then .... Read 7

---

5. Is the optic surface dirty or dusty?   YES: Read 6
                                                    NO: Read 7

---

6. Clean the optic surface with lintfree
   cloth (and alcohol, if necessary), then .... Read 7

---

7. Reinstall lamp.
   Use a card strip to ensure the gap between
   cardreader lamp and optic surface is
   between 0.13 and 0.25 mm.
   Reconnect lamp terminals, then .... Read 8

---

8. Press FAD button to signal that
   cardreader is ready for the adapter
   test.

Fig. 6.2 List-form algorithm for a maintenance procedure.

can usually be syntactically simpler than prose. They reduce distraction caused by unwanted information and reduce the load on memory because readers do not have to hold in mind previous questions or previous decisions.

Examples of a complex piece of prose, and of three algorithmic presentations of the same information are given in Figs. 6.1, 6.2, 6.3 and 6.4. The original prose text is shown in Fig. 6.1. The list form algorithm (Fig. 6.2) presents the same information using simple numbering. It is clear and to the point and takes less space than the flow chart or MAP layout. The need for the reader's eye to jump from item to item is, however, a disadvantage.

The flow chart algorithm (Fig. 6.3) is equally explicit but takes more time to prepare and more space in the document. It has, however, the advantage of using lines to guide the reader's eye from one item to the next. Also it can use different symbols (squares, rectangles, diamonds, circles) to emphasise the distinction between instructions, questions, comments and conclusions.

The MAP format (Fig. 6.4) is explicit and takes less space than a symbolic flow chart algorithm. It also has the great advantage that it can be produced entirely by typewriter. All the elements can be typed in from a normal alphanumeric keyboard. A disadvantage, however, is that it has less visual impact than a symbolic flow chart.[1]

Complex, inter-related items of information are almost always communicated most efficiently to scientific and technical readers if presented in flow charts or logical trees, but once again it is necessary to emphasise that the most suitable choice of communication tactics will depend on the aim, audience and context of the document you are writing. Research has shown that the speed and accuracy with which readers can find their way through complex information vary according to:

- whether each reader is able to decide easily which items of information are relevant and which irrelevant to his or her situation;
- whether there are so many interdependent contingencies that some display formats are automatically precluded.[2]

Wright and Reid explored the comparative effectiveness of presenting complex information in four ways – complex prose, a list of simple short sentences, a table, and a flow chart (the formats are shown in Fig. 6.5). Their main conclusion was that

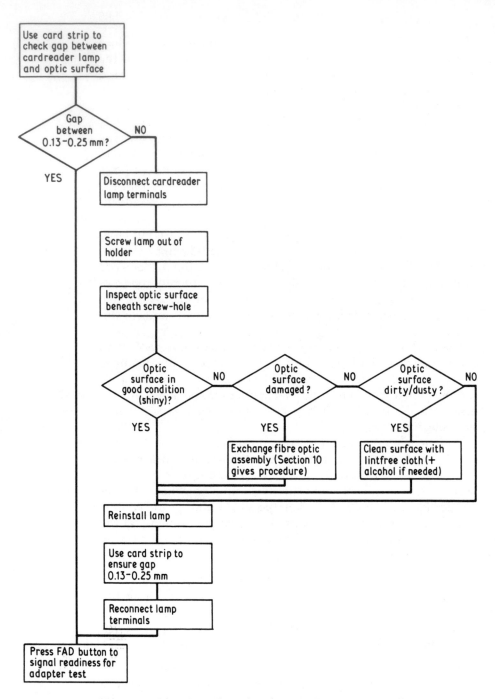

Fig. 6.3 Flow chart algorithm for a maintenance procedure.

```
01
Use a card strip to check the
gap between the cardreader
lamp and the optic surface

IS THERE A GAP
OF 0.13-0.25 mm?
Y    N
'    02
'    - Disconnect cardreader
'      lamp terminals
'    - Screw lamp out of holder
'    - Inspect optic surface
'      beneath screw-hole for
'      damage, dirt or dust
'
'    - IS THE OPTIC SURFACE IN
'      GOOD CONDITION (SHINY)?
'    Y    N
'    '    03
'    '    IS THE OPTIC
'    '    SURFACE DAMAGED?
'    '    Y    N
'    '    '    04
'    '    '    IS THE OPTIC SURFACE
'    '    '    DIRTY OR DUSTY?
'    '    '    Y    N
'    '    '    '    05
'    '    '    '    GO TO STEP 08
'    '    '    06
'    '    '    - Clean the optic surface
'    '    '      with lintfree cloth
'    '    '      (and alcohol, if needed)
'    '    '
'    '    '    - GO TO STEP 08
'    '    07
'    '    - Exchange the fibre optic
'    '      assembly (see section 10
'    '      for procedure)
'    '
'    '    - GO TO STEP 08
'    08
'    - Reinstall lamp
'    - Use card strip to ensure gap
'      between lamp and optic surface
'      is 0.13-0.25 mm
'    - Reconnect lamp terminals
'
'    - GO TO STEP 09
09
Press FAD button to signal
readiness for adapter test
```

Fig. 6.4 MAP layout for a maintenance procedure.

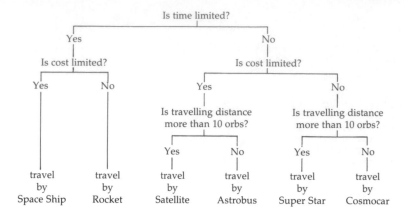

FLOWCHART – LOGICAL TREE

The Prose passage was intended to approximate the traditional bureaucratic style and read as follows:

When time is limited, travel by Rocket, unless cost is also limited, in which case go by Space Ship. When only cost is limited an Astrobus should be used for journeys of less than 10 orbs, and a Satellite for longer journeys. Cosmocars are recommended, when there are no constraints on time or cost, unless the distance to be travelled exceeds 10 orbs, when time and cost are not important, journeys should be made by Super Star.

PROSE

The list of short sentences was set out as follows:

Where only time is limited
    travel by rocket.
Where only cost is limited
    travel by satellite if journey more than 10 orbs.
    travel by astrobus if journey less than 10 orbs.
Where both time and cost are limited
    travel by space ship.
Where time and cost are not limited
    travel by super star if journey more than 10 orbs.
    travel by cosmocar if journey less than 10 orbs.

SENTENCES

	If journey less than 10 orbs	If journey more than 10 orbs
Where only time is limited	travel by Rocket	travel by Rocket
Where only cost is limited	travel by Astrobus	travel by Satellite
Where time and cost are not limited	travel by Cosmocar	travel by Super Star
Where both time and cost are limited	travel by Space Ship	travel by Space Ship

TABLE

details of the user's background experience and situation influence the relative effectiveness of the different formats. For example:

> . . . in a handbook, such as a car maintenance handbook which is to be used by trained technicians, the table may well be a more appropriate format than the flow chart. The technician's training may enable him to distinguish relevant from irrelevant factors. However, that same handbook, conveying exactly the same information, may nevertheless be better as a logical tree if it is being used on a do-it-yourself basis by the homespun car mechanic.[3]

These findings emphasize the need for writers to choose their visual tactics with as much thought about their aim and audience as they use in choosing their verbal tactics. Chapter 10 discusses visual communication in more detail.[4]

References

1. Adams, Neil, (1978) Flow Charts Versus MAPS: Which format is more efficient as an aid to fault-finding? *The Communicator of Scientific and Technical Information*, **35**, 3–4.
2. See Wright, Patricia and Reid, F. (1974) Written Information: Some alternatives to prose for expressing the outcome of complex contingencies *Journal of Applied Psychology*, **57**, 160–166.
3. Wright, Patricia, (1977) Behavioural Research and the Technical Communicator, *The Communicator of Scientific and Technical Information*, **32**, 5.
4. See also Lewis, B.N., Horabin, I.S. and Gave, C.P. (1967) Flow Charts, Logical Trees and Algorithms for Rules and Regulations *CAS Occasional Papers*, **2**, HMSO, London.

Fig. 6.5   The four formats which were compared in a study of ways of presenting complex information (reproduced by permission of Dr P. Wright).

7 Style for readability

The word 'style' is usually associated with literary writing. We are conscious that to offer to discuss style will remind many of our readers of school poetry lessons; but to have style in the sense we use in this chapter does not mean to be 'florid' or 'ornate': it is to adapt the language code to particular ends. Language can be used for a variety of purposes; it can, among other things, announce or warn (notices), instruct (operating instructions), persuade (advertising), and inform (reports and articles). What is *efficient* in writing can be measured only in relation to the purpose of the writing. If the purpose is to give pleasure, then attractiveness becomes one of the criteria of the efficient manipulation of the code; but if the purpose is to warn or to instruct, then notices like 'Keep off the grass' are admirable. They manipulate the resources of the code to achieve their ends. In other words they have good style.

There is a distinction between imaginative literature (with which the idea of style is usually associated) and functional writing.[1] We are concerned in this Chapter solely with effective style for the communication of information; what is efficient for this context is what is clearest and quickest. Elegance may or may not be a by-product; but it can never be an intention. Style for functional writing should be unobtrusive, an invisible medium, like a window pane through which the information can be clearly seen.[2] Of course, lapses from good taste, or unacceptable usage, can be unfunctional, in that they disturb and distract the reader. But equally distracting is any usage where the motivation is display or ornamentation, rather than clarity.

Effective style will contain a variety of structures and usages, and will not ban any feature of the language code. Our experience is that the poor quality of much scientific and technical writing is the result not of misguided attempts at stylishness, but of attempts to use only a restricted set of choices from the language code. Much writing is tedious because it restricts itself to passive, roundabout and impersonal constructions, and to a Latinate vocabulary. We shall not be arguing that any of these types of structure or vocabulary should be banned. But if they are used to the exclusion of many other constructions, they gradually become blunt and tasteless. If a particular feature is used exclusively, its contrastive effect disappears, and less meaning is perceived. Too many writers fail to vary their manipulation of the code; their flexibility is limited.

We would diagnose this lack of flexibility and variety as the major cause of the indigestibility of much writing. Sadly, readers get used to leaden scientific idiom. They get used to digging for meaning in the heavy soil of scientific prose; they even get inured to supplying a meaning where vapid abstraction leaves none obviously available. Sadly also, writers feel more secure if they restrict themselves to traditional phrasing and vocabulary. A stiff and formal style, lacking variety and comfort, seems to them to suit scientific truth. We hope in this chapter to show that such an unadventurous usage of the language code is unnecessary and unproductive.

Many books on writing stress that scientific style must be simple, clear and concise. Indeed our readers, most of whom must have heard such advice at some time, might be forgiven for thinking that there was nothing else to say. We intend to offer both reason and example to support our advice. We shall look first at the factors which underpin advice on effective style, and then in detail at the ways in which the language code can be handled to achieve the aim of comfortable, readable writing.

Readability research

Much research has been done to discover what it is that makes some pieces of writing more difficult to read than others. It is everyone's experience that some writing – for instance a Harold Robbins novel – is so easy to read it can be difficult to put down. But some writing is so difficult to read that as we push ourselves through it we develop a headache. Too many textbooks and scientific papers fall into the second category. There are also, of course, types of writing which fall between these two extremes.

If we want writing to be as efficient as possible, we should make reading as easy as possible, for papers that present extra barriers between their message and their readers are obviously inefficient. Equally important, they are unlikely to get promotion for the person who wrote them. It will not be his or her discoveries that the scientific community uses and is grateful for.

Each of us would like his or her writing to be readable; but how should we go about ensuring this? The first stage in acquiring an effective and readable style is to understand the factors which contribute to unreadable writing. Much work has been done on the measurement of readability.[3] We do not want to write a thesis on the linguistic discipline of stylistics (as the science of style is called), but in the following sections discussing factors that influence readability, we have tried to give brief justifications for our assertions. We give details of a well-known readability formula in the appendix.

Writer, text and reader   In analysing the factors which affect readability, we can distinguish three components: writer, text and readers. First, the writer, principally by careful selection of material, by organization, signposting and variation of emphasis, affects the readability of the text. If the writer's choices accurately reflect the interests, needs and prior knowledge of the readers, the text is more likely to be readable. Second, the text itself affects readability. Both the language (structures and vocabulary) and the physical appearance (layout, headings, white space) contribute to the efficiency of the communication. Third, the readers' motivation and attitudes contribute to their responses to the text. For example, someone with a bet on the Derby finds the racing results highly readable, though they are hardly a model of prose for report writing.

Clearly, whether readers find what they expect to find in a text affects their attitudes, and therefore the text's readability. Here, good titling and signposting will help improve the overall readability. If readers are clearly warned what to expect, and are shown frequent signposts along the way, they are unlikely to stumble over incorrect ideas about what the text is saying. The readers' mental states will also affect readability. The writer may be able to do little about distractions or tiredness, but he or she can reduce their impact. By making a text more readable, the writer reduces fatigue during reading and avoids irritating readers by inflated choices of language.

We shall not concern ourselves with questions of interest and motivation. On the whole, most scientific and technical writing is read because reading it is part of a job. Consequently, we may assume that, on average, most readers have broadly similar motivation when reading functional writing. For practical purposes, interest remains constant. Other factors become therefore more important in determining a text's readability.

Readability research shows that long sentences make texts more difficult for readers to absorb. Almost all readers experience this, although they may not identify its cause. Many readers are so generous that they attribute their growing discomfort to lack of concentration or ability. They may also think that a difficult subject, rather than a difficult style makes their task so unpalatable. But the effect of sentence length on readability is indisputable. Try reading this sentence:

Long sentences

> The coil pump supplies eluent phase at column pressure to the injection valve by way of a cut off valve activated by either a power failure or by a digital output from the computer, the digital output operating a relay switching the electrical supply to the valve, which has two solvent ($5\mu l$) passages and is arranged such that the eluent phase can flow through one whilst the sample passes through the other, injection being achieved by switching the slide valve by a pneumatic controller operated by means of a signal switch from the timer unit of the Cecil sample charger.

We doubt if many readers can grasp this without reading it through more than once. Yet it is not the technical content that is the source of difficulty, and only the word 'eluent' is likely to be unfamiliar to most technical audiences. It is the encoding, rather than the content, which causes difficulty.

Long sentences are difficult because of the way in which we read. After reading a paragraph of text, we do not remember every word, but retain ideas, facts and images. Yet as we read a sentence, we probably retain each word until we get to the full stop; only then can we confidently decode the sentence as a unit. What happens is that our short-term memory retains all the words until it can extract the content and store it more permanently in a longer-term memory. Our short-term memory for words is necessarily limited. Long sentences, such as the example we just used, overfill the short-term memory and the information is lost. As more and more words are crammed into an interminable sentence, the words we read at the beginning are forgotten.

Observe what readers do when a sentence is too long. Most go back to the beginning again, and start to re-read; but they usually do not re-read the whole sentence. They simply refresh their memory of the opening part of the sentence. If readers are in a hurry, they will not spare time to go back to the beginning of every long sentence; they take a guess at the meaning, and carry on. In this way, a fog of uncertainty builds up in their minds, and they end up with an incomplete and erroneous idea of what the text was about. All readers find continuous reading of long sentences a strain. The writer continually makes maximum, and sometimes unreasonable, demands on their short-term memories; gradually they get tired, and concentration lapses. The writer of long sentences risks making readers inattentive.

Adjusting sentence length Many writers feel that long sentences are inevitable if complex interactions have to be expressed. This is a mistake. Any subject can be broken up into longer or shorter items of information at will, and the determining factor is how much the reader can comfortably absorb, not how much information is 'logically' joined together. All the information on a complex subject is logically connected, and could therefore in theory be expressed in one sentence. It never is, because such a sentence would not *communicate*. Sentence length should be determined by what the reader can effectively decode. An example is the following sentence:

> It seems possible that the adrenergic – cholinergic antagonism may be mediated through the adenyl–cyclase system, since it is known that whereas noradrenaline increases the synthesis of cyclic AMP, acetyl choline inhibits this process, thus the acetyl choline liberated at vagal endings may decrease the quantity of noradrenaline released at postganglionic terminals and also decrease the accelerated rate of cyclic AMP synthesis in myocardial cells initiated by noradrenaline liberated during sympathetic neural activity.

For most readers this will be an unfamiliar and technical subject; it is also an enormous sentence. The writer doubtless thought that the idea expressed was all one, and certainly the logical connectors make it appear so. The logical 'bones' of the sentence are:

> It seems possible that . . . since it is known that . . . thus the . . . may decrease the . . . and also decrease the . . . in . . .

but the technical terminology with which this logical skeleton is clothed makes the sentence far too large for readers. The logic is not disturbed if the argument is broken up into stages, and sentence boundaries (and consequent breathing spaces) are provided at each small step in the argument:

It seems possible that the adrenergic–cholinergic antagonism may be mediated through the adenyl–cyclase system. It is known that noradrenaline increases the synthesis of cyclic AMP. It is also known that acetyl choline inhibits this process. Thus the acetyl choline liberated at vagal endings may decrease the quantity of noradrenaline released at postgang-lionic terminals. It may also decrease the accelerated rate of AMP synthesis in myocardial cells. This increase is initiated by noradrenaline liberated during sympathetic neural activity.

This is hardly any longer, and certainly quicker in terms of actual reading time, since it requires less back-tracking. The content remains as complex as before, but the encoding of the information does not now increase the complexity to a point at which even experts blench.

It is usually an easy matter to break down long sentences into more manageable ones. Look for connecting words, the logical 'glue' between the groups of technical words, and break the sentence at these points. Words like 'and', 'but', 'if', 'also' are often points at which the sentence can be stopped, and restarted with a pronoun like 'it'.

Flexible sentence length

What is a 'long' sentence? How many words are too many? To lay down a dogmatic length for sentences would clearly be against our advice to be flexible in the use of the resources of the language code. But it is useful to consider the problem of length in more detail. Read this sentence:

While care must be taken not to act against the provisions of the law, nevertheless certain steps can be taken to further the interests of the IBH group, and a number of discussions were held on this topic with members of IBH, Holland, and the ideas contributed by all personnel should be analysed and formed into a commercial policy which is then communicated up and down the IBH selling team so that the tactics followed by the manager, representatives, technical and administrative team follow the same lines.

Although the technical content is not so daunting, this sentence is a mind-full. We might re-write it into shorter sentences:

> Care must be taken not to act against the provisions of the law. Nevertheless certain steps can be taken to further the interests of the IBH group. A number of discussions were held on this topic with members of IBH, Holland. The ideas contributed by all personnel should be analysed. They should be formed into a commercial policy. This should then be communicated up and down the IBH selling team. This is so that the tactics followed by the manager, representatives, technical and administrative team follow the same lines.

Most readers find this 'bitty' to read. The flow of the information is constantly arrested by full-stops, and there is an uncomfortably jerky feeling. There are two reasons why such writing is not a good solution to making a text readable.

First, short sentences of similar lengths become monotonous. Readers are sensitive to repetition, whether of words, structures, ideas, or sentence lengths. Variety is valuable since it aids attention, and makes reading more interesting, so sentence lengths should vary in order to make ever-varying demands on the reader. A simple idea should be a chance to write a simple sentence. In particular, important, startling, and major facts or ideas should have simple sentences. This emphasizes their importance, and makes it easier for the reader to grasp. Thus:

> The scripset process is located at present in building 20. Raw-material and final product tankers use the road at two per week, but expansion of the plant and a higher proportion of bulk product customers will greatly affect this. Eventually, access could limit production. However, building 5 is in a far less congested area and no problems are expected with road traffic.

Access for road tankers is the deciding argument for using building 5 rather than building 20. The encoding of the information underlines this in a way which makes it easier for the reader to grasp the importance of the point.

The second reason why use of too many short sentences is undesirable is related to the complexity of the information. The passage on adrenaline contained many technical terms, and a simpler sentence structure gave more time to absorb these unfamiliar words. The passage on selling had few technical terms, and so larger sentences could be managed. The unloading rate was too high in one example, too low in the other. Thus the complexity of the information affects the length of the sentence it can be encoded in. The following sentence is not very long, but it is unmanageable because of the amount of detail:

> Crystals were grown as hexagonal plates, up to 300 μm × 100 μm thick by vapour diffusion of 2.1 M-ammonium sulphate, in tris-acetate buffer (pH 7.0), in the presence of 0.01 M-Mg as described by Rein *et al.* (1973).

Such a mass of information requires several sentences to be communicated effectively. The writer must decide if the material is familiar or new to the readers. Will they find it easy to grasp, or will it strike them as complex, and require great effort? How important is it? Will the readers need to grasp all the detail, or do they need only the overall outline? Is the information repetitive, or is it information the reader has not met before in the same passage? Does the logic of the ideas flow easily, or are there a series of complex interacting ideas? All these factors will determine how long a sentence the reader can comfortably decode. Anything unfamiliar, complex, and new will require stating in shorter sentences, while a review of familiar information can be coded in longer sentences. Here, by contrast, is an example of information which is not in itself complex, but which is unmanageable because of the way in which it is presented:

> Both sets of costs are lower than the forecast made in April 1972, since more steam was available for the turbo-alternator than was anticipated because production of nitric acid and sulphuric acid was higher than forecast and space heating requirements were lower than forecast, but less steam from Ableton boilers would have been required to keep the turbo-alternator fully loaded.

The reader has to remember a complex series of interacting relations: 'lower, more, higher, lower, less.' The demands are too great, and communication fails. The complexity of the content, in the broadest sense and from the readers' point of view, determines the comfortable length of the sentences. Complicated information should be in shorter sentences.

Where the information is complex, there are many other techniques of presentation available to the writer, besides changing sentence length. The full-stop breaks up information in a way

Using layout

which the eye recognizes. Paragraph breaks, headings, indentation, and other devices of layout act in a similar way. Where information does not fit comfortably into a sentence structure, the layout code can provide additional aids. This sentence is awkward for the reader as it stands:

> It is clear that the decay curve is a sum probably of two exponentials, a slower phase with a half time ($\tau_{1/2}$) of 4 minutes and representing 85% of the total decay – calculated from the intercept 1.15 which is where it would have been expected to originate if the fast phase were infinitely fast, and a smaller fast phase which has a $\tau_{1/2}$ of less than 30 seconds.

It can be laid out more conveniently in this way:

> It is clear that the decay curve is a sum probably of two exponentials:
>
> 1. a slower phase with a half time ($\tau_{1/2}$) of 4 minutes and representing 85% of the total decay (calculated from the intercept 1.15 which is where it would have been expected to originate if the fast phase were infinitely fast);
> 2. a smaller fast phase which has a $\tau_{1/2}$ of less than 30 seconds.

Notice that the extra white space, the list form, the underlining, and the brackets are all used to make what is still one sentence more understandable.

Sentence length and structure are important influences on readability. Because readers cannot retain large numbers of words at once, sentences must be manageable; but what is manageable depends on the complexity and density of the information and the reader's familiarity with it. Flexibility and variety in sentence length makes writing easier to read, and shorter sentences make complex, important, and arresting information stand out. Intelligent use of sentence length and structure is an important ingredient of effective style for informative writing.

Long words   The second factor that affects readability is the use of long and unfamiliar words. We must define what we mean by long words. Some words with many syllables are quite familiar – for instance 'electricity'. It is the unfamiliarity of a word in combination with its length which makes it less easy to read. Linguists have made word lists which list the frequency with which words occur. The word 'and' in one study occurred on average once every 47 words, whereas words such as 'purpose' once every 1172 words.[4] Words such as 'epistemology' occur very infrequently in ordinary language, and many readers do not understand them. Words which are infrequently used are likely to be unfamiliar; they are less easy to read for that reason. The mental pathways which decode familiar words are well-worn, but unfamiliar words make us pause very briefly, and leave a sense of extra strain in the overall effort of decoding the message.

Writing which uses long, unfamiliar words is more difficult to read:

> This work has involved the acquisition of skills and techniques required when working with . . .

Words like 'involve', 'acquisition' and 'required' are longer than are needed to do the job. The writer could have written more readably:

> In this work we have learned new ways of working with . . .

In a short example the difference is small, but when these longer words are repeated in sentence after sentence, the feeling of struggling through a morass builds up:

> The choice between alternatives must of course be influenced by the reliability of the factors which affect the savings predicted. It may be difficult to make satisfactory 'pot mend' repairs to vessels and more extensive temporary repairs could reduce sales realization in 1979, a factor which adversely affects scheme two. Also this type of limitation is more likely to be apparent in the second year . . .

The writer of this passage is inconsiderate of readers' efforts and patience. This style takes risks with readers' attention. Even more seriously, it risks readers' distaste. Words like 'alternatives', 'influenced', 'adversely', 'apparent' are not in themselves unusual, but strung together they build up an air of pompous preening. The writer sounds like a show-off; and this naturally irritates readers, especially when it is done at the expense of their convenience in decoding the information they need. So to avoid this impression, go for the simpler word. Not:

> . . . the stability of the metal-carbon bond is <u>enhanced</u> by co-ordination . . .

But:

> . . . co-ordination improves the stability of the metal carbon bond . . .

Not:

> . . . the gas cell <u>exhibits</u> an absorption profile with a 'Lamb' dip . . .

But:

> . . . the gas cell has an absorption profile with a 'Lamb' dip . . .

Long words do not impress Many unusual words are chosen by writers for the air of intellectuality they give to the writing. Yet such words are often awkward and distracting:

> . . . with <u>adequate ancillary</u> labour to <u>assist</u> . . . (. . . with enough extra labour to help . . .)

> The <u>precise mechanism</u> responsible for this antagonism cannot be <u>elucidated</u> . . .

> (We do not know what causes this antagonism . . .)

Readers are usually *not* impressed by such words.

These words are not objectionable because readers cannot understand them. First, they are objectionable because they are more difficult to decode: they take longer, and consume more mental energy because they are relatively unfamiliar. Second, they create an atmosphere of overformality.

Writers sometimes use words so unfamiliar that many readers find decoding them genuinely troublesome. They have to search their memory for the meaning, and may come up with ambiguous, or incorrect guesses:

> When the lines are symmetrically placed about the centre of the gain curve, the <u>perturbations</u> in frequency usually disappear.

> Burn and Rand have provided evidence for their <u>postulation</u> that . . .

> These results indicate that it is possible for calves . . . to become <u>refractory</u> to reinfection.

Are 'perturbations' small or large movements? Is a 'postulation' a guess, a hypothesis, or an adamant claim? Does 'refractory' mean resist slightly, or totally, or is it a place where monks eat? Before you reach for a dictionary, or smile with satisfaction at your own knowledge, remember that the case we are arguing is not that all readers will misunderstand these words. It is that *some* of them *may*. Even if most readers eventually understand, areas of uncertainty will remain; and virtually all readers find reading texts which contain such words more difficult. We are not arguing that these words should be banned from use; indeed we do not believe that any of the resources of language should be banned. We are arguing that they should be used only when required. Such words are rarely used in everyday language, and they should remain so. Where no other words will convey the exact meaning, then they have a place, but where familiar, everyday words are available to do the same job, the everyday words should be used.

Why do writers use long and unfamiliar words? Clearly, it is not in order to contribute to the convenience and comfort of their readers; readers find simple writing more readable. We have formed the opinion, from talking to many writers of reports in industry, that writers use long words for two reasons: to confuse and to impress.

Long words confuse

Long words often confuse readers. The precise meaning of each word may not be clear. The words may be high-order generalizations which have no single concrete meaning, but cover a large number of related activities. Thus 'assay' can mean to measure, estimate, weigh, analyse, try the purity of, or to attempt. By using this word, rather than any of the more exact descriptions available, a writer leaves his or her exact activities surrounded with an aura of mystery. The writer may hope to gain respect, feeling that it will be difficult for readers to criticize the work, simply because they have not been given enough clear information about it. But the advantages for readers are nil, and it is likely that the writer will produce precisely the opposite to the hoped-for effect.

Long words are also used in the hope of impressing readers. Perhaps at one time they did do so, but this time is long past.[5] In the Middle Ages, educated people spoke Latin to each other when discussing intellectual matters. They had a separate language for what they saw as a separate activity; it marked them off from everyone else, and was the badge of the educated man.

Because of the history of the language, English has two words for many things, one of Latin origin, one of Anglo-Saxon origin. 'Initiate' is of Latin origin, 'start' is Anglo-Saxon; 'commence' is of Latin origin, 'begin' is Anglo-Saxon; 'terminate' is Latin in origin, 'end' is Anglo-Saxon. Since the end of the Middle Ages, educated people have not spoken Latin, but the influence of Latin on the language has meant that they have had available a Latinate vocabulary in English. This Latin vocabulary was associated with intellectual life; it was also often not understood by uneducated people. By contrast, the Anglo-Saxon vocabulary was associated with common people. It was therefore possible to acquire the reputation for being educated, intellectual, or 'clever' by using a Latinate vocabulary. Indeed, for many this was the only way of appearing clever. Renaissance doctors could probably do very little for their patients, but by using intellectual-sounding Latin names for things, they reassured their clients, and earned large fees. We regret to say that the attempt to acquire a spurious reputation for knowledge by using Latinate words persists in many professions.

Our advice to writers is that this Latinate vocabulary no longer has the effect they want, nor is it a sensible way of communicating information. In the first place, readers are no longer impressed by Latinate writing. The research we reported at the end of Chapter 1 shows that simple writing is more impressive. Most readers react against the inflated and pompous atmosphere created by a Latinate vocabulary. They are disturbed by the suspicion of pretence; they are repelled by the unpleasant verbosity; they are doubtful of the honesty of a writer who needs such camouflage. In the second place, much technical information is so complex and impressive that there is no need to wrap it in flowery language. When professional people had little to say, they needed the cloak of intellectual-sounding language. Modern sciences and technologies are impressive enough in themselves; they do not need any adornment.

Jargon   The advice to avoid long and unfamiliar words is not a ban on jargon. Jargon is a short and convenient way to name new ideas and concepts. The phrase 'update' seems to us an excellent and brief way to say 'to revise and edit so as to bring up to date'. New ideas or new objects need names, and a new name is better than a long string of old ones. But technical words are often

used not for these reasons, but to create a spurious impressiveness:

> Each task is assigned a maximum period of time, or time
> quantum, for which it may run.

The word 'quantum' adds nothing to the content, and disturbs
the readers' trust in the writer's good intentions. A similar
'buzz-word' flavour surrounds this:

> The Scheduler, then, has to perform the dual-capability of
> scheduling timesharing tasks and real-time tasks.
> (The Scheduler, then, has to schedule both timesharing and real-time
> tasks.)

The compound 'dual-capability' adds nothing. Often a simple
idea is made to *sound* sophisticated by the unnecessary use of a
jargon word.

> Consideration should be given to the interface of the suite
> with the customer's main complex.

This was not part of a computer manual, nor even instructions
to a tailor measuring a gentleman's trousers; it was instructions
to a planner about siting rooms. Jargon used in this way is not
only unhelpful: it positively impedes communication by the
stumbling block it creates to both comprehension and trust.

Jargon words are sometimes added entirely unnecessarily:

> . . . the dilutions follow sequentially down the series . . .

where the word 'series' makes the word 'sequentially' redundant.

Mathematical terms are often candidates for thoughtless use.
The phrase 'of the order of' is used as a synonym for 'about' in
sentences such as, 'the result was of the order of 3 minutes'.
Used exactly, this means 'between 1–9 minutes' which is the
same order as 3. The next order (if we were working in powers
of ten) would be 10–99, and so on. But this quite precise
mathematical meaning is lost in the thoughtless use. The misuse
of jargon blunts a useful tool by depriving it of its exact meaning
and making it simply another synonym for a short familiar
word.

Misused jargon, especially where it is derived from everyday
language, can often lead to thoughtlessly funny statements:

> To end a terminal session, the user logs out . . .

A 'terminal session' is not the last big shoot-out in a Western, but a period of work at a computer terminal. Writers become so inured to the implications of the jargon that they cease to observe the more normal meanings of words.

Jargon, then, is an important resource; technical communication would be cumbersome and inefficient without it. But writers are often tempted to use it for wrong reasons, and seek to obtain spurious credibility from sounding 'clever' at the expense of their reader's time and patience. Where jargon is used aggressively, carelessly and unnecessarily, it impedes communication; where it is devalued it reduces the resources of the code. Wherever it is used without having a specific and real function in the communication of the message, it reduces readability, without offering any compensating gains.

Ladders of abstraction

Long, unfamiliar words are often highly abstract, and fail to communicate because they embrace too many different meanings. Readers are not able to decode clear ideas or images; they are left confused, unable to settle on a specific picture of the action involved. More mental energy is used in searching the 'file' for possibilities, and less information is extracted. Imprecise communication is made in:

> . . . and no adverse interactions have been seen . . .

The phrase 'adverse interactions' covers everything from a bar fight to a chemical explosion. A writer on economics complains of:

> The regressiveness and anomalies caused by the export duty and surcharge . . .

but leaves readers with no clear picture of what these 'regressiveness and anomalies' are in specific terms. There are hierarchies of increasingly abstract and general terms. For examples, names such as:

> Construction
> Building
> Dwelling
> House

Each term higher on the list covers a larger area.

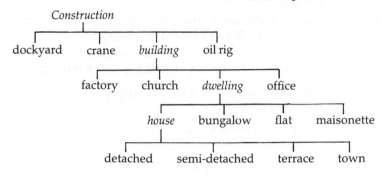

This hierarchy is called a 'ladder of abstraction'. Sometimes it is *necessary* to rise towards the top of this ladder; abstract words exist because they are a convenient shorthand to compress many particular ideas into one general statement.[6]

But abstract words are less easy to decode because the reader has to 'scan' all the possibilities subconsciously before deciding on a specific meaning. Because science often deals in generalized concepts, it is familiar with abstract words. Where these are necessary, there can be no objection to their use, but to use such abstractions where there is a more accurate, concrete word available adds unnecessarily to the readers' burden.

Unnecessary words

Phrases as well as words are often chosen for their impressive sound and massive weight rather than for brevity and clarity. We distinguish the use of unnecessary or repetitious words, and the use of whole phrases where single words will do.

Unnecessary words often repeat an idea which is already expressed in another word, and thus waste space and blunt the message. At first glance, the following phrases have an aura of technicality:

> Insert the electrodes and, stirring mechanically, titrate potentiometrically . . .
> Calculate the end-point mathematically . . .

But even an inattentive reader feels uncomfortable, since the only form of stirring is 'mechanical', just as the only form of 'calculation' normally used is 'mathematical'. A familiar example of the same looseness is:

> Potential hazards must be identified and examined . . .

Since a hazard is a potential danger, the words 'potential

hazard' support each other uneasily; 'hazards' will do duty alone, and witnesses a firmer grasp of meaning.

Simple adjectives are often turned into longer phrases by the addition of spare nouns which add nothing to the meaning:

> . . . they are not normally of a critical <u>nature</u> . . .
> (. . . they are not normally critical . . .)

> . . . ribbon showed surface roughness to a bad <u>degree</u> . . .
> (. . . ribbon showed bad surface roughness . . .)

Other words which add nothing are 'located' in:

> . . . the control room should be <u>located adjacent</u> to the scanner room . . .
> (. . . the control room should be adjacent to the scanner room . . .)

or 'visibly' in:

> . . . especially when the farmer can <u>visibly</u> see the tapeworm segments . . .
> (. . . especially when the farmer can see the tapeworm segments . . .)

Words are added which are redundant because the opposite is impossible:

> . . . the error signal is <u>suitably</u> processed . . .

Is it likely that a procedure would be designed to process the signal *un*suitably? Such words subtract from the impact of the message.

Redundant words   Sometimes writers use several words for ideas which can be expressed more clearly in one:

> This is done <u>by means of</u> inserting a Fogarty 3F arterial embolectomy catheter . . . <u>resulting in exposure</u> of the subendothelial layer.
> (This is done by inserting a Fogarty 3F arterial embolectomy catheter . . . exposing the subendothelial layer)

The phrases 'by means of' and 'resulting in' add nothing to the information in the sentence, but they do add to its length. The more economical the encoding of the message, in general, the clearer the meaning. One writer laboriously explained:

> <u>The reason for this increase</u> in tissue levels was <u>probably due</u> to de-novo biosynthesis.

instead of simply saying:

> Tissue levels increased, probably because of de-novo biosynthesis.

Another writer declared:

> If problems arise in your office <u>with regards to the completion of the CNF</u>. . .

instead of:

> If your office has problems completing the CNF . . .

Roundabout phrasing, instead of direct and simple expression, can lead to statements of elaborate tortuousness:

> He had a complaint from a customer to the effect that on consuming a drink which happened to contain Autoflav irritation of the mouth had been experienced.
> (A customer complained that a drink which contained Autoflav had irritated his mouth.)

Long-winded phrases are especially common in time references. Perhaps because we must say simple things like 'before', and 'after', and 'now' so often, the writer misguidedly looks for variety. A financial analyst once observed that the stock market can do only two things: rise or fall; but this simple fact is celebrated in a plethora of poetic metaphors. The same urge to elaborate can affect writers when they have to say 'now':

> We are at the present time in communication with the Board regarding the scheme to . . .

Or 'several times':

> On a number of occasions during the summer it was necessary to restrict or stop production . . .

Or 'soon':

> <u>Within a comparatively short period</u> they will need 15 tonnes per month . . .

Simple prepositions are often elaborated into longer phrases; for example 'near' in:

> No concentration of penthane was detected <u>in the immediate vicinity</u> of the machine.

The constant use of unnecessarily long phrases adds to the

burdens on the reader; the length of the document increases, and so does the mental effort needed to decode it. The overall impression is one of flabby wandering, rather than incisive thinking. The simplest word which will communicate the meaning accurately is the best choice for both writer and reader.

Nominaliz-
ation
A common feature of technical writing is 'nominalization'. Many books on technical style discuss it, but few name it; admittedly 'nominalization' is a technical word from linguistics, but it is not a difficult or confusing concept. Nominalization is so prevalent that it seems worth dealing with it separately even though many people are nervous about 'grammar'.

Nominalization is the habit of turning verbs into nouns, or names. For example, a simple statement might be:

The probe measured the internal diameter.

But it is common in scientific writing to think of 'measurement' as a concept, or activity, and to construct a sentence round the noun 'measurement', rather than to use the verb 'measure':

Measurement of the internal diameter was performed by the probe.

This is nominalization. Its habitual use reduces the effectiveness of writing because it requires the construction of a passive sentence, and it also requires the use of a meaningless 'general-purpose' verb. The writer cannot say 'measurement was measured' so must find another verb to replace the one that has been nominalized. Since the action is named in the noun, the verb chosen must have no meaning in the sentence. Convenient verbs are 'performed, carried out, undertaken, conducted', and a host of others. If any meaning is given to these verbs, the sentences become funny:

The experiment was carried out . . . (where to?)

The measurement was conducted . . . (with a baton?)

The treatment was undertaken . . . (in a coffin?)

Analysis was performed . . . (on a stage?)

The forces which operate to encourage nominalization are understandable. Dealing continually in concepts, scientific and technical writers tend to isolate activities such as 'experimenting', 'measuring', and 'analysing' as abstract conceptual units

in their minds. They are also pushed towards passive constructions, both by tradition and by their own desire to step
aside and allow their work to speak for itself. These forces
produce characteristic constructions such as:

A similar experiment was carried out using the material . . .

'Sigma' preparation was carried out as described . . .

So common has 'carried out' become as a general purpose verb
that it is a recognized marker of 'scientific' reporting, and
television news bulletins commonly adopt the construction
when reporting scientific work. Such constructions, with consequent nominalizations, add to the length and complexity of
statements, and rob writing of force:

The test substance is easily absorbed, therefore spillage of the
material on the skin must be avoided.

(The test substance is easily absorbed, so avoid spilling it on the
skin.)

. . . using this thin wall material a reduction in costs would be
obtained.

(. . . using this thin wall material, costs would be reduced.)

There are some cases where nominalization is a useful resource,
but these cases should be a minority. Where writing continually
nominalizes, it becomes tiring and flat: more effort is required to
disentangle the roundabout structures which result, the meaning is spread more thinly, and the passive structures with
meaningless general purpose verbs rob the writing of its impact
and energy. Linguists use the words *stative* (static) and *dynamic*
in discussing the general characteristics of nouns and verbs
respectively.[7] It is no surprise if writing that is heavily nominalized seems to lack dynamism.

Once recognised, nominalization is easy to correct. Whenever
you see general-purpose verbs such as 'carry out', 'perform',
'undertake', or 'conduct' look for the word which names the
action. Turning the name of the activity back into a verb (preferably active) will undo the nominalization, and make the sentence more direct and easier to read.

Passive structures reverse the most common order of a sen-   ***Passive***
tence. Instead of saying 'the analyser tested the sample' (the

active form), writers can say 'The sample was tested by the analyser' (passive form). The main purpose of this reversal is to provide emphasis, by bringing to the head of the sentence the thing acted on, rather than the thing doing the action. Such a simple grammatical device is clearly useful and unobjectionable. However, the average number of passive constructions in the type of language used in novels is about 6%; the total in one study of scientific writing was 32%.[8] In many cases these reversals of sentence order have no evident purpose:

> The intensities were measured on a computer-controlled densitometer . . .
>
> (A computer-controlled densitometer measured the intensities . . .)

Or:

> The benzyl solutions are decomposed by daylight . . .
>
> (Daylight decomposes the benzyl solutions . . .)

Or:

> The identification of the animals in the experiment is by cage cards . . .
>
> (Cage cards identify the animals in the experiment . . .)

In such examples, the passive structure lengthens and elaborates the sentence unnecessarily. Readers absorb active sentences more easily than passive ones, because it is easier to focus on the agent of the action if it is named first. Thus, where an action is being attributed to some person, it is usually more comfortable for the reader if the person is named first:

> The responsibility of booking the IMS Test System lies with the Chief Applications Programmer and all requests . . .
>
> (The Chief Applications Programmer is responsible for booking the IMS Test System and all requests . . .)

Or:

> This machine was evaluated by the Applications Laboratory and was found to give very consistent processing results . . .
>
> (The Applications Laboratory evaluated this machine, which gave very consistent processing results . . .)

Passive structures should be used only where they have a specific encoding function, because otherwise they add unnecessarily to the complexity of a statement. Any feature of writing which does not have a communicative function should be deleted in informative writing.

The common reason for using so many passive constructions is that they can be made impersonal. The active construction 'we started the test', turned into the passive construction 'the test was started by us', can be transformed into an impersonal structure by the simple deletion of the last part of the sentence: 'the test was started'. Because traditions of scientific and technical reporting seem to require impersonality, writers turn gratefully to the passive structure as an undemanding way of achieving the safety of facelessness. But it is a mistake to think that the passive is the only way to avoid mentioning the human experimenter. For example, a writer used a passive structure to avoid personal reference in:

In the previous report the rationale for studies in prostaglandin (PG) receptors was discussed.

He did not want to write:

We discussed the rationale for prostaglandin (PG) studies in the previous report.

But this was not the only alternative: an active construction, which would have avoided the personal reference is:

The previous report discussed the rationale for studies on prostaglandin (PG) receptors.

Where the active cannot be made impersonal, the passive is roundabout and vague:

A study has been made of the effect of storage for up to 28 days.

Who made this study? We would argue that it is more natural, comfortable and accurate to use a personal pronoun:

We have studied the effect of storage for up to 28 days.

Readers will decode the message in this way in any case. If the components of a sentence are complex, the added complexity of the passive structure can be the straw which breaks the back of readers' comprehension. They may have to go back and re-read, and their sense of progress through the technical argument is disrupted by their difficulties with the encoding of that argument. Also, if passive structures are used continually, they become obtrusively repetitive. Readers are kept alert and interested by variety in the use of the language code. Thoughtless repetition, where a structure is emphasized out of proportion to its normal frequency of use, wearies readers.

> The homogenate *was filtered* through muslin and retained material re-homogenized. The combined filtrates *were centrifuged* and the fraction sedimenting between 1000 g and 50 000 g *was collected*. The pellets *were resuspended* and stored in small aliquots at −20°C.

We are not arguing for a complete ban on passive structures in scientific and technical writing; we think their use should be restricted to places where they have a specific function. A normal variety of structures should be used, including occasional personal references, with a limited number of passives.

Personal versus impersonal During the last century, it became an accepted dogma of scientific writing that there should be no references to the person doing the work, and this is now firmly established in many writers' minds. In fact, the reporting of science prior to the nineteenth century frequently used personal structures. The formality of much Victorian writing became the norm for intellectual writing in general, and in science this has survived into the twentieth century. But there is no good reason why personal pronouns should be scrupulously avoided. Readers are aware they are reading about the work of people, and their assessment of the experimental work reported will include an assessment of the personal competence of the scientist. It is artificial to avoid personal references in scientific writing.

The organization you are writing for may try to operate a ban on personal constructions; but there are occasions where accurate reporting *requires* identification of the person who acted. The alternatives (which are often used in these circumstances) to the simple personal pronouns 'I' and 'we' are more obtrusive. More attention is attracted by the circumlocutions than by the naked pronoun. Thus:

> However, the writer's view was advised that such expenses should be included in the trading results.
>
> (However, I expressed the view that such expenses should be included in the trading results.)

Other circumlocutions are just as obtrusive:

> From the literature already published on laser frequency stabilization, the method most applicable to the author's requirements appeared to be . . .

(From the literature already published on laser frequency stabilization, the method most applicable to my requirements appeared to be . . .)

Such circumlocutions can also lead to clumsy statements which a sane reader can only laugh at:

The author was to some extent relieved to learn that similar tests had been carried out . . .

One major reason for using personal pronouns is, therefore, that the alternatives are clumsier and more obtrusive.

The following passage stumbles into another problem which is created by a blanket ban on personal constructions:

One could rationalize the asymmetric binding data by proposing a conformational change upon binding the first mole of substrate (Fersht, 1975). Recent experiments involving diffusing APT into the crystals have resulted in . . .

Readers are made uncomfortable by the rather pompous 'one' instead of 'I' or 'We'. Their discomfort when the writer is embarrassed at identifying ideas as his or her own is turned into genuine puzzlement in the next sentence. The 'recent experiments' are not attributed to anyone. Custom leads readers to think they are the author's, since such impersonal references are the norm. But the previous sentence has referred to Fersht, and doubts must enter readers' minds as to whether they are reading a continuing report of other work or whether they have just started to read about the author's original work.

A ban on personal references can therefore be ambiguous. In science, the attribution of work to named workers is an integral part of the system of reporting and publishing results. Thus the writer who reported:

From preliminary studies using the microscope, it was found that three 'passes' were required.

left it unclear whether the studies being described were his or her own preliminary studies, or those of other workers. Ambiguity which makes the source and history of the conclusions unclear, is bad; uncertainty about the claimed status of a hypothesis is often worse:

It is not possible to state the exact mode of operation of the drug.

This leaves serious doubts in readers' minds. They may well

translate this sentence, following familiar scientific idioms, as saying:

We do not know how the drug works.

But this is a different claim from the assertion that the operation of the drug is beyond any elucidation, a complete impossibility. Which did the writer intend?

Attribution of decision, as well as of hypothesis and results, requires precision. Impersonal constructions are ambiguous, and therefore introduce a worrying uncertainty. In commercial organizations, who made the decision may be important. To allow the identification to go by default is to buy anonymity at a high price.

The fear of identifying personal involvement in a scientific or technical matter extends so far that even clearly personal concepts are expressed in impersonal form:

Originally this was believed to be due to an extra production of E_2.

Belief is a personal, human, activity. But here it is not attributed to anyone, and the impersonality adds nothing. The natural structure is both easier to read, and inspires more confidence in the writer's directness, precision and honesty:

I originally believed this was due to extra production of E_2.

Impersonal constructions are not only obtrusive, and often ambiguous, but also cumbersome:

Examination and discussion of the concentrations obtained, are necessary before a decision is taken.

(We must examine and discuss the concentrations before we decide.)

Impersonal writing invites unnecessary nominalization:

The work was carried out using injection moulded containers of general purpose polystyrene.

(We used injection-moulded containers of general-purpose polystyrene.)

It seems to encourage roundabout phrasing, and unnecessary verbosity:

Finally, further attempts have been made to prepare samples of heparin.

(Finally, we have tried again to prepare samples of heparin.)

It also leads writers into pompous vocabulary:

> Current work has therefore been aimed at establishing the nature of this non-specific binding.

> (So we are now trying to find out how this non-specific binding works.)

In the examples we have been looking at so far, the use of 'I' (or the alternative 'we' where the work of a team or organization is being reported) has seemed the natural choice. We argue that to *avoid* personal pronouns where it is natural to use them is unnecessarily cumbersome, and detracts from the reader's comfort. This also applies to the other personal pronouns. The introduction to a manual read:

> The sections assume the person has a basic understanding of our AN process control computer system.

The context made it clear that 'the person' was the reader. Why therefore use the circumlocution 'the person', instead of writing:

> The sections assume you have a basic understanding of our AN process control computer system.

Our advice to use personal pronouns where they are the natural choice does not, of course, mean that they should be used indiscriminately. In normal conversation, we use a variety of constructions, and variety is always refreshing and helpful in digesting a written text. The writer who obtrudes personal pronouns at every opportunity is quite as tiresome as the writer who always conceals personal identities. It is not necessary to mention the observer of the result each time a result is reported. In conversation we do not guard every statement with the provision, 'I observe' or 'I saw that'. Someone who reported 'I went outside the door and I felt rain. By inspection I observed that the sky was overcast and I saw it was getting dark' might be correct about the source of his information, but would be tiresome to listen to. The natural structures might be 'I went outside, and felt rain. The sky was overcast and it was getting dark.' Normal decoding allows for the fact that the message depends on the reporter. We do not need to be reminded of this in every sentence. So with scientific reporting; information in a paper is encased in the inverted commas which enable us to understand the whole paper as the report of a series of observations by its writer. Within that context, facts can be reported as simple statements, and do not need the constant elaboration of 'I confirmed . . .' or 'I found . . .'.

But note, too, that normal usage *does* mix personal and impersonal statements. Our example would have seemed very artificial if it had run: 'The present writer went outside the door and rain was felt. It was observed that the sky was overcast . . .' The heavy, over-formal tone of much scientific writing stems largely from an artificial attempt to restrict expression to just one impersonal form.

The use of rigidly impersonal constructions in scientific and technical documentation is gradually dying. Both civil service and armed services writing now contain personal pronouns. If you belong to an organization which still bans personal pronouns in its documents, or if you have been convinced that they are inappropriate in scientific writing, we would ask you to rethink your reasons for this belief. You may think that personal pronouns are obtrusive and unscientific, yet our examples show that the impersonal alternatives are often more obtrusive, and less precise. Readability research shows that writing containing personal pronouns is, on the whole, easier to read. The circumlocutions, passive constructions, and omissions required for impersonal writing absorb extra energy in decoding the message.

Conclusion

We have dealt in this Chapter with some of the most distracting stylistic habits of scientific and technical reporting. There are obviously many other identifiable habits which are undesirable or awkward. We make no pretence at completeness. Indeed, it is the nature of language to offer almost endless variety and complexity; the ways in which ideas can be clumsily expressed are as diverse as the ways in which they can be precisely expressed.

But effective style is felt by many to be the key to good writing. Certainly, readers' sense of the quality of a writer's mind, of the precision, grasp and exactness of his or her thought processes is often derived from the style of the text. For this reason, we think you may want to read further about effective style for informative writing. We recommend Sir Ernest Gowers' *The Complete Plain Words*, and John Kirkman's *Good Style for Scientific and Engineering Writing*.[9]

When writing, and especially when editing, bear in mind the basic points made here. Avoid over-long sentences, try to use a vocabulary which is simple while still being exact, avoid misuse of jargon and thoughtlessly abstract words where concrete ones convey the exact meaning. Think again about roundabout, wordy phrases, the over-use of passive structures, and the temptation to use regular nominalization. Try also to use personal pronouns where they are appropriate.

Draft your documents, and then read through, looking for the types of clumsiness we have identified in this Chapter; it is possible to acquire considerable skill at seeing and correcting stylistic ineptitudes. Our chief advice is to be varied and flexible in the use of the wide resources of the language code, but you must also recognize that the precise and incisive encoding of information is a difficult achievement. Even for experienced writers it is not always, or even often, achieved first time. Learn to be a critical editor, as well as a thoughtful writer, and the quality, and impressiveness, of your documents will undoubtedly improve.

References

1. See Kapp, R.O. (1948) *The Presentation of Technical Information*, Constable, London, p. 9.
2. See Orwell, George (1968) Politics and the English Language. *The Collected Essays, Journalism and Letters of George Orwell*, Secker & Warburg, London, Vol. **IV**, p. 156.
3. See Klare, R.G. (1963) *Measuring Readability*, Iowa State University Press.
4. West, Michael (1953) *A General Service List of English Words*, Longmans, Green, London.
5. Kirkman, J. (1975) Readable Writing for Scientific Papers. *Bulletin of the British Ecological Society*, **VI**, (1), 5–9. 57.4% preferred 'Direct, verbs mainly active, minimum of special vocabulary, judicious use of personal and impersonal constructions, sentences of varied length but mainly short and not complex.' The five alternative versions, using less simple style, scored between 1.1% and 16.4% preference.
6. See Mill, J.S. (1879) *A System of Logic*, London, Vol. **I**, p. 213.
7. See, for example, Quirk, R., Greenbaum, S., Leech, G. and Svartvik, J. (1972) *A Grammar of Contemporary English*, Longman, London, p. 46ff.
8. Svartvik, Jan (1966) *On Voice in the English Verb*, Mouton, Paris (1966), p. 46; see also Huddleston, R.D. (1971) *The*

Sentence in Written English: A Syntactic Study Based on an Analysis of Scientific Texts, Cambridge University Press, p. 172.

9. Gowers, Sir Ernest (1954) *The Complete Plain Words*, HMSO, London (also available in a Pelican edition); Kirkman, John (1980) *Good Style for Scientific and Engineering Writing* Pitman, London.

Writing with a 8 computer

The majority of writers now use computers (as word-processors) for their writing. The use of computers does not change the principles of good writing, but it does make achieving them easier in many ways. It also calls for extra care over the writing process. We are sometimes told that the so-called 'electronic office' will make our advice on writing unnecessary. We doubt that. Indeed, we think *more*, not less, training of 'authors' will be required as new technology makes it easier to prepare and duplicate 'texts'. **Using a word-processor**

Word-processing changes the way text is created and extended, and the ways in which writers think and work. At the simplest level, a word-processor is little more than a clever typewriter, with electronic correcting fluid. The main advantage of the word-processor is the ease with which mistakes can be corrected. Clean copies can be produced without the need to re-type the whole document. The labour of typing several drafts is eliminated, and the temptation to let a draft through with small mistakes disappears. Final copies are cleaner, neater, and should be error-free. Revision, that corner-stone of good writing, becomes a regular practice rather than a distant ideal.

With a manual typewriter, revisions *are* possible; but to see their effect properly requires complete retyping. The word-processor makes it possible to revise documents bit by bit, and to see the effect of each batch of alterations without having to go through the labour of re-typing the whole text.

We recommend that you use the same technique of rapid writing when you revise, as when you write the first draft: read rapidly, and mark passages, words, and sentences that need looking at carefully. If you stop for too long to wrestle with a hydra of a sentence, you will distort your memory of the overall shape and flow of the writing. The techniques that we have found useful are to mark the passage with a row of stars, or to have a quick shot at drafting an extra sentence or two to clarify the point. We do no more until the next clean print-out is ready. Then, what is needed is usually clearer.

Typically, we find one of three things becomes obvious:

- the original sentence can be deleted, leaving the new sentence(s) to sit among the rest;
- half of the new sentence can be deleted, together with half of the original sentence, and the halves welded together to make a reshaped whole;
- a few more sentences are obviously needed, and they can be drafted in.

Which of these three will be needed cannot be seen easily until the text is reprinted, and one can read and revise a clean copy. The process of revising is reiterative; repeating it again and again can refine the text into something quite different from the opaque and sloppy original.

Easy and repeated revision is an enormous benefit that word-processing confers on the writer. But it is important to see that the new technology changes the *processes* of writing, not its principles.

Computers make many of the mechanical aspects of writing easier, and increased ease and speed (once the necessary keyboard skills have been learned), help writers overcome the difficulties inherent in composing coherent and cogent text. But externalizing thought in an orderly and stylish form is still not easy. For all their automation, computers are not thinking machines. They make it easy to take words out and put words in, but *you* still have to make the judgements about which words must be changed. The machines can save some time and much of the boredom involved in repetitive work. But they cannot compose texts for you. They cannot decide what information you need in a letter replying to a customer's enquiry. They cannot decide how much data to include in your progress report. They cannot choose the most persuasive way to organize and express the information you know will be needed to convince a finance committee to give you capital for a project.

A word-processor makes it easier to plan a document. Your first thoughts about the sections required can be typed straight into a 'file'. If another arrangement of material subsequently seems better, you can shuffle those thoughts around easily. New notes, ideas, details, facts and figures can be inserted under appropriate headings. Do not worry about making final decisions about order in the early stages. A heap of notes can be put in one section in the order in which they are discovered. Then, you can use a print-out of that section to work out an order of sub-sections. The notes can be allocated to sub-sections by pencilled directions in the margin. Back on the word-processor, you can re-arrange the notes quickly, and produce another print-out, if necessary.

Using word-processors to plan and organize documents

Of course, it has always been possible to modify typescripts by the 'scissors and paste' method; but this produces a scruffy-looking text, in which it is hard to see, literally, the form and force of your argument. If you use a word-processor, it is easier to add notes about points that have occurred to you during a study-session in a library or while you were listening to a talk. Ideas and facts scribbled on the backs of envelopes, and in the margins of books and papers, can be inserted quickly into the appropriate section of your document. As soon as the new information has been inserted, the scribbled notes can be torn up and thrown away, so that there is no build up of untidy fragments. Another print-out will enable you to see what you have achieved, and help you to see what further modifications and alterations are needed.

As we have said in Chapter 7, style is not just a literary idea: good style in informative writing is efficient use of words to communicate meaning. The word-processor encourages revision of style, because it shows the writer *immediately* on the screen the effect of breaking long sentences or reconstructing clumsily expressed phrases and clauses.

Revising style

It becomes much easier to use a policy of writing rapidly, ignoring problems of precise phrasing during the creation of the first draft. Writers creating a text in handwriting or on a typewriter are tempted to pause and try to get things 'right' the first time through, because they know the labour of re-writing or re-typing will be so great. This interrupts the flow of ideas. Writers using a word-processor do not feel so inhibited by the labour that will be involved in revision. They know that it will be easy to insert and re-arrange words, and to re-print the whole or part of a page or chapter. Thus, the use of a word-processor encourages flow in writing, and rigour in reviewing the readability of text.

Disadvantages in word-processing

What are the disadvantages in using a word-processor? Strangely, the main one may be the sheet amount of writing one is encouraged to do. Word-processors are revolutionary tools that help in the creation of readable text; but they can just as easily help in the proliferation of mindless drivel.

Another disadvantage can be the ease with which documents can be revised by the process of 'cutting and pasting'. After a cutting and pasting operation, writers *should* re-read the whole section of text to check for awkward joints and unexplained references. However, we see an increasing number of documents that show signs of crude word-processing, where chunks have been cut out or carelessly shifted to other positions, without careful adjustment of the surrounding text. Probably, this happens because it is tempting to restrict one's review of the quality of a rewritten section to the limited number of lines that can be seen on a single screen. Often, this is not adequate: it is essential to re-read and revise a much larger stretch of text, to ensure that the argument of a section or chapter remains coherent, and that the views expressed remain consistent.

We think four other points need to be emphasized:

- word-processors can encourage monotonous repetition of words or whole chunks of text;
- the ease with which the machines can revise and reprint text can lead to uneconomic use of their capacities;
- the ease with which the machines can up-date and add to texts can lead to verbosity;
- constraints imposed by the programs of word-processors and computers can cause writers to put the convenience of their machines above the convenience of their readers.

One of the chief enemies of good style is lack of variety. A feature of many word-processors is the ability to reproduce at the touch of only a few keys whole paragraphs of standard text, for insertion in a range of letters and documents. It is tempting for writers to 'make do' with wording they have used in a previous text to save themselves the trouble of thinking out the best way of expressing slightly changed ideas. The result is text that is monotonously repetitive and sometimes inexact.

Most word-processors enable writers to specify that given words are to be altered to different words throughout entire texts. For example, the word 'initiate' might be identified, and the instruction given to replace this word throughout with the word 'start'. This could be a useful change; but lack of variety usually makes text indigestible, and there are many occasions on which 'start' is not a direct equivalent to 'initiate', especially in texts on computing. Editing should usually be done with a rather more delicate touch and greater sensitivity to the precise nuances of each word in its immediate context. Word-processors can produce uniformity effortlessly and at staggering length: that is the danger. Used intelligently, they can save time; used thoughtlessly, they can increase the unreadability of texts.

We want to warn against the ease with which word-processors can revise and reprint text, leading to uneconomic use of their capacities. One great advantage of word-processors is that they relieve typists of the need to retype every word in successive drafts of texts. The financial investment in equipment is more than balanced by the saving of typists' time, as the machines quickly make minor adjustments to rough drafts and then reprint the text accurately and in correct format. Unfortunately, however, speed and ease of revision can tempt writers to become increasingly slipshod in the composition of their first drafts. The number of drafts increases; eventually the overall cost of the completed document is as high as, or higher than, that of a normally typed document.

Another warning is against verbosity. Probably, in the next decade, computer manufacturers will perfect voice-recognition programmes. It is likely to be possible to dictate text, which the machine will reproduce in printed form. As so often, such a development has been anticipated in creative fiction. The hero of Lawrence Durrell's *Tunc* and *Nunquam* has such a machine, called Dactyl. In the novels, as real life will doubtless verify, the result is sinister. Most everyday chat is, thankfully, ephemeral. It is easy to talk at length; anyone who dictates to a secretary or to a dictating machine knows that it is difficult to be brief and incisive while talking. In some ways, the sheer laboriousness of hand-writing is a saving grace: it forces the mind to think slowly and deliberately about the use of words, since each word written costs time and effort. Dictation tempts us to be expansive. But even as we dictate we are conscious of the human effort that will be required to transcribe these minutes of tape into pages of script. The ease with which machines will convert our ramblings into text will seduce us into undue loquacity. Although the invention of printing was a great triumph for civilization, few writers would deny that the speed, ease and cheapness of modern printing has produced an avalanche of vacant and repetitive books on every subject. The electronic revolution is undoubtedly as important as the printing revolution. There is an obvious danger that there will be an equivalent avalanche of vacant and repetitive business and research documents.

Finally, a warning against a shift in outlook that word-processors encourage. Already, in many companies, debates on writing techniques are stopped by comments such as 'but our word-processor/computer will not accept that'. Mainly, these comments apply to points of physical layout such as the best hyphenation of word-breaks at the ends of lines, or the indentation of segments of texts for emphasis or listing. We have found that even professional technical writers are beginning to think primarily of the convenience of their machines, and only secondarily of the convenience of their readers. The constraining influences of word-processor programs have an insidious effect.

Frequently, too, we have discovered that the word-processors that have been blamed *would* have allowed writers to do what they wanted to do, but to do that precisely would have required the writers to change the 'default values' – the settings for margins, line-spacing or other features that a computer program uses unless it is modified by the user. In truth, the writers could not be bothered to make changes, so texts that were less than optimum were produced because of the writers' laziness, and/or because operating a word-processor often requires a little more conscious effort than simply wielding a pen.

This catalogue of the 'shortcomings' of word-processors may suggest that we are hostile to the introduction of new technology to the writing process. Most emphatically, we are not. Every aid to efficient acquisition, manipulation, storage, retrieval and transfer of information should be used to the full. We wish simply to warn against the belief that electronic equipment will bring to the task of 'composition' the savings of time and effort it has brought to mechanical tasks like riveting or calculation. Regrettably, many people who ask us about word-processors seem to imagine that they represent a dream come true – entirely effortless writing. But one of the oldest sayings in computing applies to word-processing as much as to 'number-crunching'. That saying is 'GIGO' – garbage in, garbage out. Word-processors may save a typist's time in drafting and final typing of a text: but if badly organized ideas, formulated in a verbose and vague style, are put into the machines, then the final text may *look* superficially attractive but it will be just as tedious for readers as any manually retyped text.

The computer can speed up, and even automate, many of the routine checking tasks in writing. We are likely to see a growing range of computer-based 'tools'. These tools (or programs) will lighten the burden on writers, and improve the quality of administrative and technical documentation generally. Their great advantage is their ability to help inexperienced or inexpert writers to produce more readable text. They act, in effect, as extensions to word-processors, and operate as simple sub-editors. The tools query parts of the text that do not conform to norms that have been established by the tool-creators.

Computer-aided writing

The most obvious computer-based tool is a spelling-checker, now almost universal in word-processing software. In practice, most writers can spell most complicated words, but have a random set of minor errors in their spellings. And they make far more typing errors than spelling errors. Unfortunately, this means that a program to check spelling *reliably* must be very sophisticated – which many are not. Since a typing error is often very different in kind from a spelling error (as in the difference between *spearate* and *seperate*), different tactics are needed to correct it. An intelligent spelling-checker would have, for example, to notice when *and* has been mis-typed as *an*, since both words will be correct as far as the checker knows.

Another 'tool' is a program that looks for clumsy or cliche-ridden phrasing. In essence, what this tool does is very simple. For instance, *'dict'* is a program built into the UNIX (TM) computer-operating system. It contains a list of phrases considered disagreeable – phrases such as 'in this day and age', 'at the present moment', and 'in the author's opinion'. The program has a device known to computer scientists as a 'pattern matcher'. This recognizes the pattern of letters which make up one of these banned phrases, whenever it appears in a text, and prints a list of the banned phrases it has found, asking the writer to change them.

Later generations of tools have improved on the simple lists of errors made by early spelling-checkers and diction-checkers. Now, they use more sophisticated presentations, and make it easier for writers to insert corrections. They are extremely convenient to use, and we are confident that they will be improved to give increasing help in the campaign to improve the quality of documentation.

No doubt we shall soon have grammar-checkers available to support word-processing programs. Grammar has proved difficult to define with the logical exactness required by computer programming, as linguists working on automated translation between languages have discovered. But in principle there is no reason why a machine should not in the end be programmed to recognize, for example, every passive construction and convert some into active ones.

These new aids to writing could be sadly misused. The more powerful the mchines to aid our minds, the more they separate users into the dull and the imaginative. A machine-user could decide to edit a text so that it contained nothing but active constructions or nothing but passive constructions. This would produce a dull, repetitive piece of reading. However, the ability to recognize grammatical features could also be used intelligently; for example, to give writers information about the *proportions* of different structures in their texts, so that they could see if they were leaning too much towards one or the other. But the ability to manipulate language in word-processors will never relieve writers of the ultimate responsibility for writing varied, interesting and intelligent texts.

Undoubtedly, programs that will produce coherent commentaries on the style of texts are on their way. We urge writers to make maximum use of all the aids available to them, thereby releasing maximum time and energy for the 'unautomatable' activities of thinking, composing and re-appraising that underlie all effective writing.

In summary   Our contention, then, is that the development of word-processors will not remove the need for attention to basic techniques of writing. It will not bring magic formulae to make writing suddenly effortless. The real effort in writing is in the thinking required for planning and preparing, in the judgement required for organizing and laying out, and in the continual need for sensitivity in the encoding of ideas in words and phrases. In comparison, the mechanical labour of producing and sub-editing texts is small. Electronic devices can reduce this mechanical effort many times, and therefore release energy and time for thinking. But they cannot reduce the effort of thought.

Informative 9
summaries

Most reports and papers need an informative summary. But, as in all writing decisions, there are no rigid rules. To decide if a summary is needed and how to write it, we must think first about the purpose of the summary, and then about how the reader is going to use it.

First, a summary acts as an extended title. It helps readers to see if the report or paper contains information they need. A manager taking a first look through a pile of reports in the morning mail, a researcher looking through a shelf of papers in the library, and a reader turning over the pages of a journal, all want an extended title. No-one can read everything, and few people have time even to read all that is written on their own specialization. From a summary, a reader can answer such questions as:

An extended title

- Which part of the subject area is this paper about?
- Does the writer cover any special areas I am interested in?
- What line does the writer take with the subject?
- Is this a survey, or a report of new research?
- Is this new to me or am I already familiar with the information?
- Are there unusual methods or techniques that I might be interested in?
- Does the writer come to clear-cut conclusions and how important are they to me?
- Do I need to read this?

The reader is then able to define more closely what the paper is about, and can make an informed decision about whether to read the whole paper.

It is in the writer's interest to tell readers exactly what the paper is about. Writers do not want to lose even a part of their target audiences, or their work will be less well known, less discussed, and less influential. But equally, they do not want to be read by people who are not interested. These readers may become disappointed or confused as they go through the paper, and they will not respect the work.

A short version Second, the summary is a short version for people who do not have time to read the whole paper. Time is always the important factor. New ideas and new facts are interesting, and people enjoy reading to explore and discover; if they had enough time, most scientists, engineers and managers would read much more than they do. The reason why more people do not read your paper from beginning to end is not that they are uninterested in what you have to say, but that there is so much else to read, and so much else to do. If they are to survive, physically and mentally, in a world which produces more and more writing every year, readers must be increasingly selective.

There are two main groups of people who want a short version of the report: first, senior managers, research supervisors, and others who need to have an overview of a large area of work; second, those who are marginally interested in your subject, because it uses the same methods or assumptions as their own work, although its aim and results are different. Both groups form an audience which probably will not read the whole paper, but who want to be told the essence of the matter.

Speed-reading has been advocated to cope with the problem of having too much to read. The teachers of speed-reading techniques say in effect, you *want* to read more, but time is inexorable. Therefore you must read faster. Speed-reading teaches readers to skim rapidly through material; when they find something they are closely interested in, their minds light on the passage and devour it. For those who can use this technique it is a great time-saver, a great boost to their efficiency as human word-processors. It is partly to help skimmers find their way that a paper needs clear, informative titles and sub-headings.

But speed-reading has a disadvantage: it is a little haphazard. Which key words the readers pick out depends partly on chance, since the readers are making a rapid sample of the text, and that sample must be to some extent random. They may miss important details, and they may see a different balance in the information from that which the writer intended. How much better for *the writer* to make the selection. A summary picks out for the reader-in-a-hurry just those key words, phrases, facts and conclusions which the author *knows* are the ones which matter.

Third, a summary also helps readers who are going to read the whole report, to start with an overview of the subject. A summary gives those readers a map. As they go through the report, they can mentally tick off the stages of the argument. Readers can best absorb information, facts or evidence, if they know the conclusions they are being led to; they are able to assemble the details in their minds in a rational way. Without a summary, any digression may mislead the readers into thinking it is the main road. Only if they know where they are going can they keep their sense of direction and balance. The summary focuses their attention on the main direction of the argument. A mystery tour along a dry, dusty road, with more work at the end of it is no-one's idea of fun.

A 'map' of the paper

Fourth, a summary helps readers to remember the paper. If they are asked to join in a discussion of a paper they read weeks ago, the summary is their life-line. It helps them hook out of the recesses of their memories all the forgotten details. Summaries also help the memory because they provide repetition and reinforcement. By reading the summary and the report, readers get the key information twice, and their chances of remembering it are multiplied.

An aid to memory

Here then are four major uses for a summary. It:

- helps readers to decide if they need to read the whole paper;
- enables readers who are short of time to get the key points reliably and quickly;
- focuses attention on the aim of the paper;
- reminds everyone after reading, and reinforces learning.

What is the best style, organization, balance and selection of material? What sort of summary does these four jobs best?

A *precis* is a compressed version of a paper, and keeps the information in the same order. The precis is a school exercise,

A precis is not a summary

and it usually has a fixed word length, into which the given passage is compressed. It does some of the jobs of a summary, but it has two disadvantages for the reader. First, in a precis, writers work within an arbitrary limit on the number of words; but in a good summary, the length should be a balance between the amount of important information and the reader's available time. In other words the length should be conditioned by the reader's needs, not by an artificial limit.

Second, a precis reduces length in proportion; if half the paper is on theory, a quarter on methods, and the last quarter only on results, a precis should preserve the same proportions. But a good summary of the same paper might have only one sentence on theory, and three-quarters of the summary devoted to the conclusions. Readers of a summary want to know what conclusions have been reached; if they want to check up on the theory or work through the method, they can read the full paper.

Generally, readers trust the writer's results and conclusions. They are not examiners of the work, but users. If we buy a washing machine, we are mainly interested in finding out if it will do its job, not in spending time considering the theory behind its design, and the methods of manufacture. Were we looking at the machine as the product of a student engineering project, we would want to know about these things; but if we simply want to use the machine to achieve other ends of our own (like clean socks), then the theory and methods are of very marginal interest. Similarly, information to use, not a way of checking up, is what the reader of a summary wants.

Notice that we are not saying that readers never want the full evidence or the detailed arguments which support the conclusions; we are saying that readers of the *summary* do not want these things. If they do, they can read the whole paper. In saving themselves time by reading only the summary, they trade trust of the writer's expertise, for quick access to the results: a reasonable compromise between time and knowledge. The precis does not make this compromise; it shortens everything equally.

So the difference between a summary and a precis is that a summary is designed to help the reader do a job; the precis is an exercise for the writer. In practice, people often use the word *precis* when they are talking about a summary, but it is less confusing if we think of *precis* and *summary* in the terms we have discussed.

In some organizations, the word *abstract* is used in place of *summary* to describe the same thing: an attempt by the writer to draw out and state succinctly the essence of the subject-matter in the text, especially the new information. In particular, collections of summaries in book form or in computer storage often have the term *abstract* in their titles, even though they contain the type of concise, condensed version of the essence of a text that we are calling a *summary*.

Abstract or summary

In other organizations, the word *abstract* is used to describe something halfway between a title and a summary – an extended title, giving extra details of what is included in the text.

As you read the following two summaries, think which you find more helpful. Since you are reading only a summary of the paper, which is all the reader-in-a-hurry would read, you are in the same position to judge the summaries' effectiveness:

Descriptive or informative

1 Phosphate production planning

Summary:

This report describes the production problems, raw material supply difficulties, and changes in the sales pattern which require a reappraisal of the production and packaging plan for phosphates.

We have examined the likely dispatch pattern and propose a production and packaging plan to meet this situation. The aim is to keep the maximum availability for as many products as possible for as long as possible.

Varied estimates are made for the forward dispatch pattern, and ideal review intervals are calaculated.

2 Reducing process water usage

Summary:

We are installing a re-circulation unit and cooler for the water used on the injector inter-condensers. This system will reduce the injector usage by 30% and so offset the need for expansion of the Process Water Facilities.

The system will circulate and cool 9500 litres/hour. Probeck Engineering Ltd., of Leicester, have been chosen to supply and install the major items of equipment, which consist of a forced-blast condenser, pumps, filters, and associated instrumentation.

The capital cost is £84 500, which is only 56% of the cost of the alternative expansion of Process Water Facilities.

Notice that the first summary describes what is in the report, but does not give any details. If readers want information about the new production plan, they have to read the report. The second summary, by contrast, does not simply describe what will be in the report: it gives a selection of information. It is useful to distinguish between these two kinds by calling the first a *descriptive* and the second an *informative* summary.

The descriptive summary starts 'This report describes . . .' but the informative one starts 'We are installing a re-circulation unit . . .' Which of these two types is more useful to the reader? Both do the first job of a summary, which is extending the title. They both describe the specific areas of work to be found in the report. The descriptive summary explicitly says, 'this is what is in the report'. Although the informative summary never uses the words 'the report describes . . . it extends the title because the reader knows that the information it gives is typical of what is in the report. We are clear that if we did read the whole report, we would be told more about the new re-circulation unit. As extended titles, both summaries are effective.

Which summary is more helpful to readers who have no time to read the whole paper? The descriptive summary leaves readers guessing; they are told there are 'production problems', but not how bad they are, or even of what kind. Readers of the informative summary, in contrast, are not left guessing; they are told what will be installed, by whom and at what cost. The descriptive summary is coy; readers' curiosity is aroused; but only by reading the whole report can they get any facts. The informative summary is complete in itself; it does not point outside itself, promise what it does not deliver or arouse questions and expectations in the reader's mind. Readers who have not got time to read the whole report are given hard facts by an informative summary; readers of the descriptive summary are given fewer facts. So the informative summary does the second job of a summary much better.

The third use of the summary is to focus attention, and the fourth is to help everyone remember what was in the report. Both the descriptive and the informative summary do these jobs to some extent, but again the informative summary has the advantage. It is specific while the descriptive summary only promises. Descriptive summaries have an element of the mystery tour about them, and are not much help in reminding readers of the detailed contents. They tell them that there was something about a new production plan. But what were the main priorities of that plan? If they cannot remember, they have to read the whole paper again.

Why are not all summaries written informatively? One reason is that writers are often subconsciously protective about their results; they do not want to give them away too easily. They think that readers should go through the fire and brimstone of reading the whole report before arriving at the prize. It is perhaps natural to feel that hard work for the writer must be made hard work for readers. More charitably, the writer probably wants the readers to share his or her adventures, to go through the process of discovery at his or her side. So the readers must stumble, sweat and struggle, until they too can feel the joy when the answer becomes clear. But the readers want information, not excitement. The writer is offering a product – results. The consumer of these results wants them as conveniently accessible as possible.

People also write descriptive summaries because they are afraid of misinterpretation. Writers think that if their results are expressed in brief form, without all the qualifications, doubts and warnings which the full text contains, the reader will seize on half-truths and misuse them. This can happen; but there are better ways of guarding against misunderstanding than simply withholding information. Information in a summary can be expressed in a way which makes its limitations clear. Thus, if a summary said, 'the tensile strength of the new fibre is 3.6 kg mm^{-2}' but the report said that this was a maximum and only under specific conditions, then the summary would seriously mislead the reader. The summary should say: 'the new fibre has a maximum tensile strength of about 3.6 km mm^{-2} in favourable circumstances . . .' Anyone designing with the new fibre knows that it will be essential to read the whole paper and take into account all the circumstances before using the material.

Information in summaries will often be prefixed with 'approximately', 'about', 'typically', 'a maximum of . . .' But in a descriptive summary, the sentence 'the tensile strength of carbon steel is described . . .' would give no idea whether this strength was comparable to that of steel or cotton. Readers will ask, in what range is the strength, and what sort of materials does it compare with? They do not know whether it is high or low. The report *may* say: 'the new fibre won't hang a flea . . .' or it *may* say: 'the new fibre is used to string up battleships for keel inspection'. A descriptive summary gives no clue. Fear of mis-understanding may be a motive for writing descriptive summar-ies, but it is a false fear. Some information, properly expressed as 'typical' or 'average', is better than no information, and precise figures are best of all.

Informative summaries use words efficiently   A third reason why people avoid writing informative summaries is that they assume they must be longer. They expect informa-tion to take up more space and more words than general description. Surprisingly, this is not always true. Here are two different summaries of the same paper, both the same length. As you read them, think which is more useful to a reader who is never going to read to the whole paper.

Reactor Vessel Jackets

Summary:

The report describes an apparatus built to measure the resist-ance to the flow of heat through various thermal-insulating reactor-vessel jackets, under conditions simulating those obtaining in practice. The effects of a variety of thick, and thin-film materials were studied, and the decrease in thermal resistivity of foam due to ageing was quantified. The relative resistance of thicker foamed polymers and glass fibre blankets is shown and the cause of the enhanced resistivity of glass-fibre combinations is suggested. Observations confirm a signi-ficant improvement in thermal resistance by placing thin-layer materials on top of polystyrene.

An alternative informative summary:

Thermal-insulating reactor-vessel jackets were tested on an experimental 50 litre vessel, kept at 500 K internally, and atmospheric temperature externally. Foamed polymers and glass-fibre in layers of 5 cm gave resistivities of about 2.7. Thin films of aluminium foil and PVC gave resistivities of about 1.3. With foam, ageing reduced resistivity by about 7% per year. Thicker glass-fibre blankets, up to 15 cm, were about

17% better than the same thicknesses of foamed polymers. We think this is because the multiple irregular surfaces within the glass-fibre blanket trap more air. A thin layer of aluminium foil on the outside surface increases the resistivity of polystyrene by up to 30%.

The informative summary is more useful. But why is it no longer, since it contains more information? The answer is that many of the words in the descriptive summary are redundant. Either they say what we assume anyway, or words are used to avoid saying things, to cover up instead of simply leaving unsaid. Words are also wasted in passive, roundabout constructions. By contrast, the informative summary is written in a lean, active style. Let us give examples of these points:

The descriptive summary uses phrases like:

The report describes . . .
The effects . . . were studied . . .
. . . the causes . . . are suggested.

But the informative summary does not use any of these words. It goes right ahead and *does* the describing. The descriptive summary has:

The decrease in thermal resistivity of foam due to ageing was quantified.

While the informative summary has:

Ageing of foam reduces thermal resistivity by about 7% a year.

It is shorter to give a figure than to say that a figure is in the report. '7%' is shorter than 'was quantified'. Similarly 'a significant improvement' takes up as much space as 'increases by up to 30%'. The descriptive summary has:

. . . the cause of the enhanced resistivity of glass-fibre combinations is suggested.

whereas the informative summary has:

We think this is because the multiple irregular surfaces within the glass fibre blanket trap more air.

Few more words are needed to give the cause than to promise to give it later. By using active, rather than passive sentence structures, the informative summary reduces redundant words.

A summary can contain numbers

In an informative summary, the facts are stated with whatever qualifying word is needed, and these facts should, as far as possible, include numbers. Even though they may be approximate numbers, they are more useful than evaluative words. For example, if we told you that the rewards for being an engineer who writes well were 'high', you would not have a clear idea of what sum we had in mind. All the other words available to say the same thing, such as 'substantial', 'significant', 'elevated', or even the simple 'large' are equally unhelpful. Qualitative words are vague, and leave different readers with different impressions. Unless specifically told otherwise, readers naturally allow their own expectations to be confirmed by what they read. Some engineers may think that being able to write well is so important that, having read and studied this book, they would double their salaries. For them, 'high' and 'substantial' are a polite way of saying 'double'. If you asked them a few weeks later, they might say, 'and the book I've just read said that salaries were twice as much for engineers who can write'. Because their assumption has not been corrected, they assume it has been confirmed. Equally, other engineers, who believe that it is technical skill, not 'frills' like good writing, that affects earnings, may think that 'high' means 'more than it's apparently worth'. A high reward for them would be 10% more, and this is what they will probably think they have been told.

To avoid this sort of variation in understanding, use a number not a word. We should have written, 'engineers who are good writers receive, on average, about 30% extra salary . . .' Notice again that the number is qualified so that it does not claim to be an exact figure. It is a simplification, 'about 30% . . .' Readers will accept it as a typical value, a guide which is better than nothing, and will not feel cheated if the report itself refines this as, 'surveys show that the range of increased earnings was between 16% and 49%, with a median value of 31.7% in the period 1985–87'.

Helpful approxima-tions

It is best, then, to use numbers, and qualify them as necessary to show that they are typical, average, or characteristic numbers, approximations for guidance only. Here, for example, is a summary with no numbers in it:

Modifications to Renclor 406 Process

Tighter BPC specifications on pharmaceutical grade Renclor 406 require operational changes to improve our product. High temperature chlorination tests have been performed and have given improved results, but the chlorinator jacket had to be modified before even higher temperature tests could be made.

High temperature chlorination results in excessive carry-over of Renclor to the off-gas system. So we had to modify the system to cope with this excessive entrainment. A cooler from salvage was modified to pass the gas downwards through the tube side, and the water temperature was increased above the melting point of trimenyl. Purity is now satisfactory.

Although the summary is informative, not descriptive, we are still left wondering. How much was the specification changed? What is a 'high temperture'? What is 'excessive carry over'? What is the 'melting point of trimenyl'? Such a summary is unsatisfactory because it leaves us guessing. Here is another summary of the same text with some numbers in it:

Reducing Renclor 406 impurities below 4.5 ppm

BPC specifications for pharmaceutical grade Renclor 406 now restrict impurities to 4.5 ppm, instead of 6.0 ppm. Chlorination tests at 195°C improved purity, but the chlorinator jacket had to be modified to test at over 200°C.

Chlorination at these temperatures results in up to 10 ppm Renclor being carried into the off-gas system. So we had to modify the system to cope with this excessive entrainment. A cooler from salvage was modified to pass the gas downwards through the tube side, and the water temperature was increased to over 78°C (the melting point of trimenyl). Impurities are now less than 4.0 ppm.

This summary gives a clearer picture of the problems, and we are not left wondering. Notice too that the summary with numbers is no longer; in fact it has fewer words in it. Generally, the numbers in the summary should be only a proportion of those in the report, not all or none of them. The figures in the summary do not have to be the same as the figures in the report. You are trying to give typical, not exact, figures so you may want to use approximate figures for the summary, which never appear as such in the report itself.

Because the summary has a different *readership* and *purpose* from the paper itself, it must have its own organization and style. While the audience of a summary overlaps that of the paper itself, some readers of the summary will not read the paper; the

The organization of a summary

aim of the summary is also different from that of the paper. Therefore decisions about style and structure have to be re-thought for the summary.

The paper's aim might, for example, be to tell fellow special-ists about a new measurement method, to record in detail the theory behind it, and to give examples of the new method applied to a project of current interest. Part of the audience for the summary will be the fellow specialists; but it is likely that there will be an additional part of the audience who do not want the details of theory and method. They want to know what is new, so they want only the name of the method, and why it is an improvement. The questions they will ask are: Is it more accurate? How much more? Is it cheaper, quicker, or safer, and by how much?

As in all informative writing, the important facts must come first; but what is important will vary for different readers. If the paper is for a journal, the general interest of the new method may come first; the fact that it is, for example, a fresh application of a new fibre may be most important. But if the reader is the Works Manager of a chemical plant, stress first the achieve-ments and advantages of the method. One sentence for a brief description of the techniques used is enough; readers who want the whole story will read the report itself.

In writing a summary, think of all the key facts and ideas in the report, grade them in order of importance for the readership of the summary, and then write them in that order. Give the fact which is most interesting or most advantageous to the reader first, and then go down the scale of importance towards smaller and less important details.

Some writers are afraid to organize a summary like this. First, the order is different from that in the report, and they are afraid it is not 'logical'. Second, they are left with all the excitement at the beginning of the summary, and a 'weak' ending which runs into the sands of increasingly less important detail. These wri-ters feel it is more satisfactory for the summary to follow the structure of the report, and for it to work up to some sort of final revelation. They are wrong. Let us look at their reasons one by one, and test them against the principles discussed earlier.

What is a logical order?   'Logical' can be a misleading word. As we suggested in Chapter 4, what is logical to the writer may be the opposite of what is logical to the readers. This is especially true in a summary. The readers are looking at the first words they have seen on a new topic, and they are short of time. For them, the 'logical' order is to put what they are most interested in first; the best order is the order of *announcement*, not the order of *discovery*. Neither the logic of argument, nor the logic of discovery is appropriate to the summary.

A summary can end in smaller and smaller details; there is no need to finish with a crash of cymbals. Summaries are not forms of entertainment, or substitute circuses; they are ways of doing a job. Here, as so often in writing, half-remembered and unanalysed ideas derived from writing for pleasure (whether the reader's or the writer's) are mistakenly applied to the very different job of writing to inform. Reading a summary is not an experience which must end with a sigh of satisfaction. It is a way of saving time, no more. So concentrate on saying the most important thing from the reader's point of view at the beginning, and realize that what happens at the end is less important.

Getting the right balance

The order of information in a summary will probably be different from that in the report itself; so will the balance between different facets of that information. Readers of most summaries want conclusions from a piece of work; they do not need the detailed evidence, or the full method by which the results were achieved. Some writers feel they have to prove everything, and display each step of the argument for inspection. While this may be true of the paper itself, it is certainly not true of the summary. Readers of a summary often do not have time to check through the detailed arguments; they regard the writer as an expert, and trust him or her. Only if they have doubts need they read the whole paper. In the summary itself, neither methods nor conclusions need detailed discussion.

The bulk of the summary will be a statement of conclusions. As a rule of thumb, something like half the summary may be a restatement of the most important conclusions or recommendations. Only one or two sentences are needed to summarize the introduction (i.e. the problem the paper solves), and a few sentences to summarize the methods on which the conclusions are based. The order in which these sections are written will depend, like the order of the paper itself, on what the purpose is. A report recommending specific actions will have a summary which puts the recommendations first. For example:

Replacing Florite with Hillpore

Summary:

Hillpore H6 additive should be purchased instead of Florite-9 after June 1980. Supplies of the Florite additive will become uncertain by then, and will cease altogether within two years. But Hillpore is available at the rate of 2.6 mt/month from S. Hill and Co. Ltd and supplies will remain firm. Both additives have similar properties.

The manufacturers of Florite, E.C.D. Ltd, supply their product only to us. They find this uneconomic, and when their present plant requires replacement in the next two years they will cease production. The present plant will be run as long as possible, but our experience suggests that they will face increasing down-time as the plant becomes unreliable. This will seriously affect the regularity of our supplies.

Our laboratory tests of the recommended product, Hillpore, show a fire-retardency in fibre-board using this additive of 12 mins/cm at 600°C. The impurity level is less than 80 ppm in typical samples. Moisture content and granule size are all suitable for our plant.

Notice that the final recommendation of the report comes first in the summary; the main reasons are given next. The second paragraph gives more details of the reasons, and finally details of the laboratory tests. The summary then ends, without any further generalization.

A summary of a paper written for record, with only provisional or marginal conclusions would have a different order. For example:

Dumping at Sea

Summary:

Although small compared with atmospheric fallout, river and direct coastal discharge, dumping in the open sea has grown ten times in the last two decades. It is now 10% of total waste disposal into the sea.

The 1972 Oslo convention prohibits the dumping at sea of some materials, and requires a permit for others. In deciding the suitability of sites and materials, dispersion rates and biological effects are considered. Dispersion after dumping is in two phases: initial dilution (typically 1/1000–1/100 in dumping from tankers and barges), and subsequent spreading.

The use of marine eco-systems for recycling must be further investigated. The retention of harmful wastes in the bottom sediments, and the transport paths of certain substances such as DDT must also be studied. Ocean dumping may provide an alternative to over-loaded coastal zones and vulnerable rivers and estuaries, but it is clear that persistent bio-accumulable substances should not be released into the sea at all. Proper management must be based on understanding, achieved through basic research.

Notice that the conclusion comes last here; the first thing is the arresting fact that dumping at sea has increased alarmingly. Details of the controlling convention, and of the research needed follow. The summary is designed to focus the reader's attention on a problem of wide general interest, but half of it concentrates on the conclusion that more research is needed.

As a general rule, start planning your summary round these structures: **Rules of thumb**

Reports for Record

One or two sentences to summarize the introduction
A few sentences only to summarize the method and results
The last half of the summary to state the main conclusions

Reports for Action

Recommended action stated first
Main reasons for this recommendation given
Statement of costs, savings, timings and more detailed evidence

Unlike a precis, a summary has no fixed length. It does *not* have to be under 10% of the report, or 500 words, or any other arbitrary limit. It should be as long as necessary. This necessity is not that felt by the writer, but by the readers. The proper length of a summary is not what is needed to summarize everything in the report: it is what is needed to tell the readers what they want to know. Not everything in the report will be mentioned in the summary. Especially if it is a long report, large sections may not be mentioned at all in the summary. **The length of a summary**

Many summaries are of similar length, because most readers

are prepared to spend just a few minutes reading a summary. A summary of only two sentences is too short and they will supplement it by leafing through the report. A summary which goes on to a second page will probably irritate them by taking too long, and they will not read all of it. So for reasons connected with the reader, not the report, most summaries will fall between a quarter and a full page.

What needs to be summarized will also affect the length of the summary. For example, an accident investigation which found no single cause, but twenty-three minor contributing causes all of which needed attention in plant safety, would probably put all twenty-three things in a long summary, covering a full page. In contrast, a report which has only one recommendation ('we should not buy this machine') and only one reason ('it is erratic in its production performance') will need only a short summary. The account of how the machine works and the tests which showed its performance was inadequate, may take up many pages in the report itself. These details are needed in the full report for anyone who wants to check or repeat the work. But in the summary, to be read by the executive and senior manager, the simple fact is enough, and there is no need to elaborate on it.

Does it need a summary?

Not all reports need a summary, either because they are short enough anyway, or because they have no readers who will want a summary. If the report is only one or two pages, there is little point in making it three pages by adding a summary. Equally, if it is going to be read only by two colleagues, both of whom want to follow through all the details of the work, a summary is probably not needed. But these are extreme cases. They are reports which are verging on memoranda or letters. Most reports *do* need a summary, if only because it helps to focus attention, and to remind readers what the report was about.

Place the summary first

What is the correct position for the summary? At what stage of the report should it be written? The answers are, first and last.

The position of a summary is conditioned by how readers use it. Some will read only the summary, and will not want to look through any of the rest of the paper to find it. Others will use it to give them an over-view before starting to read the whole paper. The summary should therefore always appear first, before even the contents page, and it should not be included in the numbering system or the list of contents. In effect, the title page and summary form a separate short report on their own.

Some papers put the summary at the end. This is useful only to remind people what they have already read, and does not do any of the other three jobs of a summary. The place for the summary is either on the front page itself, or on a separate page after the title page. If the summary is short, it is best on the front page, preferably in a block about two-thirds of the way down the page. Fig. 4.3 shows a page laid out like this.

Some organizations ease the readers' job by putting the summary on coloured paper. For example, the summary page may be always yellow paper, and executive readers go first to this colour-coded page. Other organizations save time, and paper, by circulating only the title page and the summary. If readers want the whole paper, they ask for it. The technique has the advantage of reducing the amount of paper circulated, and making the work load look less. But the other advantage is that readers have to take positive action, so that they have put themselves in an inquiring state of mind before they start to read the paper.

The summary should be put at the very beginning of the report, but it should be written last of all. Writing the summary should not be an opportunity to make points which were not made in the paper itself. Nor should the summary contain information which is not discussed in the paper, since this would be most confusing for the reader. The summary is not a chance to make up for the failures of the paper.

Write the summary last

The best way to write a summary is to read through the draft paper after completing it. Have a spare copy, and underscore the key points and information while reading through. Then go back, looking at these key points, trying to number them roughly in the order you think they will be of importance to the reader. Write the summary from these notes. You will have ensured that the summary is a helpful selection from the paper, and that the decisions about order have been made afresh for the particular job the summary has to do.

Summaries, like all informative writing, should be written in a style that communicates effectively. As we saw in Chapter 7 on

Style for summaries

Style, this means short, simple and active sentence structures, using the most familiar words which convey your meaning correctly. There are also some special aspects of style which must be thought about when writing a summary.

In a summary, the temptation to write 'observer-centred', not 'fact-centred', sentences is strong. When drafting papers, writers frequently think of themselves as abstract 'experimenters' observing events. So they write, 'It was observed that the column rose rapidly . . .'. When they come to write their summaries, they see themselves as in turn describing these observations. They are tempted to write, 'The report describes observations on the rate of rise of the column . . .' instead of 'the column rose rapidly . . .'.

To writers, the longer 'observer-centred' version somehow seems a more accurate description of the reality of the situation. But to readers, the extra information is redundant. It is unnecessary to remind them that they are reading a summary of observations of events; they want to look straight over the writers' shoulders, as it were, at the events themselves. But writers who obtrude between the readers and the events block the view. Not only do they use more words, but also they confuse and tire readers, who have to 'unpack' all the wrapping before they get the facts. Summaries should be direct, active statement of fact. Write:

The tracker bar measured 21 cm . . .

Not:

The report describes measurement of the tracker bar

Similarly, write:

We modified the return valve . . .

Not:

The report describes modifications to the return valve . . .

Another example of unnecessary wrapping-up of information is the sentence:

The importance of international cooperation is emphasized in the report . . .

It should be:

International cooperation is important . . .

The first version describes the emphasis; the second version enacts it.

A summary contains a number of simple statements of fact: therefore it is likely to be in a series of short sentences. We saw in the chapter on style that too many short sentences can obstruct the reader's progress, and that constant repetition of similar sentence lengths can be irritating. Because a summary is short, this is less important, and you should aim to write shorter sentences in a summary. Thus, do not write:

> The collapse of the element was for two reasons, of which the first was the increase in pressure, and the second the high temperature.

write instead:

> The element collapsed for two reasons. The pressure was increased, and the temperature was too high.

It is easier to absorb closely packed information in small units.

Do not write a summary like a telegram. Try reading these two different versions of the same summary. The first is in 'telegram' style: *Telegraphese*

Pallet air-cushions

Summary:

> Pallet movability poor with 'glide-air'. Air cushion should work, but system cannot adapt to air pressure variation. Also problems with small ground irregularities. Regulating system for separate control of each of four pads needed. System designed and demonstrated. Two pallets adapted, and remainder planned. Theory of system complex.

The second is in a normal style:

> The movability of pallets is poor with the 'glide-air' system. The air cushion method should work well, but the system cannot adapt to the variations in air pressure. There are also some problems with small irregularities in the ground. A regulating system which can control each of the four pads separately is needed. Such a system has been designed, and successfully demonstrated. Two pallets have been adapted, and adaptation of the remainder is planned. The theory of the system is very complex, however.

Notice that although the normal style uses more words, it is easier to read. From our first principles, helping readers is most important, and shortness is only a means to that end. Usually, it helps to be as compact as possible in your writing, but 'telegram' style is an example of unhelpful compactness. The readers have to make guesses about the missing words; they have to reconstruct each full sentence for themselves and this naturally takes longer than reading a ready-made one.

A summary of summaries   Here are two ways of summarizing what has been said in this chapter. As you read them, think which you find the most helpful:

Summary D

This chapter describes the nature and function of summaries. The ways a reader uses summaries are discussed at some length. The differences between abstract, precis, and summary are described. A distinction is made between descriptive and informative summaries, and the advantages and disadvantages compared. The use of numbers in informative summaries is considered, together with relevant examples.

Differences in organization between a summary and a report are suggested, and the reasons discussed. General rules for the organization of a summary are offered. Whether all reports need a summary is discussed, and the positioning of the summary investigated, as well as the order in which it should be written. The appropriate style for a summary is discussed with examples, and comments made on telegram style.

Summary I

Summaries have four uses. They are as an extended title; a time-saving short paper; a way of focusing attention on the main information; and an aid to remembering the paper. An abstract is usually only an extended title, while a precis is an exercise in shortening, not reorganizing. Descriptive summaries do not help the reader who wants the facts; informative summaries contain facts, and should have some numbers in them.

The organization of a summary differs from that of the paper it summarizes, because its aim and readership are different. Most of a summary should be conclusions and recommendations. Most reports need a summary, and it should be placed first in the report, although written last. Summaries should avoid 'observer-centred' style, and use short, active sentences. Telegram style is less helpful than a normal style.

The first summary is descriptive, the second informative. Informative summaries are always more helpful to the reader.

10 Choosing and using tables, illustrations and graphic presentation techniques

Visual signalling In turning to consider the use of tables, graphs, diagrams and other illustrations in the presentation of information, we are not changing our topic. Our subject is still clear communication, and we are still discussing how to make precise, manageable statements using language. Words, graphs and drawings are all visual patterns used to symbolise or represent meaning. In both graphic statements and verbal statements, we use a variety of hieroglyphics – dots, dashes, and other marks on paper – as symbols to carry information. Words, after all, are made up of letters which are composed of combinations of lines and circles; for example, the difference between 'o', 'p', 'd', and 'b' lies only in the positioning of the line tangential to the circle. So words and drawings are not conflicting or competing modes of expression. They are, at most, extremes on a continuum, with words at one end making minimum use of the visual appearance of the signals, and with drawings and graphic presentations at the other end making maximum use of the visual appearance of the signals.

In earlier chapters, we have discussed how statements in words often cause difficulty for receivers because they contain unfamiliar vocabulary or signals, because they are too long and complex, or because they require the reader to hold in mind too many inter-related clauses and conditions. Visual statements can be difficult for the receiver for similar reasons: they may contain vocabulary or signals with which the reader is unfamiliar; they may be too long or too complex; they may contain too many inter-related items and conditions for the reader to absorb. So, just as writers must be skilful in selecting words and sentence structures from the verbal code, they must be equally skilful in selecting and handling the elements from the visual code.

Thinking about the task

All that we have said in earlier chapters about tactics for selecting and handling information applies equally to the choice of visual techniques. As always, aim and audience are the governing factors in this choice, and it is especially important to consider two questions:

- What is the precise function of the table or illustration?
- Will the readers of the paper receive this information more readily in verbal or in numerical/visual form?

We have argued earlier that the way a text is organized and laid out, and the rate at which information should be 'unloaded' or packed into our pages, must be varied according to the function of the text. In a dictionary or a parts list, it is effective to pack together a great deal of information tightly and economically, because these texts are designed for reference, for scrutiny and cross-checking of particular items. We must make it easy for 'readers' to find their way into and around the assembled information, but we do not have to construct a coherent discourse; the entries are not statements in a connected argument. Tactics of selection and organization are different from those used in a report or an instruction sheet.

In just the same way, tactics in using tables and graphic techniques must be related to the precise function of the document as a whole and of the visual items in particular. Distinguish between tables and charts that are to be used for reference, as stores of classified and juxtaposed information, and visual statements that are to be used to make a point in an explanation or argument. Tables and drawings designed as reference material (such as wall-charts or timetables) can be packed tightly in the equivalent of dictionary or parts-list form. They are usually best separated from the main text of a report or paper so that they are not an obstacle to the readers' smooth progress through the argument. Tables and drawings that are designed to make a point as part of an argument should have simple structures and

METHANE

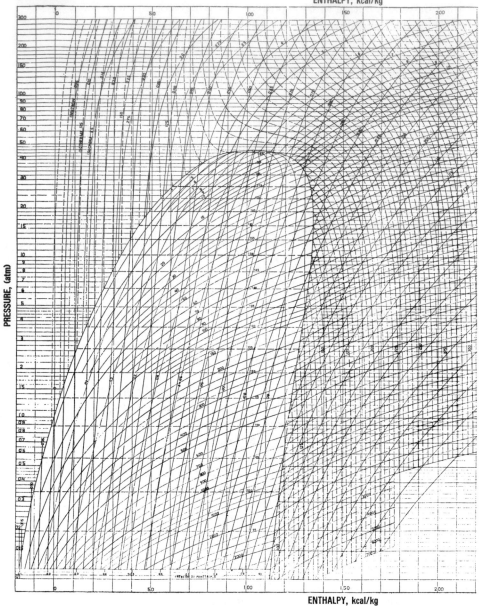

ENTHALPY, kcal/kg

PRESSURE, (atm)

ENTHALPY, kcal/kg

Fig. 10.1 A detailed graph for reference, best placed in an appendix (reproduced by permission of Philips Components).

carefully judged information-loads. They should be placed as close as is physically possible to the point in the prose text at which you want readers to take in the information they provide. For example, Fig. 10.1 shows a very detailed chart, providing a mass of information about the enthalpy of methane for reference and for scrutiny of detail. In most circumstances, it would distract the reader if it were part of the text, and it would be best placed in an appendix. Fig. 10.2 shows a specially drawn graph, based on the same information as Fig. 10.1; but it is a simpler statement designed to make one particular point. It was placed within the prose text of a report, close to the point in the argument at which the visual point was needed.

A practical tip: abstractions of information like this can often be made simply by putting tracing paper over a complicated original and inking in the significant lines. The traced outline can

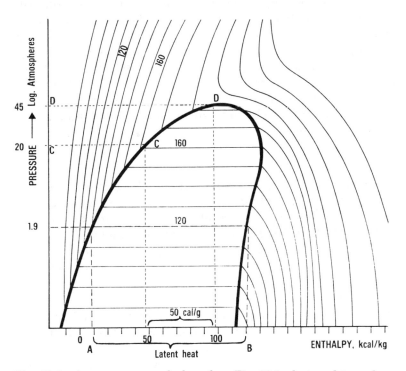

Fig. 10.2 A summary graph, based on Fig. 10.1, designed to make a point in the argument, best placed in the text of the document (reproduced by permission of Philips Components).

then be photocopied (perhaps even reduced) and included conveniently within a typewritten report or paper.

The second important question – will the readers receive the information more easily in verbal or in numerical/visual form – is of particular concern to writers who must communicate to specialists from a wide range of backgrounds. It is well established that readers will take more information more rapidly from documents if they know what to expect from the document and where in the document to look for it. It is also well established that some people are by nature and training more inclined to be 'verbalizers' and others are more inclined to be 'visualizers'. Some readers will find it easier to assimilate the verbal statement, 'Output falls to half within the first hour, to a quarter within the next hour, and then stabilises at one tenth for the remainder of the run'; other readers will absorb that information more rapidly if they are shown a simple graph that shows output plotted against time.

In writing for engineering and scientific readers, you will probably decide that they will usually be helped by the use of tables and graphic presentation techniques; but *which* technique still requires careful thought. Readers who like block diagrams may be bemused by complex drawings of electronic circuits. In debates with engineers and scientists about the relative effectiveness of different algorithm layouts (discussed in Chapter 6), we have been surprised to find how powerful is the influence of 'what they are used to'.

The resources and techniques available to the writer

In this chapter, we shall discuss only the best use of resources and techniques usually available to writers who have *by themselves* to produce internal reports and papers, articles for journals, instruction sheets and other similar documents. This is not a chapter for professional illustrators. If you are fortunate enough to have access to experts who can produce exploded drawings or use airbrush techniques, always involve them as early as possible in your planning and preparation for a report or paper. But most engineers and scientists have to rely on their own resources to produce the graphic presentation of their data. What is the best way of doing this?

First, review the 'language' elements available. The main symbols in visual presentation are:

● numbers (used mainly in tables);

- words (used in tables, algorithms, or flow charts);
- lines (used in graphs and drawings to symbolise paths, links, a lapse of time;
- shapes (used in symbolic charts, drawing and photographs).

These symbols constitute the equivalent of the verbal 'vocabulary'. This vocabulary is put together into the visual equivalent of sentences and paragraphs, and as in your choice of verbal 'style', it is vital to:

- consider carefully the length and complexity of the statements you ask your reader to digest;
- be sure to conform to conventions of 'word order';
- avoid the visual equivalent of wordiness and waffle;
- control the use of jargon.

In visual signalling, you also have available important cues that you cannot use in verbal signalling:

- spatial cues (alignment in columns and rows, grouping);
- typographic cues (size, design, and weight of type);
- colour cues (shading, colouring, colour of paper as well as of print);
- ruling (use of lines not as symbols in themselves but as a framework to separate, group and relate information);
- use of 'white space' to group or emphasize items of information.

Perhaps the greatest advantage of visual presentation is that it is possible to represent three dimensions. Prose restricts information to a one-dimensional linear sequence: visual presentation enables you to show shapes, to show activities going on in parallel, to show movement in varying directions. Your reader can take in all these things 'at a glance', because the human eye can use a span of awareness much wider when looking at visual presentations than when looking at words (focus on any word in this sentence, and notice how much of the surrounding text you can see without changing your point of focus). By presenting information in tables or in graphic forms, you can often make much more efficient use of your readers' perceptual abilities than by presenting information in prose.

But remember that perception and comprehension are not the same. Your readers must not only *perceive* your visual presentations but also *understand* them. So beware of complication and overloading. Give readers the minimum data needed to make your points, not the maximum data available to justify your existence. And make your visual statements self-sufficient, so that readers can comprehend them without continuous cross-reference to the prose text.

Just as it is desirable to coin a new sentence each time you want to say something, it is wise to try to produce a fresh illustration each time you decide you want to make a visual statement. Automatic re-use of pre-packed words and phrases frequently produces only approximations to the intended meaning of a statement: likewise, apparently time-saving (and thought-saving!) use of ready-made graphs or photographs frequently presents only an approximation to the point intended. As you work at communication tasks, you will constantly be tempted to trade-off efficiency against convenience. Often, you will be able to use existing visual material very effectively; but sometimes you may be tempted to write a text that fits the available visual material rather than to take extra trouble to produce visual material to suit your text. Resist this temptation.

The great advantage of using visual presentations is that they give all readers the same visual image to look at. But notice that we are not saying that readers will all see the same thing: each illustration must have a caption or heading telling readers what you want them to see in the illustration. Imagine two identical pictures of a boy kicking a ball along the pavement of a busy suburban street. One caption reads: 'Road-safety training teaches children to stay safely on the pacement'. The other caption reads: 'We need parks to keep our children away from dangerous roads'. Readers see different points made by the same picture in the two illustrations. You might be entertained by taking any drawing or photograph designed for inclusion in a report without its caption, and asking your colleagues to tell you not only what it shows but also what *point* it is making about its content. We suspect you will rarely get a clear or unanimous response.

Tables   Tables give a systematic and orderly arrangement of items of information. Tabular layout has the particular virtue of juxtaposing items in two dimensions for easy comparison and contrast. Tables eliminate tedious repetition of words, phrases and sentence patterns that can instead be put at the tops of columns or at the sides of rows in the table. Although tables do not make much impact by visual display, it is possible, by careful arrangements, to emphasize and highlight particular items or groups of information.

There are several ways of arranging information within a table and no one way is always the best. As usual, we must return to our basic questions: what are we trying to achieve with this table? What is the required emphasis? For whom are we presenting the information? What are the interests and needs of those readers?

Tables can be organized with the information in numerical order, in alphabetical order or in an order which groups items according to common features or common values. Normally, however, readers expect the elements or entities which are being compared to be grouped or listed vertically, and to find variables, qualities or performance details listed horizontally. Readers expect to move from known material on the left to new information on the right; known (or base) information should therefore appear on the left, with explanatory, conversion, or derived material on the right.

We find it helpful to distinguish two broad types of tables: *dependent* tables and *independent* tables. A dependent table is placed in the text and is an integral part of the prose statement. It continues the sentence or paragraph in just the same way as a mathematical or chemical equation that is included in a sentence, and it needs no title or caption because it is a continuous part of the text. It follows that it must be restricted to a small amount of information, probably a maximum of two or three columns and rows, a dozen or so numbers in all. An example of a dependent table is shown in Fig. 10.3. The reader can read through this table as a continuation of the sentence that it completes.

The table shown in Fig. 10.4 is too large to be presented as a dependent table. It is not reasonable to expect readers to absorb the information presented within the table as though they were simply continuing to read through the paragraph. The amount of information presented in that table requires readers to stop and reflect on the arrangement of facts. Since the writer wanted the readers to absorb this information at this point in the account, it should be left in the place that it occupies on the page; but it would have been wiser to have separated it from the text more clearly by surrounding it with white space, and by giving it a table number and a caption. Even more effective, probably, would have been to make prose summaries of the

They were anxious to know our plans and how we saw growth, particularly with respect to increasing governmental pressure, towards better and improved run characteristics in products

2. EUROPEAN PRODUCTION REQUIREMENTS

The forecast provided by Production Planning, London was tabled as follows:

Requirement(Mt)	1988	1989	1990
Min	1.9	3.5	4.8
Max	2.9	5.4	7.2

It was explained that these are min-max numbers and that the use of the average would be most realistic. With these numbers plus US requirements, the present plant design capable of 2.5-3.0 Mt with small-scale de-bottlenecking, would be outstripped in 1989. Thus, a European site would provide the added volume plus provide the safety of a second source.

Exploratory discussions on the concept of buying product in Europe and on stock procedures at the sites was accepted without commitment for further study. Technology was via denitrogenation, by the route:

$$NaCl + C_2H_6N_2 \longrightarrow 22H_4Cl + NaN_2 + H_2O$$

This process yields a serious loss of nitrogen via salts and it is a very important economic facet of this process that any nitrogen loss is fully recovered. Initially, the raw material is transported to site in single-load tankers to

Fig. 10.3 A summary table, brief enough to be included in the text.

significant points that emerge from the data and to have put the full table in an appendix.

An independent table may be placed physically within the text – be surrounded by it – but should be clearly distinguished from it. In an independent table, you are inviting your readers to look at a visual display of the information separate from their reading of the text; the amount of information being presented will require a conscious step by the reader from the text to the table and back again. Minimize the size of that step if you can, by placing the table as near as possible to the text that discusses it (often this will be difficult in a typescript report and it may be necessary to collect the independent tables at the end of the report). Clear captions focusing the readers' attention on the

The following table, derived from H.A.A. for the year ended
31st December 1988, illustrates the long-stay nature of these
hospitals:

Speciality	Discharges 1986	1987	Av. No. beds occupied	% occupancy 1986	% occupancy 1987
Moreton					
Geriatrics	553	579	475.3	91.6	92.9
General Med.	2126	2215	227.6	81.5	95.3
Gen. Surgery	429	388	34.8	54.5	58.8
Mental	210	224	204.3	85.0	83.1
Others	2312	2923	?	?	?
Total	5630	6329	942.0	78.2	82.6
Woring					
Geriatrics	221	212	266.4	86.5	88.2

Even for non-geriatric beds at Moreton the average length of
stay is much longer than at say Widepark where, for example,
general surgical patients stay for an average of 8.9 days. This
is because the majority of all Moreton patients are old and are
kept in after acute treatment is completed, often for social
reasons. Thus the atmosphere at Moreton and Woring is very slow
compared to a General Hospital.
Moreton General Hospital was formerly a workhouse but became
a chronic sick hospital in 1944. After the formation of the N.H.S.
many improvements were carried out and a programme of ward
up-grading is now virtually finished. There is also a new
assessment wing, mainly for "Eastern" patients, which has
improved staff morale which is generally low, because the rest of
the wards are in three-floor blocks most of which have no lifts.
The wards are not very wide but patients do have lockers, though
not individual clothing. In general the wards are light and clean
and the blocks are arranged as follows:
Ground floor: Patients attending treatment departments such as
Physiotherapy
Middle Floor: (sister's office) - Admissions and Patients
requiring active nursing.
Top Floor: Long stay, convalescent and social cases awaiting
discharge.
It has only been possible to provide day rooms on the ground
floors so non-ambulant patients higher up cannot use them.
Brownpath Wing, where over 100 male psychogeriatrics live has
proved unsuitable for the type of patients because not all

Fig. 10.4 Table which is too large to be included as part of the text.

significant facts or inferences that you want them to see are also important.

Ruling   The design of the ruling in independent tables presents choices: an *open* design, a *semi-closed* design or a *closed* design. An open design is one which has no vertical or horizontal rulings in it at all. A semi-closed design has just some vertical lines and/or some horizontal lines. A closed design has a complete array of both vertical and horizontal lines separating virtually all elements from all others.

Consider the examples in Figs. 10.5, 10.6 and 10.7. Which of these helps you to see most readily the information that the writer is trying to present with particular emphasis? Even if you do not know what information the writer wants to emphasize, it is possible to sense the difference of impact of the various ways of ruling a table. Most readers find an open table (Fig. 10.5) is confusing, giving too little help to the eye. A fully closed table (Fig. 10.7) is also difficult to use because the apparatus of lines seems to overwhelm the information that is being presented. Most readers prefer a semi-closed design (Fig. 10.6), with some horizontal and/or some vertical lines to help signify the importance of the piece of data.

Are vertical lines or horizontal lines preferable in semi-closed tables? There can be no over-all rule, because the lines in the

TABLE 2

Test Conditions on Luwa Evaporator

Run No.	1	2	3	4	5	6	7
Pressure mm/Hg	275	275	275	275	275	275	275
Feed Rate Lb/hr.	66	–	44	37	37	27.7	29
Product rate lb/hr	39.5	–	28.6	23.1	23.1	18.5	18.5
Product % of feed	60	64.2	65.2	62.2	62.2	66.6	63.6
Product temp $^{\circ}$C					102	102	
Vapour temp $^{\circ}$C	25	25	25	25	25	26	25
Rotor Speed R.P.M.	1500	1500	1500	1500	1500	1500	1500
Jacket inlet $^{\circ}$C	200	200	200	200	200	200	200
Analytical result % t.s.	97.3	97.8	97.5	97.8	98.2	97.9	98.4

Fig. 10.5   An 'open' table, with no ruling.

RESULTS

3.

3.1   TABLE 1   Degradation of Compound A with HF and HCl

Acid	Solvent	mls Solvent	Percentage loss after:		
			1st Treatment	2nd Treatment	3rd Treatment
Hydrofluoric	n-Propanol	10	80.4	99.1	99.1
	i-Propanol	10	14.9	35.4	59.7
	i-Propanol	20	32.0	94.3	--
	n-Butanol	10	98.0	--	--
	n-Butanol	20	98.0	--	--
	i-Butanol	20	98.0	--	--
	t-Butanol	10	10.2	16.0	22.3
	t-Butanol	20	36.6	79.2	94.0
	Amyl Alcohol	20	98.0	--	--
	2-Ethyl Hexanol	10	99.0		
Hydrochloric	n-Propanol	10	19.2	24.0	27.3
	i-Propanol	10	9.4	11.1	not done
	n-Butanol	10	35.6	94.6	98.0
	n-Butanol	20	93.0	99.7	--
	i-Butanol	20	93.9	98.0	--
	t-Butanol	20	5.7	16.4	23.4
	Amyl Alcohol	20	97.5	--	--
	2-Ethyl Hexanol	10	96.0	--	--

N.B. Treatment is not continued after >94% loss in weight.

Fig. 10.6   A semi-closed table, with some ruling.

tables may be doing two separate things. They may be helping the readers' eyes with the simple business of seeing the figures in the table, and they may be stressing the significance of particular groupings. They may be guiding the eye *across* the page or *down*. Most readers are accustomed to looking up and down columns of figures without too much difficulty, provided

Shutdown Causes		Jan.	Feb.	Mar.	Apr.	May	June	Total	Monthly Av.
Decompositions	No.	5	7	23	54	24	10	123	20.5
	Hours.	9.3	9.8	43.1	76.8	50.5	22.6	212.1	35.4
Reactor Leaks		3	-	1	5	5	1	15	2.5
		73.4	36.0	56.2	41.4	85.3	10.1	302.4	50.4
Blockages		3	1	1	0	2	2	7	1.2
		96.9	2.1	10.2	0	32.6	9.6	151.4	25.2
Pretreatment Faults		1	1	3	4	10	2	21	3.5
		2.0	2.0	30.3	7.9	78.9	4.7	65.8	11.0
Fresh Gas Compressor Faults		0	0	0	0	0	0	0	0
		0	0	0	0	0	2.5	2.5	0.4
Precompressor Faults		3	5	3	4	6	4	25.0	4.2
		44.4	28.0	12.5	21.5	13.7	29.0	149.1	24.9
Hypercompressor Faults		8	8	5	5	6	2	34	5.7
		41.4	46.1	23.2	65.6	15.0	4.0	195.3	32.6
Instrumentation Faults		2	2	2	0	0	1	6	1.0
		12.4	7.8	2.0	0	0	1.4	23.6	3.9
Electrical Faults		1	1	1	1	3	0	7	1.2
		8.6	13.5	2.2	2.6	5.9	0	32.8	5.5
Utilities Faults		0	0	0	1	1	0	2	0.3
		0	0	0	1.5	4.5	0	6.0	1.0
E/F, F/E Jet Changes		-	1	0	0	0	1	3	0.5
		18.3	40.0	0	0	40.0	48.0	146.3	24.4
Planned Maintenance		0	0	1	1	0	0	2	0.3
		0	0	48.2	50.6	0	0	98.8	16.5
Others		2	2	14	5	18	30	71	11.8
		3.9	11.2	74.8	6.3	40.1	124.0	260.3	43.4
External Causes		1	0	0	0	0	0	1	0.2
		51.0	0	0	0	0	0	51.0	8.5
Total No. of S/D		29	28	53	80	76	51	317	52.8
Total Hours Down		361.6	196.5	302.9	274.2	306.5	255.9	1697.6	282.9
Percent Downtime		16.7	9.3	14.1	12.3	13.7	11.5	12.95	12.93

Fig. 10.7 A 'closed' table.

the figures are carefully aligned by the typist. They need more help when they have to compare figures in horizontal rows. That might seem to suggest that in semi-closed tables, the normal use of lines should be horizontal.

But you must also take account of the second function of ruling within a table. That function is to stress the significance of particular groupings. It may be that you wish to stress groupings that are horizontal or vertical. In those circumstances you have to weigh up whether readers will need more help in seeing

I   Improvements in Operating Rates

This report is based on actual operating conditions and the calculated rates have been demonstrated in the plant.

The report reckons to have 31 days shutdown in January for major repairs (motor overhaul, drive and mounting repairs etc.) and a 15 days shutdown in June for part overhaul. Therefore, all rates include 5% downtime for the two yearly shutdowns,

Table 2: Individual Equipment Capacities

Equipment	presently	June/July	after minor debottle-necking
HOV reactor	3.5 Kg/day	3.80	3.80
Dissolution vessel	*	2.46	2.86
Storage tanks	3.00 Kg/day	3.20	3.30
Mixer	7.15 Kg/day	7.80	7.80
Heater	5.26 Kg/day	5.26	5.26
Reactor	4.43 Kg/day	4.23	4.27
TDE	$	$	$
Chlorination	2.10 Kg/day	2.14	2.14
Washing	5.32 Kg/day	5.17	5.17
Colour-fastening	2.98 Kg/day	2.97	2.97
Mixing	3.50 Kg/day	3.50	3.50
Recovery	5.20 Kg/day	5.20	5.20

*   The present dissolution vessel consists of three temporarily linked tanks. It would be misleading to cite its capacity. The June/July figure is based on a new single vessel to be installed in May.

$ Precise capacity measurements of the TDE have been mislaid: details will be made available at the co-ordination meeting on April 1st.

Fig. 10.8   Table without ruling.

the significance of groups, or more help simply in following the rows of figures across the page. In general, however, the eye more often needs help with horizontals than with verticals. We more often use a ruler, or a finger, to run across a line than down a column. Fig. 10.8 shows a table with open ruling. The same table in Fig. 10.9 is easier to use because the ruling gives

I   Improvements in Operating Rates

This report is based on actual operating conditions and the calculated rates have been demonstrated in the plant.

The report reckons to have 31 days shutdown in January for major repairs (motor overhaul, drive and mounting repairs etc.) and a 15 days shutdown in June for part overhaul. Therefore, all rates include 5% downtime for the two yearly shutdowns.

Table 2:   Individual Equipment Capacities

Equipment	Presently	June/July	After minor debottlenecking
HOV reactor	3.5 Kg/day	3.80	3.80
Dissolution			
vessel	*	2.46	2.86
Storage Tanks	3.00 Kg/day	3.20	3.30
Mixer	7.15 Kg/day	7.80	7.80
Heater	5.26 Kg/day	5.26	5.26
Reactor	4.43 Kg/day	4.23	4.27
TDE	$	$	$
Chlorination	2.10 Kg/day	2.14	2.14
Washing	5.32 Kg/day	5.17	5.17
Colour-			
fastening	2.98 Kg/day	2.97	2.97
Mixing	3.50 Kg/day	3.56	3.56
Recovery	5.20 Kg/day	5.20	5.20

*   The present dissolution vessel consists of three
    temporarily linked tanks. It would be misleading
    to cite its capacity. The June/July figure is
    based on a new single vessel to be installed in May.

$ Precise capacity measurements of the TDE have been
    mislaid: details will be made available at the
    co-ordination meeting on April 1st.

Fig. 10.9   The same table as Fig. 10.8 with semi-closed ruling.

some help to the eye. However, some lines are redundant, and Fig. 10.10 shows how these can be removed. Note that the double line under the headings helps the eye to separate heading and content. This method of ruling looks neat, and has the advantage that it can be produced on a typewriter without taking the paper out and ruling it separately.

I   Improvements in Operating Rates

This report is based on actual operating conditions and the calculated rates have been demonstrated in the plant.

The report reckons to have 31 days shutdown in January for major repairs (motor overhaul, drive and mounting repairs etc.) and a 15 days shutdown in June for part overhaul. Therefore, all rates include 5% downtime for the two yearly shutdowns.

Table 2: Individual Equipment Capacities (Kg/day)

Equipment	Presently	June/July	After minor debottlenecking
HOV reactor	3.5	3.80	3.80
Dissolution vessel	*	2.46	2.86
Storage Tanks	3.00	3.20	3.30
Mixer	7.15	7.80	7.80
Heater	5.26	5.26	5.26
Reactor	4.13	4.23	4.27
TDE	$	$	$
Chlorination	2.10	2.14	2.14
Washing	5.32	5.17	5.17
Colour-fastening	2.98	2.97	2.97
Mixing	3.50	3.56	3.56
Recovery	5.20	5.20	5.20

*   The present dissolution vessel consists of three temporarily linked tanks. It would be misleading to cite its capacity. The June/July figure is based on a new single vessel to be installed in May.

$ Precise capacity measurements of the TDE have been mislaid: details will be made available at the co-ordination meeting on April 1st.

Fig. 10.10   The same table as Fig. 10.8 with horizontal ruling only.

In designing a table, you must consider how readers will use it. Is their main objective to find a single item of information in a single 'cell' of the table (for example, the arrival time in Cardiff of the 1400 departure train from London); or is their main objective to compare the lists of figures in two columns (for example, the comparative times at various stopping points for two trains on the journey between London and Cardiff); or is their main objective to appreciate generally the over-all pattern (for example, the existence of faster trains at 'peak' hours compared with 'off-peak' hours)? To help with the first objective, more lines would probably be effective. To help with the second, fewer lines, emphasizing complete columns rather than individual numbers would probably be better. To help with the third objective, perhaps a bar-chart would be better than a table; at least the table should make use of some means of emphasizing starting and finishing times, perhaps by using heavier print.

You can obtain the effect of ruling without the use of lines by using white space to separate groups or blocks of information.

Switching

Junction

			RATINGS			CHARACTERISTICS						
type	status	case	$\pm V_{DS}$ V	$P_{tot} @ T_{amb}$		$-I_{GSS}$ max.	$-I_{DSS}$ min.	$-V_{(P)GS}$ max.	$r_{ds\,on}$ max.	C_{rs} max.	t_{on} max.	t_{off} max.
			V	mW	°C	nA	mA	V	Ω	pF	ns	ns
BSV78	D	TO-18	40	350	25	0,25	50	11	25	5	10	10
BSV79	D	TO-18	40	350	25	0,25	20	7,0	40	5	15	15
BSV80	D	TO-18	40	350	25	0,25	10	5,0	60	5	15	25
2N3966	D	TO-72	30	300	25	0,1	2	6	220	1,5	120	100
2N4091	D	TO-18	40	1800	25[1]	0,2[2]	30	10	30	5	25	40
2N4092	D	TO-18	40	1800	25[1]	0,2[2]	15	7,0	50	5	35	60
2N4093	D	TO-18	40	1800	25[1]	0,2[2]	8	5,0	80	5	60	80
2N4391	D	TO-18	40	1800	25[1]	0,1	50	10	30	3,5	15	20
2N4392	D	TO-18	40	1800	25[1]	0,1	25	5,0	60	3,5	15	35
2N4393	D	TO-18	40	1800	25[1]	0,1	5	3,0	100	3,5	15	50
2N4856	D	TO-18	40	360	25	0,25	50	10	25	8	9	25
2N4857	D	TO-18	40	360	25	0,25	20	6	40	8	10	50
2N4858	D	TO-18	40	360	25	0,25	8	4	60	8	20	100
2N4859	D	TO-18	30	360	25	0,25	50	10	25	8	9	25
2N4860	D	TO-18	30	360	25	0,25	20	6	40	8	10	50
2N4861	D	TO-18	30	360	25	0,25	8	4	60	8	20	100

1) T_{case} 2) $-I_{GSO}$

Fig. 10.11 A well-blocked table, white space used for 'ruling' (reproduced by permission of Philips Components).

When you do this, restrict your groups to blocks of five at the most. The eye can discern easily the top, bottom and centre rows within a block of five, but once you provide six or more rows in a block, it is difficult for the eye to move through the figures without help. We can 'see' a group of up to five objects (such as marbles on a table) at a glance; six objects tend to be counted as two groups of three, and so on. This may be the reason why five is a convenient maximum in any one grouping. Fig. 10.11 shows an example of a well-blocked table.

However, take care if you introduce blocking. Arbitrary arrangement of rows into blocks may suggest a special relationship between the rows in each block, and differences between the blocks.

Figure 10.5 makes another important point about the design of effective tables; there are blank spaces in some of the columns and rows, and some items are marked simply with dashes. Presumably, the writer wished the blanks to signify something different from the dashes, but it is not clear to readers what a blank space signifies or what a dash means. The principle that emerges is that there should never be blanks or other unexplained signals in a table. If you have no reading (if there was a nil value or if it was not possible to make a measurement for a particular reason) you should place either a nil within the table or some hieroglyphic such as an asterisk or dagger and explain the significance of that hieroglyphic at the foot of the table.

Clarity and manageability

Figure 10.12 emphasizes the difference between tables designed to make a point in an argument and tables designed to make available masses of information for scrutiny. It is far too large to be included within a text or even within an argument. You may find, however, that there are occasions on which you feel it is necessary to invite your readers to examine a mass of facts and figures at a central point within a report. In such a case, it may be necessary to use a table such as is shown in Fig. 10.12. But recognize the overwhelming impact of so much information presented in that way. If possible, provide some small steps by means of which your readers can approach the mass: for example, provide two or three smaller tables in which you separate some of the variables or groups of information, so that the final presentation of all the information seems less daunting. Also, summarize key information in words or small tables as you discuss it in the text.

Fig.1 Results of tests on treated and untreated samples of
Material X at varying temperatures and frequencies

Sample			Port	Below Freezing						Above Freezing					
				−15°C			−05°C			+05°C			+15°C		
	Temperature	Frequency MHz		600	700	800	600	700	800	600	700	800	600	700	800
1	Treated		1	1.14	1.14	1.14	1.16	1.14	1.15	1.15	1.14	1.16	1.24	1.12	1.10
			2	1.18	1.16	1.05	1.17	1.17	1.14	1.17	1.16	1.06	1.20	1.16	1.05
			3	1.17	1.16	1.04	1.11	1.17	1.12	1.17	1.17	1.06	1.17	1.17	1.05
	Untreated		1	1.13	1.14	1.15	1.11	1.19	1.14	1.16	1.16	1.14	1.22	1.14	1.11
			2	1.17	1.15	1.10	1.14	1.15	1.16	1.20	1.15	1.06	1.21	1.17	1.07
			3	1.18	1.17	1.06	1.14	1.12	1.15	1.16	1.17	1.11	1.19	1.19	1.06
2	Treated		1	1.09	1.12	1.14	1.11	1.15	1.16	1.11	1.15	1.16	1.22	1.14	1.11
			2	1.05	1.12	1.14	1.09	1.08	1.07	1.20	1.19	1.06	1.22	1.13	1.11
			3	1.18	1.11	1.05	1.10	1.16	1.14	1.17	1.16	1.06	1.17	1.16	1.05
	Untreated		1	1.10	1.11	1.06	1.15	1.12	1.11	1.09	1.14	1.18	1.23	1.14	1.12
			2	1.06	1.12	1.06	1.13	1.14	1.13	1.19	1.17	1.07	1.14	1.14	1.07
			3	1.21	1.14	1.07	1.19	1.19	1.20	1.21	1.16	1.05	1.15	1.16	1.08
3	Treated		1	1.13	1.16	1.13	1.14	1.15	1.12	1.13	1.15	1.14	1.22	1.13	1.09
			2	1.18	1.16	1.05	1.15	1.11	1.04	1.19	1.15	1.06	1.23	1.16	1.05
			3	1.25	1.14	1.06	1.22	1.21	1.07	1.21	1.14	1.06	1.24	1.13	1.06
	Untreated		1	1.16	1.16	1.12	1.14	1.11	1.17	1.12	1.16	1.13	1.21	1.12	1.07
			2	1.17	1.15	1.04	1.11	1.17	1.06	1.20	1.17	1.07	1.22	1.12	1.04
			3	1.24	1.16	1.08	1.19	1.15	1.09	1.21	1.13	1.05	1.20	1.14	1.09
4	Treated		1	1.08	1.08	1.21	1.09	1.11	1.05	1.08	1.13	1.19	1.12	1.13	1.20
			2	1.08	1.11	1.11	1.08	1.14	1.07	1.09	1.15	1.16	1.06	1.16	1.18
			3	1.13	1.09	1.09	1.11	1.09	1.06	1.13	1.14	1.15	1.14	1.15	1.15
	Untreated		1	1.04	1.07	1.20	1.10	1.11	1.19	1.07	1.16	1.20	1.13	1.14	1.16
			2	1.04	1.10	1.20	1.08	1.11	1.15	1.11	1.17	1.21	1.07	1.14	1.20
			3	1.09	1.19	1.18	1.09	1.17	1.08	1.12	1.13	1.16	1.16	1.14	1.20
5	Treated		1	1.14	1.06	1.24	1.18	1.17	1.20	1.13	1.07	1.29	1.14	1.07	1.20
			2	1.11	1.06	1.24	1.11	1.11	1.10	1.08	1.09	1.29	1.07	1.06	1.22
			3	1.15	1.06	1.13	1.08	1.15	1.12	1.13	1.10	1.20	1.11	1.11	1.20
	Untreated		1	1.12	1.07	1.25	1.12	1.09	1.16	1.12	1.09	1.28	1.15	1.10	1.19
			2	1.16	1.04	1.20	1.14	1.05	1.21	1.10	1.07	1.20	1.07	1.09	1.23
			3	1.14	1.08	1.17	1.11	1.18	1.20	1.15	1.14	1.27	1.16	1.14	1.18

Fig. 10.12 A very large table, best kept in an Appendix for reference, with smaller tables or summaries in the main text.

QUALIFICATIONS OF ENTRANTS TO EACH SECTION OF
HIGHER EDUCATION (ENGLAND AND WALES, 1961)

Type of Institution	Percentage with qualifications of:			
	3 "A" levels or more	2 "A" levels	1 "A" level	ONC & other qualifications
Universities	82	14	1	3
Teacher Training	12	28	20	40
CAT's (Full-Time)	23	37	15	25
Other Further Education (Full-Time)	10	20	20	50
Part-Time Day	3	10	11	76
Evening	1	5	6	88

Fig. 10.13   Table giving information in bare numerical form.

Bar charts are often better ways of presenting numerical data **Bar charts**
than tables. Frequently it is necessary to show several different
variables or relationships within overall totals. In these circumstances, the use of a table does not make this information as
clear as the use of a bar chart. Consider, for example, the table in
Fig. 10.13. It shows the number of students who have various
types of qualifications in different types of higher education. But
the presentation of raw numbers does not make an impact
quickly. The figures in the first column (82, 12 and 23) are not
very different in shape and size. Readers draw information
from these numerical signals only after mental addition or
subtraction.

If, however, the information is presented in bar-chart form, it
offers an immediate visual impression of the different proportions of students with various qualifications in various forms of
higher education. Fig. 10.14 shows this. Notice that it is possible
by joining the various levels within the bars to get some of the
sense of movement usually associated with the drawing of
graphs. Also, note that it is possible to use bar charts horizontally, as well as vertically. If, for example, you are showing
braking distances for various types of cars, it is valuable to show

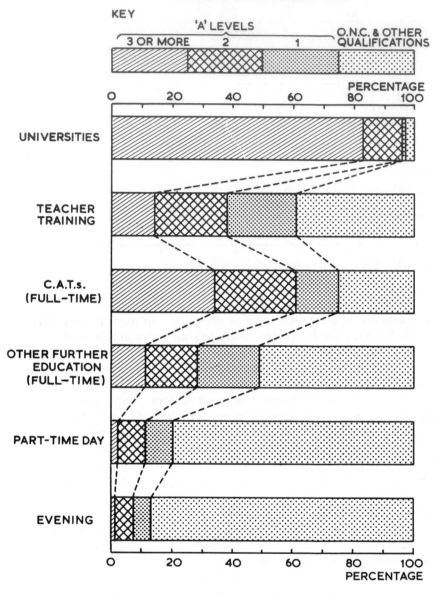

Fig. 10.14 Bar chart giving the same information as Fig. 10.13, with greater visual impact (reproduced by permission of HMSO).

these horizontally because the bars reflect the spatial point you are making.

It is helpful for your readers if you label the tops of the bars in your chart either with a number or with an identifying word. Since it is mainly the top of the bar that interests readers, that is naturally the first place they look. The value of labelling the tops of bars is shown in Fig. 10.15. This figure also shows a dangerous practice: the suppression of zero in a chart in order to emphasize some difference in levels. The designer of Fig. 10.15 was not necessarily wishing to distort his or her information, but the visual impression made by the bars would have been very different if the bars had been shown in their totality, rather than starting at 80%.

Visual comparison of performance data is often much easier if a bar chart is used. But notice that bar charts are not limited to comparing one quantity only, and that the bars in the chart need

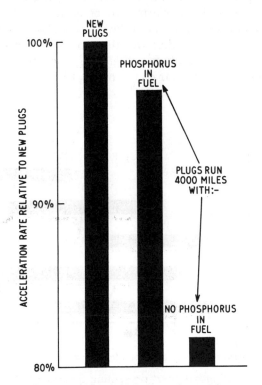

Fig. 10.15 Bar chart with helpful labelling, but with a suppressed zero.

TABLE 7: Performance of "Teemin" samples in TK test rig

Sample	Start x (gm/cm)	Theoretical End-Point (gm/cm)	Test End-Point (gm/cm)	Crosses 4a=0?
A	4.7	5.1	6.5	yes
B	2.6	4.3	6.6	yes
C	1.2	4.5	4.3	no
D	1.8	5.1	6.7	yes
E	0.9	3.7	5.2	yes

Fig. 10.16   Presentation of test results in bare numerical form.

not be anchored to either axis. The table in Fig. 10.16 gives information about five different sample materials. It gives details of performance figures and, in particular, emphasizes whether or not the performance of each sample crosses an important boundary. After a few moments of scrutiny and mental calculation, readers *can* discern the differences in performance from the numbers presented in the table and select the 'best' sample. But the bar chart in Fig. 10.17 shows how much

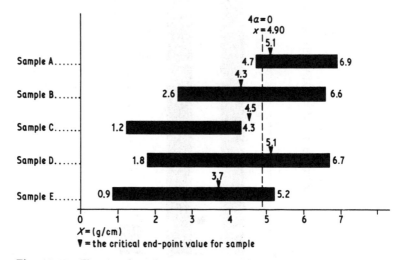

Fig. 10.17   Floating bar-chart presenting the same test results as Fig. 10.16 with greater visual impact.

EXPERIMENTAL SECTIONS ON RW 15 NEAR TIEL

Experimental Section No.	Gravel Asphaltic Concrete (mm)	Sand (mm)	Sand Cement (mm)	Slag (mm)	Sand Asphalt (mm)	Total Depth (mm)
1	60+60	-	400	-	-	600
2	60+60	-	300	-	-	500
3	60+60	-	150	-	-	350
4	60+120	-	150	-	-	410
5	50+70	210	100	-	-	510
6	60+60	100	100+100*	-	-	500
7	60+60	-	-	200	-	400
8	60+60	-	-	-	100	400
9	60+60	-	-	-	100	300

* Either side of sand layer

Note: All sections topped by 40mm Open Texture Asphaltic Concrete and 40mm Coarse Dense Asphalt.

Fig. 10.18   Tabular presentation of data in bare numerical form.

more effectively the same information can be presented. It makes an immediate visual impression on the reader. The performances of the different samples are seen at a glance and it is immediately clear which of the ranges cross the important boundary and which do not.

Our examples so far have shown bar charts with horizontal bars, vertical bars and 'floating' bars. One more example shows bars being used with telling effect by being taken across the horizontal axis. The table in Fig. 10.18 gives details of various types of under-surface for experimental roads. The variations can be grasped by a scrutiny of the tabulated figures, but the presentation in Fig. 10.19 using bars above and below a single axis, makes a more immediate impression upon the reader and enables comparison and contrast to be made much more readily. It is particularly easy to interpret visually because the spatial disposition of the bars echoes the subject it is illustrating –

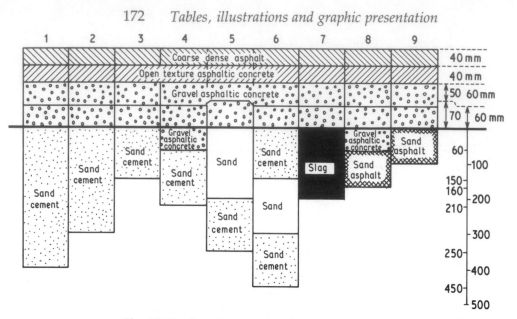

Fig. 10.19 Bar chart, presenting the same data as Fig. 10.18 with greater emphasis (reproduced by permission of TRRL).

sections of road foundations. Looking like what is being represented, in this simple geometrical sense, is a great help in visual communication.

Readers may be beginning to think that we are giving undue stress to very minor points in urging attention to how a table is ruled, how bars are labelled and the effects of presenting bar charts horizontally or vertically. Indeed, these matters *are* quite minor in themselves; but it is the cumulative effects of a number of small tactical decisions that influence whether a presentation will have immediate visual impact, and therefore be easy or difficult for a reader to use. And writers must always recognise that the comprehensibility of a presentation cannot be considered without reference to the context in which it is being received. As Patricia Wright explains:[1]

> When things are easy, when there are few distractions, when people are highly motivated, then the better of two formats shows only a slight advantage, but as working conditions become less optimal the disadvantages of a poorer format become considerably greater. This is a point of particular relevance to technical communicators who are often designing information in relatively ideal conditions. Hence their

intuitive feel for the differences between alternative formats may suggest that such differences are marginal. Indeed the differences may not even be available to intuition. This is why there is an advantage in having a body of research findings to which the technical communicator can turn.

Dr Wright's article, *Behavioural Research and the Technical Communicator*, from which this passage is taken, is a valuable record of that body of research.

Pie charts and surface charts

Another type of chart, the pie chart, is useful for presenting information that is related to time or proportions. For example, the table in Fig. 10.20 presents the results of an analysis of outgoing telephone calls made by an organization during the first hour of a working day. The table certainly makes all the details available for scrutiny; but the clock-face analogue of the pie chart in Fig. 10.21 shows with greater impact the proportion of long-distance calls to local calls throughout the hour, especially the 'rush' of people who made long-distance calls as soon as work began.

In drawing pie charts, remember that it is easiest for readers to read clockwise from the twelve o'clock position. Also, it is normally most effective to place larger segments first, provided that does not distort a time sequence.

Another chart that is useful for showing proportions within rising figures over a period of time is a surface chart. A surface chart is a cross between a chart and a graph. The example in Fig. 10.22 shows how a visual impression can be made, emphasizing not only development over a period of time but also the proportional changes within the totals over that period of time.

Graphs

Graphs (line charts) need to be composed with as much care as any other type of verbal or visual communication. Unfortunately, it is common to find that little thought is given to choice of scale and to emphasizing the precise point which is to be made. Fig. 10.23 shows many of the weaknesses in graphs that occur in too many scientific and technical reports. It is mystifying, designated simply Graph A. As there is no explanatory caption, readers are required to remember what Graph A was supposed to be showing or have to refer back to the text to remind themselves. The line of the graph is scarcely visible, and

Table 1: Outgoing calls initiated per 5-minute period
between 0900 and 1000, Monday 13 June 1988

	Number of calls			Percentage of calls	
	Long distance	Local	Total	Long distance	Local
0900-0905	8	3	11	72.73	27.27
0905-0910	6	9	15	40.00	60.00
0910-0915	10	12	22	45.45	54.55
0915-0920	10	16	26	38.46	61.54
0920-0925	8	16	24	33.33	66.67
0925-0930	14	13	27	51.85	48.15
0930-0935	9	19	28	32.14	67.86
0935-0940	16	14	30	53.33	46.67
0940-0945	8	15	23	34.78	65.22
0945-0950	18	16	34	52.94	47.06
0950-0955	16	21	37	43.24	56.76
0955-1000	15	20	35	42.86	57.14

Fig. 10.20   Tabular presentation of data, which makes data available for scrutiny, but does not make a point.

it is not at all easy to see how many changes of direction there are in the line as it moves forward in time. It may be that the writer's intention was to emphasize that the results scarcely rose above the bottom axis. But it would probably have been better to emphasize the flatness of the graph in general, and the small

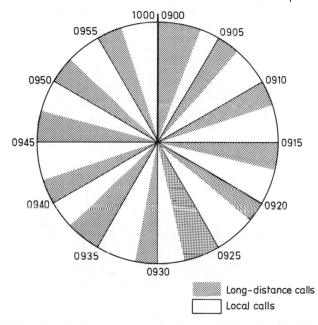

Fig. 10.21 Pie-chart presentation of part of the data in Fig. 10.20, using the clock-face analogue to emphasize the proportions of long-distance calls to local calls in each five-minute period throughout the hour.

changes in movement in particular, by choosing a different scale.

What we see here is the equivalent of thoughtless choice of words in making a verbal statement. Fig. 10.24 seems to show a similar carelessness in putting together a statement, but this time it seems to go to the other extreme by having not too little information but too much. However, this graph was not designed to make a single point within an argument. It must be seen as a 'reference' graph, equivalent to the large table shown in Fig. 10.12. Once again, we must distinguish between tactics chosen to make a point during an argument, and tactics used to present masses of inter-related data for readers to scrutinize at greater length. The graph in Fig. 10.24 fits the second category. But even so, it would probably help readers if that graph were approached by means of two or more steps presenting smaller elements of the information and gradually building up to the composite package provided in the massed detail in Fig. 10.24. As John Parry puts it:

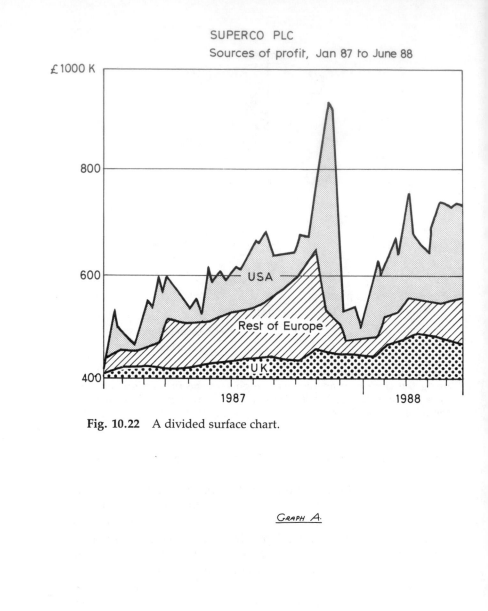

SUPERCO PLC
Sources of profit, Jan 87 to June 88

£1000 K

800

600

USA

Rest of Europe

UK

400

1987   1988

Fig. 10.22 A divided surface chart.

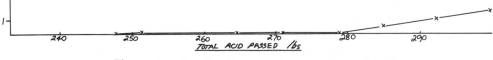

GRAPH A.

10
9

7

5

3

1

240   250   260   270 *TOTAL ACID PASSED* /bs   280   290

Fig. 10.23 Graph with mysterious caption and badly chosen scales.

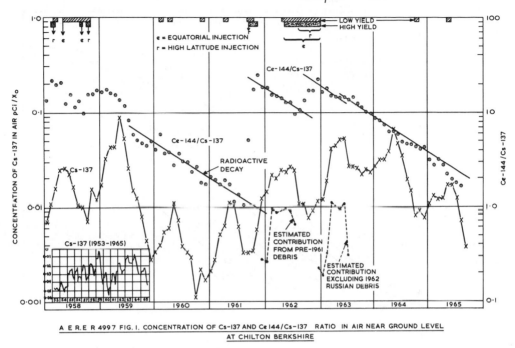

A E R.E R 4997 FIG. I. CONCENTRATION OF Cs-137 AND Ce 144/Cs-137 RATIO IN AIR NEAR GROUND LEVEL
AT CHILTON BERKSHIRE

Fig. 10.24 Heavily loaded graphic presentation (reproduced by permission of the UKAEA).

Visual presentation can . . . be overdone; the inexpert user of charts and diagrams often fails to resist the temptation to try and say too much at a time. The keynote of nearly all successful diagrammatic presentation lies in simplicity of design and absence of cluttering detail. A sequence of logically developed charts is invariably preferable to a single monsterpiece, which in saying everything conveys nothing.[2]

How many lines is it possible to accommodate comfortably on a graph? Once again in discussing effective communication, there is no single correct answer. Everything depends upon the precise objective of the graph that you are drawing. For example, the graph in Fig. 10.25 has six lines on it, and yet it is not too cluttered because the principal objective of presenting that graph is to show that the lines all move almost in parallel. But if those lines had begun to move across one another, the load of information would have been too great to absorb.

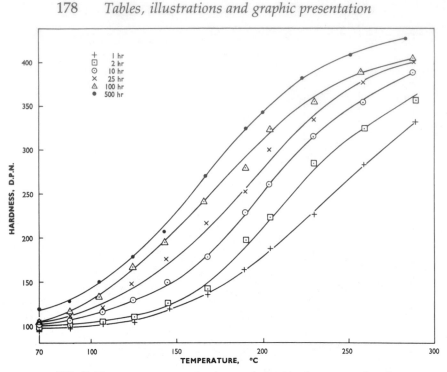

FIG. 2—Time-temperature-hardness relationship for copper-beryllium

Fig. 10.25 Graph showing the clear use of several lines but poor labelling (reproduced by permission of Shell Research Ltd).

In Fig. 10.25 the different lines are labelled by means of small symbols and a key is provided in the top left corner of the graph. Most readers find this an irritating practice, since they are obliged to move their eyes frequently from the identifying symbols on the lines to the keys in the top corner and back again to ensure that they are not misunderstanding the information being presented. Wherever possible, it is desirable to put the label at the ends of the lines so that the reader does not have to keep moving to and fro across the graph to find identifying information in a key. Figure 10.26 shows a graph labelled in this way. Notice, however, that the label for the left-hand curve seems to be in the wrong place. It would be better on the left of the curve. A moment's thought shows that in fact all the labels are on the top right-hand end of the curve; but this 'verbal' logic conflicts with the visual logic of the eye. Visual logic should always take precedence.

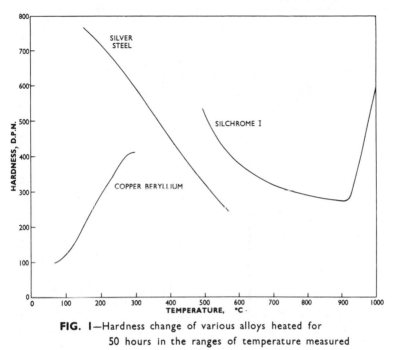

FIG. I—Hardness change of various alloys heated for
50 hours in the ranges of temperature measured

Fig. 10.26 Graph showing logic of labelling of curves (reproduced by permission of Shell Research Ltd).

Flow charts

Flow charts use lines to help readers see sequences and movements through a process or a set of facts or possibilities. Lines are used to enable each reader not only to follow a path, but also to ignore information which might be relevant to other readers but is not relevant to him or her. Normally, in creating an algorithm or a flow chart, the writer wishes to make it easier for readers to decide which details, circumstances or conditions relate to their interests and needs. The information is arranged in a hierarchy, enabling each reader to start by asking the most important overall question, and subsequently to follow a decision-taking sequence through a number of points at which simple decisions between two paths are possible. The paths normally represent a sequence in time or priority in physical or mental operations.

But not all flow charts are algorithms. A conventional circuit diagram can be described as a flow chart, as it shows all the paths or flows in a circuit without necessarily emphasizing any

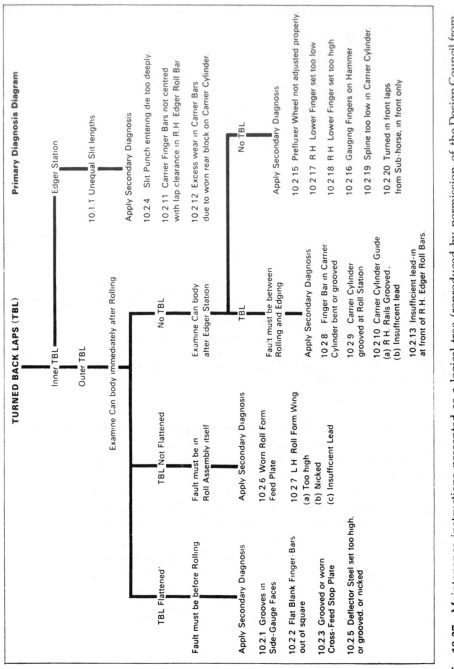

Fig. 10.27 Maintenance instructions presented as a logical tree (reproduced by permission of the Design Council from *Engineering*).

principal flow. But the best circuit diagrams, too, are structured to help the reader recognize groups of operations, sequences, primary and secondary flow, or feedback.

The simplest type of flow chart is a logical tree (otherwise called a family tree, or a genealogical tree). Figure 10.27 shows a logical tree used to present a fault-finding procedure. By reducing the information to a series of questions and comments, the writer has managed to avoid generating dense paragraphs of prose setting out various possibilities, and the actions that should be taken in the light of those possibilities. This enables readers to concentrate on the particular faults they identify in the apparatus before them.

Logical trees

The flow chart in Fig. 10.27 guides the reader simply by the use of lines. All other information is provided in words. It is possible to use flow charts to reduce the number of words as well. This can be done by introducing pictorial representation into the presentation as well as words. Figure 10.28 is a representation of the procedure for producing technical literature in a company. By use of recognizable symbols, the writer has managed to give an impression of the various stages in the process, culminating in the production of the literature and its dispatch from the factory.

Use of symbols

Not many flow charts go this far in pictorial representation. Most rely on the use of well-known symbols to add information to that which is written in words within the various elements on the flow chart. Fig. 10.29 shows some of the most familiar symbols in use. A circle indicates a starting or finishing point, a diamond or lozenge shape indicates a question and a rectangle indicates an instruction or decision point. Figure 10.29 shows use of conventional symbols, and reliance on readers' recognition of information conveyed not by words but by the use of symbols. However, this practice can become dangerous because some readers may not recognise the significance of the symbols used in the presentation.

Particularly, readers in other countries may not understand symbols that are very familiar to you. Most British readers understand the meaning of a tick ($\checkmark$) as used in Fig. 10.30; in many other countries, the ($\checkmark$) symbol is not used.

In some countries, too, a cross (x) customarily signifies a

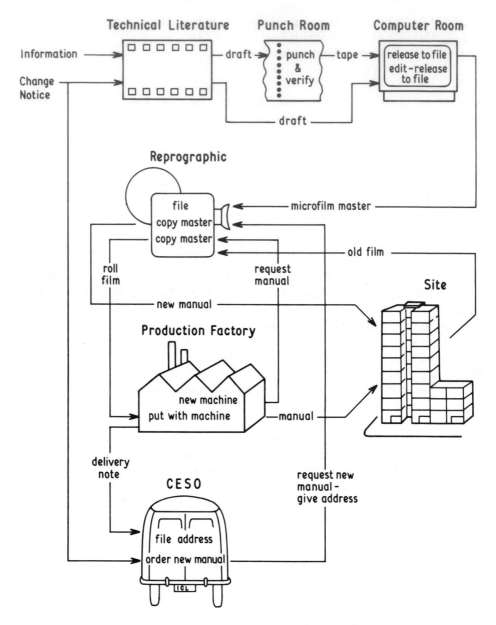

Figure 8 Film & Paper Flow (Future)

Fig. 10.28 Flow-chart using semi-pictorial symbols (reproduced by permission of ICL).

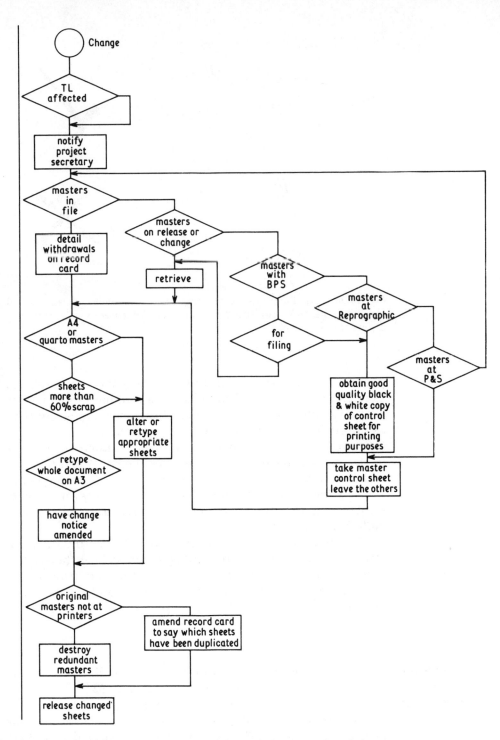

FLOW DIAGRAM FOR CHANGE PROCEDURES WITHIN TECHNICAL LITERATURE

Fig. 10.29 Flow-chart using conventional symbols (reproduced by permission of ICL).

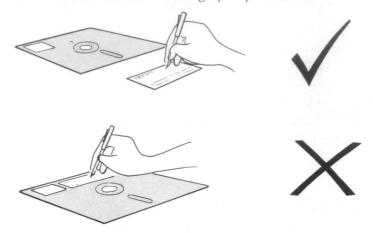

Fig. 10.30   An illustration that may cause confusion by its use of symbols (the tick and the cross may be interpreted differently in different countries).

positive response (not, as in Britain, a negative response). For example, in a register of attendees at a meeting in France, the secretary puts a cross by the name of each person present (not, as in Britain, by the name of each absentee).

So, when you use symbols in your illustrations or text, try to choose symbols that are in use everywhere. Avoid the confusion that arises when organizations create different ways of symbolizing a single meaning. Fig. 10.31 shows seven ways of symbolizing the earliest and latest times of an event in a Critical Path Analysis network!

Of course, the safe way to proceed is to use international standards and to give readers a key to symbols at the start of each document. But remember that your readers may not be using the document as frequently as you are, and extensive use of symbols identified by keys may place heavy loads on your readers' memories.

Emphasis on flow and functions   A common fault in flow charting is to make all movement or flow seem to be of equal importance. Figure 10.32 is an example showing a flow chart in which it is difficult to see the relative importance of different pieces of information and different movements. Figure 10.33 is a simplified and clarified flow chart

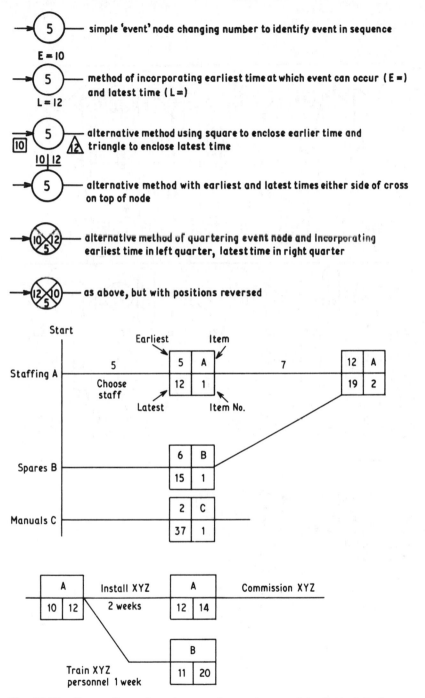

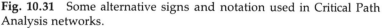

Fig. 10.31 Some alternative signs and notation used in Critical Path Analysis networks.

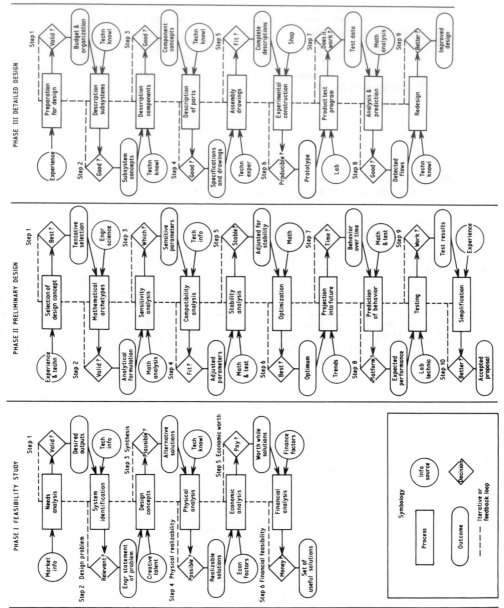

Fig. 10.32 Flow-chart where flow-lines are confused by symbols.

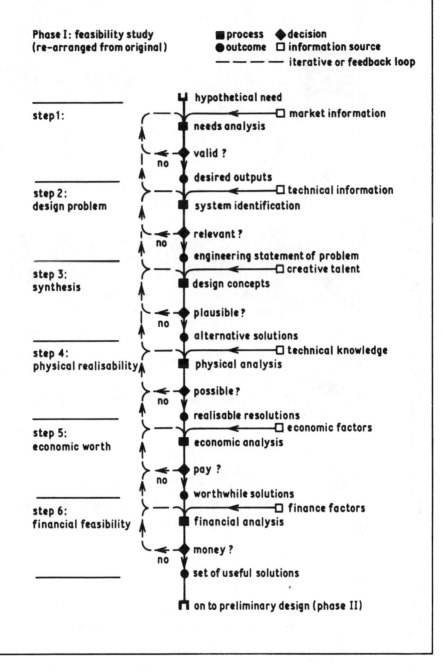

Fig. 10.33 Re-drawing of Fig. 10.32 with clearer flow-lines (reproduced by permission of Ken Garland Associates).

TYPICAL PRODUCTION PROCESS

QUALITY – THE UNIFYING BOND FROM SILICON TO SALES

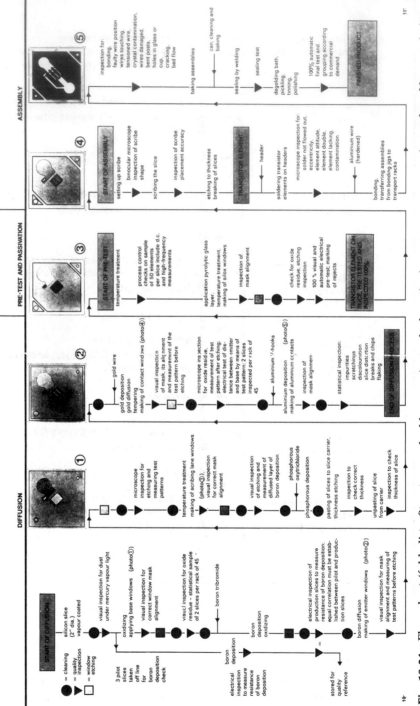

Fig. 10.34 Flow-chart 'folded' to fit onto one double page, instead of continuing over many pages (reproduced by permission of Philips Components).

TR22 TR23
COMPLEMENTARY
EMITTER FOLLOWER

INVERTER
output at
logic 0 when
sync input to
unit is absent

IC4 RETRIGGERABLE
MONOSTABLE
C17, R40 determine unstable
period. Sync pulses to pin 1
maintain unstable state. If
sync pulses fail cycle
completes and output pin 8
goes to logic 0. On restoration
(of sync pulses) triggering
through pin 1 is delayed until
pin 2 goes to logic 1 after
5–7 s

INTEGRATOR/COMPLEMENTARY EMITTER
FOLLOWER
fault signals charge C11 via R30 and D5, output
follows C11 potential. SA enables fault
indicator action to be checked.
Procedure is detailed below.

IC2 COMPARATOR STAGE
input to pin 3 is compared with
fixed potential on pin 2. Output
from pin 7 goes to logic 0 when
threshold is reached from fault
integrator. R206 provides +ve
feedback to speed-up transition

Fig. 10.35 Block text supporting the block circuit diagram shown in Fig. 10.36 (reproduced by permission of S.W. Amos from Wireless World).

emphasizing by different weights of line and symbols the main movement and the feedback within the flow.

Sometimes flow charts become long and complex if you attempt to show all possible paths, branches and outcomes on a single chart. One way of reducing complexity is to have a 'family' of charts – a main chart showing an overall flow, indicating branches to lower-level charts that give more detail of specific decision-points or procedures. Another helpful technique for reducing the length of flow charts is to 'bend' them, as is shown in Fig. 10.34.

Block diagrams can be used particularly successfully to indicate the linking of functions or other structural entities in scientific and technical work. Figure 10.35 shows a simple display of functional blocks in electronic equipment. The con-

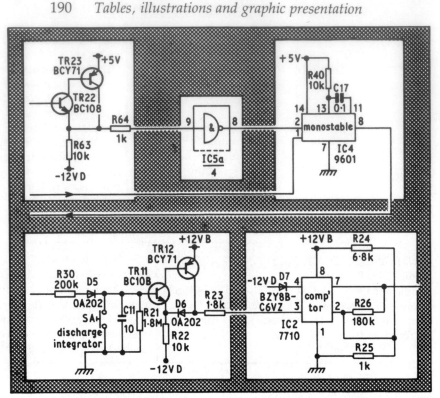

Fig. 10.36   Block circuit diagram supported by block text shown in Fig. 10.35 (reproduced by permission of S.W. Amos from Wireless World).

tent of the functions is explained in words. Figure 10.36 shows a parallel illustration, emphasizing the circuit layout that matches the explanation in the functional blocks in Fig. 10.35. And if the information is not too complicated, it is possible with benefit to superimpose the two functional layouts one upon the other, to produce a flow chart which shows functional blocks with the explanation in words and the circuit diagram all in one presentation.

Skilful use of   In this discussion of graphic presentation techniques, we have
lines, shapes   not included analysis of the advantages and disadvantages of
and tones   different types of specialized technical drawing such as ortho-

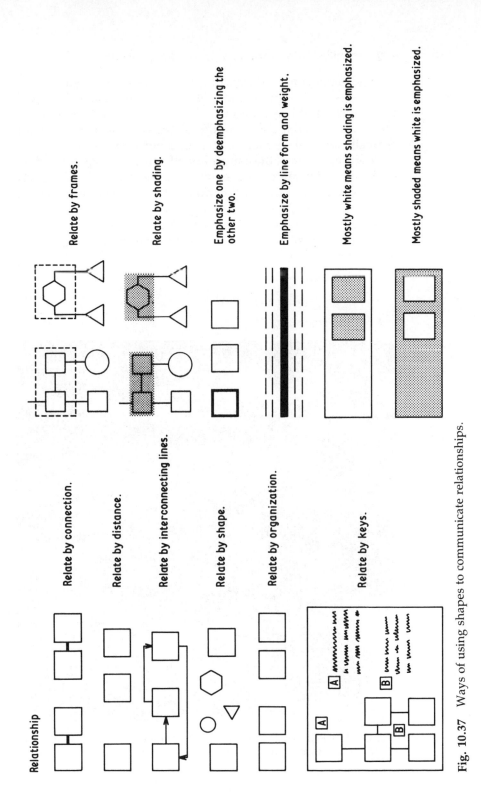

Fig. 10.37 Ways of using shapes to communicate relationships.

graphic projection, isometric projection and so on. Neither have we discussed the production of illustrations using air-brush techniques, multiple colours and other specialized techniques. These are beyond the scope of this textbook because they are not normally available to most writers of reports and papers.

However, some of the simple but effective techniques used by professional illustrators *are* available to the producer of reports and papers. For example, you do not have to be a professional illustrator to use lines, shapes and shading effectively in your presentations. Figure 10.37 is a valuable summary of the tactics the non-specialist illustrator can use to show relationships.

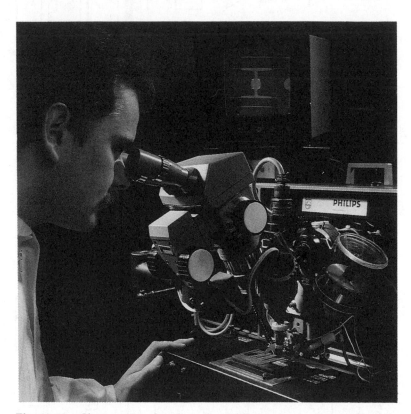

Fig. 10.38 Clear sense of scale and orientation in simple photograph of equipment (reproduced by permission of Philips Components).

Simple photographs, emphasizing size, scale and position can be used effectively in reports and papers at low cost and without specialized help. Figure 10.38 shows the skilful use of a photograph to emphasize the position of controls. Note particularly the effective introduction of a human figure, to give a sense of scale.

Finally, let us emphasize that although the presentation of factual information in diagrams or even in pictorial charts can ensure that it will be understood and remembered better than when it is presented in a table, much depends on the skill with which the presentation is matched to its aim and audience. Indeed, for some readers, the inclusion of graphical illustrations in a text may *decrease* accuracy of recall and grasp of an argument over-all. Much seems to depend on the intelligence of the readers and the extent of their training in how to interpret visual presentations.   *A word of caution*

Audiences for most scientific and technical papers are likely to have a reasonable amount of experience in interpreting visual presentations, so it should be possible to use many of the tactics discussed in this chapter. Nevertheless, if you have frequently to write for audiences with little or no scientific training, we recommend that you read M.D. Vernon's *The Psychology of Perception*[3] (especially Chapter 7); and in particular, if you have to write for audiences in a non-Western cultural setting, you should be aware of the ways in which cultural backgrounds and formal education influence interpretation of visual presentations. We recommend *The Span of Visual Perception in Engineering Drawing* by T.N. Davies[4] and *Perception and Cognition* by Barbara Lloyd.[5]

1. Wright, Patricia (1977) Behavioural Research and the Technical Communicator. *The Communicator of Scientific and Technical Information*, **32**, 6.
2. Parry, John (1967) *The Psychology of Human Communication* University of London Press, p. 114.
3. Vernon, Magdalen D. (1965) *The Psychology of Perception*, London, reprinted (1971) by Penguin, Harmondsworth.   *References*

4. Davies, T.N. (1976) The Span of Visual Perception in Engineering Drawing. *The Communicator of Scientific and Technical Information*, **27**, 2–10.
5. Lloyd, Barbara B. (1972) *Perception and Cognition: A Cross-Cultural Perspective*, Penguin, Harmondsworth.

Writing **11**
instructions

What we have been saying about general principles applies to all types of informative writing, but there are specific writing tasks which we want to discuss as special cases, requiring their own special skills. Two types of writing with specialized aims, and therefore specialized tactics, are instructions and descriptions, which are the subjects of this and the next chapter.

Much writing is difficult to use because it fails to make clear decisions about what its aim is. This extract is from a document that was intended as an *instruction*:

> The computer and the external equipment are placed in operation by procedures which incorporate loading magnetic tape, making certain manual selections, and starting the program. The operator first makes sure that all the equipment which is to be used by the program in store is properly prepared: that is to say that there is paper in the typewriter, that its margins are correctly adjusted, that its switch is set to COMPUTER, and that the power is on. If magnetic tape is to be used, the door of the tape handler is opened.

Difficulty is not caused by unreadable style. It is caused by the writer's confusion between the task of *describing* the process, and that of telling the reader how to *operate* the equipment.

Writers must be clear about the differences between these two modes of writing. *Instructions* enable the reader to do something with minimum hesitation. They do not necessarily require him or her to *understand* the operation; indeed to try to make the reader understand as well may interfere with the sequence of operations. A description, we shall argue in the next chapter, progresses from external overviews, through descriptions of the function and purpose, into detailed discussion of the components. Descriptions tell the reader how something is constructed, how it works and perhaps why it is used. They fit a machine or process into a context of previously understood tasks and needs; but they do not necessarily tell the reader how to *operate* the machine or process. Instructions, however, have a simply defined aim, and the definition of failure is exact; if the process or equipment fails to operate correctly, the instructions have failed as communication.

We have emphasized throughout this book that decisions about the selection, arrangement and presentation of information depend on decisions about the aim and the audience. For operating instructions, the aim is to make possible confident and correct operation, so the content must be the complete information needed to do this. Careful thought about the audience is needed in deciding how to spell out fully an action which may be familiar and routine to some readers, but not to others. The layout of the text is also conditioned by the aim. Instructions should use the most convenient layout for the operator to follow through the sequence of operations with text and machine side-by-side. Finally, the tone created by the style must not interfere with the willingness, understanding and confidence of the operator, as he or she carries out the sequence of operations.

Are the instructions complete? Incomplete instructions can be disastrous. For example, an electricity generating station installed a new generating set, costing millions. During the bedding-in period, the operator was instructed to measure the temperature of the bearings every 15 minutes. His instructions were detailed and specific, and required him to plot a graph showing these temperatures; the graph showed the temperature steadily rising until after several hours the bearing melted, destroying the generator. At the inquiry, the operator pointed out that he had done exactly what the instructions required. His employers could not blame him because the instructions had not told him to do anything *about* the rising temperature.

The most difficult task of all for writers is to ensure that they have not left out a vital instruction. They must judge how much routine knowledge their readers already possess, and how much they need to be told. Thus, this instruction:

The reactor jacket may need manual draining of the condensate during warming up.

fails to give enough detail. We are not told how to drain the condensate manually, and in any case we seem to be given the option of draining the condensate or not. What will we see, feel or hear if there is condensate which needs draining? How much condensate must there be before it is worth draining? What will happen if we do not drain it? Instructions do not need to specify all the things which can go wrong if they are not followed. But if they invite us to make our own decisions, they must supply information on which to base sensible decisions. It is quite acceptable to have another source of information elsewhere to give this information, but the instructions must then have a clear exit loop. We must be in no doubt as to *where* we must go to find the additional information, and under exactly *what* circumstances. In practice, it is usually easier to give operators a complete instruction:

> Read the level of condensate, shown on the eye-glass. If it is above the 1.5 cm^3 mark, open valve 3 (diagram 2) and allow the condensate to drain away. Close the valve when steam, not water, comes out.

Explicitness and exactness are paramount: spell out every detail which could cause doubt. This need not be cumbersome if it is done succinctly and sensibly.

Writers of instructions often seem too afraid of being thought pedantic by their readers. Their image of the readers is fixed on experts; afraid of irritating those experts, they put summaries of the complete action in the instructions. There are indeed operators who think they know everything; some even do. But it is a mistake to be too concerned to avoid offending this class of reader, while leaving the beginner to flounder. For readers who *do* already know the procedure, complete instructions are still a useful 'check-list': they can work through the instructions and fill gaps in their knowledge. But the writer should forget the 'bored experts'. These readers will not use the instructions anyway; and in any case, their boredom is their own problem; the writer's problem is the inept non-expert. Remember that legislation throws a heavy responsibility on the writer of instructions.

Writers of instructions must make some assumptions about the operators, such as assuming that they know the meaning of every-day words (though writers must always be careful about

What assumptions do you make?

using technical terms, and about using familiar words that have specialized meanings in particular contexts). Thus, it would be unreasonable to assume that the instruction 'switch on' needed to specify how to operate an electrical switch (but if the switch had an unusual action it would need to be explained). To write instructions so complete that a robot could follow them would be immensely laborious and would fail in the task of communicating with human beings. Some assumptions about readers must be made. The art of successful instruction-writing is to make the correct assumptions, and to do this, writers must put themselves in the receivers' frames of reference. Do the readers know the terminology? If not, information transfer is at an end. Decisions *must* be made about what to leave out; wrong decisions about selection are disastrous.

The major problem is the writer's own over-familiarity with the material. For the writer, the operation may be automatic; but he or she must deliberately bring the operations into full consciousness, inspect each action in turn, judge what the readers will know and will not need to be told. Assumptions must be made; but they should be made consciously, not by default. It is a feat to imagine what it is like *not* to know what we already know; err, therefore, on the side of completeness. Finally, as a last check, get some people who are unfamiliar with the operation to see if they can perform the operation following the instructions, but using no other information.

Ambiguity   Assumptions which cause trouble are not just those about what the readers know: writers also make assumptions about how readers understand ambiguous words. If someone shouts 'run', he or she may mean 'run away' or 'switch the machine on – run it'. Usually, the context makes it clear. In speaking, communication takes place when both speaker and hearer are in the same context; but what is written in one context may be read in another. Consider, for instance, these instructions for changing a plug:

> The domestic plug consists of two parts: the back part which is the main body of the plug and covers up the connections inside, and the front part which supports the three metal projections which fit into the socket.
> In order to change the plug firstly unscrew the screw which enables the back part to be removed. Looking inside the plug,

i.e. on the back part of the front part, one sees the back part of the projections.

These instructions are confusing because the writer imagines the plug in use, plugged into a wall-socket. In this position the cover of the plug faces the observer, and is the 'front' part. But a reader who is about to change the plug would probably have it on a table, lying with the prongs upwards. In this position, the cover is the back part. The context of the writer is different from the context of the reader. Words which mean one thing in one context, can mean quite another in a different context.

We would distinguish five sources of ambiguity: *relative words*; words with *double meanings*; *unusual* words or unusual usages of familiar words; *grammatical* ambiguity; and *ellipsis* or compressing a sentence by leaving out parts of the grammar.

Words such as 'back' and 'front' are relative to the position of the reader. Better names to choose in the instructions for changing a plug we have just discussed would have been 'cover' and 'body'. Another example from the same set of instructions is:

Relative words

> With the earth pin at the top, the live pin is bottom right, and the neutral is bottom left, looking into the plug from the top.

'Left' and 'right', like 'top' and 'bottom', are relative words and are decoded by each reader by reference to his or her own position. Unless writers can be quite sure that readers will be looking at the equipment from exactly the same position, they should avoid using such words. Similar problems occur with words like 'hot' and 'cold', 'large' and 'small', and any other word which is relative rather an absolute.

Another confusing instruction is:

> Select a suitable amount of choke for the weather conditions and temperature of the engine.

'Suitable' means 'appropriate to the context'. Readers may not know what is suitable, and the word does nothing to help them decide. Many similar words appear in careless instructions, such as 'enough', 'about', 'insufficient'. Completeness in instructions must include precision. The writer of this instruction tried to be more specific:

> Check that the proportional band setting, already made, gives lively but stable operation of the actuator.

Just what 'lively but stable' means depends on the context. If it is the impression of a new friend just made at a party, it means something different from the description of a Channel ferry on a rough night. The writer tried to be specific but chose adverbs from deep in the territory of the relative. He or she should have looked for specific words – for example, 'deflects to follow the signal, but does not waver'.

Words with double meanings   The effect of words with two meanings is often funny:

> Set the temperature control to 20°C (68°F) and run up the transmitter to normal working.

We can imagine the operator running up the ladders to a working platform high on the aerial. Other ambiguities are less funny. An aircraft fitter was instructed, during an undercarriage overhaul to:

> Check undercarriage locking pin. If bent, replace.

He took out the pin, and examined it. It was indeed bent, so he carefully put it back into the mechanism. The aircraft subsequently crashed.

Words such as *replace, refit, reconnect* can mean either 'fit a new part', or 'put back the old one'. Writers must take precautions to define these words in servicing instructions to avoid this mistake. Definition may seem cumbersome, but ambiguity is never obvious to writers; they know what they mean, and often find it very difficult to see the alternative meaning. Safety and efficient operation lie only in knowing that the readers will understand the same actions as the writers. It is wise to look for trouble – to look deliberately for words that could be ambiguous, and either define these words, or choose a structure, context, or alternative word which cannot be misunderstood.

The instruction to 'check', in particular, is often a source of confusion:

> Check reading of thermocouple read-out.

Does this mean record it, or remember it, or does something else have to be done? The writer must specify what action to take if the condition is *not* as it should be, and therefore there should usually be an 'If not . . .' clause in the instruction. Even where the action is considered self-evident (such as closing a valve if it is not already closed) it is best to make the instruction positive:

Ensure that drain valve at top of column is closed.

How easy to use is the following instruction?

Check that unit is to total reflux.

Will readers know what 'reflux' is, or know the difference between 'total reflux' and plain, ordinary 'reflux'? These are technical terms, and the use of technical terms in instructions must be controlled and deliberate. If there is any doubt, the writer must either find a more explicit – if longer – phrase, or list definitions at the start of the instructions. Thus a car manual instructed the reader:

The battery tray should be removed from its mounting which will be found on the offside of the car on the wheel valance.

We doubt if all readers would know that the valance is the inside of the wheel arch. The danger is not just that a technical term will be opaque, but that the reader may half-know it, and make a (misguided) guess with disastrous results. Only when quite certain that the technical word will be understood can you use it. When you only *think* it *may* be understood, it is safer to define it or choose a simpler alternative.

Problems are also caused by familiar words used with unusual meanings. Because readers know the word, they will guess at what it means in the context:

Pump up Chemical 1 until scale reading is 2000 lbs, after awaiting for siphoning back of water to break.

The common usage of the word 'break' in a similar phrase is to 'break wind', and since 'break' here means 'stop' the operator may find this a disturbing image. Some unusual uses come from a desire to sound technical, but they can arouse irrelevant associations:

Two or three wires can now be seen to be stemming from inside a wider tube.

The thought of the wires like a bunch of flowers is pleasant, but distracting. Computer jargon very often makes a similar use of familiar words in an unusual way:

After the program has been entered, the software pilot lights are displayed.

Because computers run automatically, there is confusion between a passive and an active meaning of 'enter'. The irrelevant image is of the operator carefully squeezing into the program, and holding up the pilot lights for everyone to see. Here is another unusual use:

> Apply punched cards to be listed to the hopper of the punched card reader.

'Apply to' probably here means 'put in', but the phrase has more familiar meanings in 'apply for a job' and 'apply paint to a wall'. These possible meanings are searched, and discarded in the de-coding process, but a residual insecurity of meaning is left.

Ambiguous grammar

Ambiguities can also arise because the syntax of the sentence can be decoded in alternative ways. Even if the right meaning is made obvious by the context, mental energy has to be used disentangling the ambiguity; and because instructions are usually short sentences, there is less context to help in the decoding of meaning:

> The screws on the connections must be loosened to enable the cables to be entered.

The first verb (loosened) is a passive construction with the implied subject 'by you'. Therefore we naturally read the second verb (entered) in the same context. The result is funny, but not dangerous.

In some cases the structure is so complicated that the reader cannot readily decode it:

> Set variable speed floating control to damp fast movement of the damper and provide a safety margin for the stability of the air conditioning control system at positions of the controlled elements where the system amplification is greater than at the positions at which the proportional band setting has been made.

Another cause of grammatical ambiguity is the omission of some part of a sentence. We do this frequently to save time in speaking (it is known as *ellipsis*) but it can lead to misunderstanding. For instance, the following instructions appeared on a packet of spaghetti:

> Cooking spaghetti: Put three pints of water on the cooker – drop in spaghetti – stir.

The ways in which instructions can be misunderstood are many and various. We would counsel you to develop a lively sense of humour in spotting the ambiguities in your own instructions.

An exercise we often use is to ask students to write instructions for driving a car. It is a familiar operation and it is therefore easy to make incautious assumptions. It is also an activity usually described in common words, with various kinds of ellipses. The results, not all from one writer, make a compendium of ambiguities: *Instructions for driving a car*

1. Sit behind the steering wheel.
2. Adjust mirror for best rear view.
3. Ensure handbrake is on.
4. Put gear lever into neutral.
5. Pull choke knob right out.
6. Turn key to right.
7. Rotate engine until it fires.
8. Depress accelerator until engine can be heard running fast.
9. Select first gear.
10. Allow clutch pedal to gently rise while depressing accelerator yet further.
11. Take off handbrake.
12. Wink in the direction you are going.
13. Grip steering wheel at ten to two.
14. If you need to brake read the following instructions . . .

We leave our readers to work out in how many ways these instructions can be misunderstood!

As important as the completeness and comprehensibility of instructions is their sequence. Many instructions fail because they are out of sequence, or contain gaps or loops. Instructions must follow exactly the order of the various operations required: *Correct sequence for faultless operation*

> Adjust flow through valve 4.23. This requires a check on temperature, and before adjusting the valve, opening briefly the cylinder drain valve.

Not only may this lead to a mistake, but also it is difficult to read. The operator has to remember the three steps all together, and then do them in reverse order. Sequence is the responsibility of the writer; the advice to 'read through instructions to end before starting work' is a writer's exemption clause, but it is poor tactics. Users are confused by reading all the instructions: they cannot remember all the details, and they will probably be appalled at the complexity of the instructions, upset by the unreadable and indigestible style, and worried by their inability to understand. Instructions are not explanations or descriptions and are certainly not meant for reading through. The user should be able to trust the writer for the correct sequence. Thus the instruction above should read:

6. Open the cylinder drain valve for five seconds.
7. Is the temperature between 180° and 220°C? If not, adjust control 4.27 and pause until the temperature is within limits.
8. Adjust the flow through valve 4.23 until the meter reads between 4350 and 4450 litres/minute.

Such a sequence does not require users to hold more than one action in their heads at once. Note also that each instruction gives specific values, not vague approximations.

Instructions must contain no gaps in the sequence. If it is necessary to switch on auxiliary test gear before using it, the instructions must specify this. The sequence must provide for rapid, confident operation. The logic of instructions should be as rigorous as the logic of a computer program.

These instructions invite expensive disasters:

3. Start the vacuum pump from the START button local to the pump.
4. Before starting, check that cooling water flow and return valves are open (CW1 and CW2) and that the trade water feed valve is open.
5. The trade water control valve (TW3) is pre-set and should not be adjusted.

An operator, following these instructions one by one, would fail to make the necessary checks first.

These instructions failed not because of gaps, but because they contained an endless loop:

13. Run in 900 lbs of Chemical 1 into reactor until scale reading is 1100 lbs.
14. Repeat 11, 12, and 13.

A conscientious operator would never get to 15. The writer probably meant 14 to apply only once or twice, but there is no indication how often the user should go through the sequence. Such logical loops are gateways to disaster; the writer should specify under what conditions the 'repeat' instruction is cancelled:

13. Run in 900 lbs of Chemical 1 into reactor.
14. Note the scale reading. If it is less than 1800 lbs, repeat 11, 12 and 13. If it is 1800 lbs or over, continue to 15.
15. Turn on . . .

Sometimes instructions also cover situations where there are a series of points at which alternative sequences divide, or come together. Simple sequential written instructions can cope with these situations only in a very limited way. If the logical sequence contains many alternative, it is wise to use an algorithm. These are discussed in Chapter 6.

Check your instructions

We have said so far that instructions must in the first place be accurate and complete, and with enough information for the user to do the job. They must be comprehensible to every member of the likely audience, and contain no ambiguities of usage or of grammar. They must be in correct and rigorous sequence, with no gaps and loops, and they must be safe and readable.

To confirm that all these complex requirements are met, get instructions checked by another person. Try to find a friend or colleague who is *not* familiar with the equipment to work through the instructions. He or she must have the equipment there and follow the operations right through to see if the instructions are complete and accurate. If you cannot find another person to do this, your only choice then is to put the instructions aside, and some time later work through them with the equipment. Cultivate a lively sense of humour, and a sharp eye for the ridiculous; in many ways, these are useful skills for an instruction writer.

The layout of instructions

Layout greatly affects the ease with which information is assimilated. Letters are geometrical shapes with conventionalized meanings; the layout of a letter is the core of our communication code. Equally, indentation, spacing, underlining and the layout of blocks of type are a geometry which communicates. To see what effect these factors can have, read these instructions:

Although removing power from the equipment is primarily a maintenance responsibility, the operator can ensure that the system is inoperative by taking several steps. Firstly the reader motor is turned off from the console, and then the magnetic tape is unloaded by pressing the REWIND UNLOAD button whereupon the tape reverses to a point where the tape can be removed. The tape leader is clamped, the door closed, and the power OFF switch pressed. Finally, the following switches are pressed in turn: typewriter OFF switch, MASTER CLEAR switch, and computer OFF switch, and the computer and peripherals are now shut down.

Laid out in a solid block, they are difficult to use. Readers must make their own decisions where to stop reading and start doing. But look through the same instructions again, this time using the layout code as well:

Removing power from equipment

The main responsibility for removing power is with the maintenance engineers, but the operator can shut down the computer and peripherals by following this procedure:

1. Turn off the reader motor at the console READER switch.
2. Press the REWIND UNLOAD button to unload the magnetic tape (the tape will reverse to a point where it can be removed).
3. Clamp the tape leader
4. Close the door
5. Press the power OFF switch
6. Press the typewriter OFF switch
7. Press the MASTER CLEAR switch
8. Press the computer OFF switch.

Notice that the sequence becomes simpler and clearer. Graphic signs (separate sentences, new lines, and numbers) replace groups of words like 'Firstly . . .' 'and then . . .', 'Finally . . .', 'in turn . . .' The information about sequence is contained in the layout, rather than in the text, which makes it quicker and easier to absorb. It is less effort to *see* the relationship between actions by their layout on the page, than to *decode* it from groups of words. Notice, too, that the heading focuses attention on the purpose of the section and makes the reader's task easier. So does the layout of the introductory explanation. Separating explanations visually from the sequence of instructions assists the reader to perceive them as different sections.

Explicitly laid out instructions are easier to use than continuous prose. Prose adopts one set of conventions for layout (for example, that white space is used only at the end of a meaningful group of sentences called a paragraph). These conventions are convenient for continuous reading, because they assist the action of the eye, which only pauses for a rest at the end of the group of sentences. Instructions are used in a different way. We read then by sorting the information into kinds (explanation, description, instruction, etc.) and then dealing with each instruction in turn. Therefore instructions adopt a different set of layout conventions to emphasize the separate steps.

Instructions are normally best arranged in a sequence of sections, identified clearly by headings which identify the purpose of the action, and do not simply name the equipment. Subheadings help readers divide a long sequence into smaller stages, and provide a resting place. They help to accentuate the stages in an activity, and to identify sub-routines as parts of a whole sequence. Such headings may be numbered using the decimal numbering system, explained in Chapter 5.

Sequence of sections in instructions

A common sequence of sections is as follows:

1. **Introductory explanations.** Explanations help the operator by giving an over-view. These explanations should be short, since users of instructions do not necessarily want a full understanding of how the equipment works; but they may want to know why they are performing the operations. Therefore an introductory paragraph may give the purpose of the action, what it will achieve, and why this is a useful result. It can also tell them how much ground the instructions cover.

2. **Tools required.** It will save time if the operator can select any special tools required *in advance* and take them to the job. But if only standard tools are required, a list is a cumbersome irrelevance.

3. **Materials required.** If the materials required are unusual, and require finding in advance, they should be listed also.

4. **Definitions.** Definitions may be needed if the text contains words which may not be understood. Every-day words with special or restricted meanings must also be defined. Definitions of terms are no use in an appendix; they will already have caused problems. Even though users may not remember

all the definitions as they work through, they will remember that there were some definitions, and when they meet problematic words in the instructions, they will turn back.

Some writers re-define all standard terms in every set of instructions. This wastes space and time; and as in all information transfer, redundant information increases the chance of real (i.e. new) information being missed. Do not create a haystack of familiar information in which to lose the needle of a new fact. For a regular group of users, restrict the list of definitions to giving a reference to a standard list elsewhere, and note only new or unusual words or usages.

5. **Overriding instructions.** Next give any overriding instructions that apply throughout the sequence. They should be repeated in the body of the instructions wherever they apply to a specific operation.

6. **Warnings.** The writer of instructions is responsible for safety. He or she must always choose a sequence which is as safe as possible, and warn readers about possible dangers. Because of the way instructions are used (each action is read, then done, before the next sentence is read), warnings which come after the instructions are useless. Inevitably, even if *most* readers notice them, there will be one who does not. One is enough. Warnings about a particularly dangerous process should be given twice; once in the preliminaries, and again just *before* the instruction to which they relate.

The wording of warnings   It is important to make warnings stand out. Therefore, both in the preliminaries and again in the body of the instructions, use capitals, bold type, or if possible a different colour.

It can help to use standard names for the level of risk:

NOTE: for background points
CAUTION: where the equipment of property could be damaged
WARNING: where life or limb (the operator's or others') could be at risk
DANGER: for inherently risky operations which require special precautions.

Warnings should be given in simple, clear imperatives. This warning is so wordy that the point is blunted, and the reader's attention wasted by the time the point appears:

Do not forget however, under any circumstances, that it is imperative that . . .

Equally, polite hints are useless:

It is considered advisable to . . .

Warnings must use imperative verbs:

WARNING: Keep naked flame away from the evacuator
pump.

It adds to the force of a warning if a brief explanation is given. In
a safety-conscious world, operators get tired of reading warnings, and in fairness they are often given warnings for operations which are not very dangerous. Therefore when they meet
a real risk, where a small mistake could run a chain reaction
through a complete chemical plant, they may treat it lightly. If
told the scale of the risk, they can respond reasonably. This does
not mean a lengthy account of the sequence of events, or an
actuarial statement of the statistical risk. One reason only
should be given – more is overkill – and the reason should be a
good one.

WARNING: Keep naked flame away from the evacuator
pump: ammonia gas is explosive.

Make sure the warnings are explicit and relevant. The following,
like all our examples, is real. It is difficult to believe anyone with
a sense of humour could write it:

When there is only about half an inch of clutch-pedal left, the
car will be about to start moving. When it is safe to set off,
gently release the rest of the clutch pedal. Although the
instructions seem long-winded they are done in a very short
interval, and after some practice you can watch the road
throughout the exercise.

Warnings are an important part of the task of an instruction
writer. They must be prominent, bold, and sensible.

Numbering instructions

Various numbering systems are possible, but the clearest is
probably the use of continuous numbering throughout the
major sections of the instructions, and the placing of sub-
headings between the blocks of instructions.

If you break the instructions down with sub-headings, do not
necessarily start numbering again from '1' in each small section.
The reason for this is that in looking away to do the action,
readers lose the place. If there are two instructions numbered '4'
on the same page readers can easily go back to the wrong

sequence. Instructions which number through, past the sub-headings, look logical and avoid this difficulty.

Roman numerals (I, II, III, IV, V, VI, etc.) are confusing – people can confuse IV and VI, and with large numbers (e.g. XXXIV) confusion is almost universal. Using letters can also be confusing, and there is difficulty when more than 26 instructions are needed. What comes after 'z'? There are no disadvantages in using simple Arabic numbers. There is no need to use brackets, dashes, or anything but a simple full-stop between the numbers and the instructions.

Because the user has to remember an instruction while turning from text to equipment, each instruction should be manageable. How easy would you find it to use this instruction?

> Shut toggle valve G and remove blanking union from secondary column 1 and set PR1 to a pre-determined pressure to give the required linear gas rate (40 ml min^{-1}) for a non-retained component down this system at 130°C. Note the pressure on PG3 when at equilibrium (allow at least 10 minutes). This is the back pressure due to column 1.

Such a block of instructions is thoughtless, and unlikely to produce satisfactory operation of the equipment. Because of the way the reader uses them, each instruction should contain one action (or group of actions if they are done together). When writing, imagine the user looking to and fro between text and machine. If the instruction runs to several lines, it is almost certainly too long.

Figure 11.1 shows an example of instructions with sections divided by sub-headings, but with the numbering continuing throughout.

Decimal numbering can also be effective, especially in very long sets of instructions, that consist of many sections. In such sets, continuous numbering leads to instructions with numbers in the hundreds. Decimal numbering helps to reinforce the sense of stages in long procedures, and keeps the numbers manageable.

Style for operating instructions

Our advice on the most effective choice from the language code throughout this book has emphasized the need for an intelligent matching of resources to task and audience. Language is used for a large variety of different purposes. Statement is only one; there are also questions, assertions and what are called phatic

ADJUSTMENT AND TESTING

Adjusting Brake

1. Attach a load of 1140 kg to the single cable and raise the load about 1 m.

2. Adjust the brake until it just holds the load, by turning the brake adjuster with a 2 BA socket spanner.

Adjusting the Handle Clutch

3. Attach a load of 1100 kg to the single cable end.

4. Insert a 2 BA Allen key through the two holes in the end of the handle boss, to engage in the adjusting screws.

5. Adjust the handle clutch so that it just releases when the handle is turned vigorously to raise the load. The slippage is increased by turning the screws anti-clockwise.

Adjusting the Governor Brake

6. Attach a load of 915 kg to the single cable end, engage the winding handle, and raise the load 1.5 m.

7. Press the brake release trigger and check the time required for the load to reach the ground. This should be less than 8 seconds.

8. If the lowering speed is excessive, dismantle the governor assembly, wash all parts in trichlorethylene, and re-assemble.

PREPARING FOR USE

Precautions

9. When a hoist has been in storage for a long period, ensure that the winding mechanism operates freely.

10. Ensure that the cable does not show signs of fraying or distortion. Do not wind a damaged cable into the hoist.

11. Before winding out the cable from the hoist, fit the extension tube and top sheath.

12. Ensure that all accessories are correctly fitted and secured.

Preparations

13. Engage the operating handle on the intermediate drive dog (A).

Fig. 11.1 Instructions showing sub-headings and continuous numbering of individual instructions.

uses (which carry attitudes but not information), and instructions. Here are some examples:

STATEMENT: The chuck locks the bar in place.
QUESTION: Is the machine ready to start?
ASSERTION: We definitely did complete the tests.
PHATIC: Good morning, how are you?
INSTRUCTION: Turn the inlet valve to the 'off' position.

This list by no means exhausts the possible functions of language; we may also wish to express doubt, hope, sympathy and many other things. With this range of types of meaning to communicate, and the variety of ways of expressing each function, the possible choices of structure are very large indeed. This is why any advice on style which tries to restrict choice is misguided; indeed for continuous reading, variety of structure is refreshing. Instructions, however, are a special case, and it is worth surveying the available choice of structures in some detail.

In social interaction, if we have to instruct someone, or request or ask (all versions of the same language action), we have a number of ways of doing so:

Please . . .
Could you . . .
Would you mind . . .
You are to . . .

and so on. In writing technical instructions, our choice is more limited. To begin with, structures which start with 'please' would get tedious, and eventually absurd. Having abandoned politeness as a valid aim, there remain two major areas of choice in structures: first, the name used for the person addressed; second, the variety of verb form chosen. Thus instructions can start:

You must close the valve   (second person)
The operator must close the valve (third person)
He must close the valve   (third person pronoun)
The valve must be closed   (impersonal)

The verb form which follows this choice of name can also vary:

You *must* close the valve
You *ought* to close the valve
You *should* close the valve

You *will* close the valve
You *are* to close the valve

These two types of variation can be mixed and combined, so already we have 20 varieties, and of course there are many more. Having such a wide choice available may seem desirable, but both areas of choice create problems. Naming the reader raises questions of authority. 'He', 'she' or 'the operator' sounds coldly impersonal; 'you' sounds over-friendly. We do not want to raise issues of authority in instructions; it is better to keep them as business-like as possible. This means that it is best to avoid all forms of address to the operator, since they all carry overtones of one kind or another. The exception is that sometimes it is necessary to specify who is to do something. Thus an instruction might read:

The supervisor must check the setting before the next operation is begun.

Problems are also raised by the use of verbs like 'ought', 'will', 'shall'. This group are known as *modal* verbs. The exact difference of meaning between 'must' and 'ought' is uncertain, yet if someone wrote the following phrases, we would understand:

Modal verbs

'I should, but ought I to?'
'I have to do it, but am I to?'
'I must do it, but do you think I ought?'

But although we perceive a difference of meaning, it is not consistent. Certainly, the difference of obligation expressed by these words is not reliable enough for technical instructions.

Modal verbs raise other problems too. Verbs such as 'should' reduce the instruction to the status of an observation. They appear to be passing information, rather than instructing. Many modal verbs carry less than total obligation, because they express shades of obligation. The instruction 'the valve should be closed' is less precise than the instruction 'close the valve'.

A further disadvantage of modals is that they introduce an extra verb in the structure. This can produce complications:

The valve should not yet have been closed.

The verb 'should' blunts the impact of the instruction verb 'close'. Modal verbs also cause problems of repetition. A list of instructions might read:

1. The valve should be closed immediately.
2. The steam should be blown-off by opening vent C.
3. The boiler casing should be drained.
4. The oil supply should be switched off.

This is unacceptably repetitious. The writer is therefore tempted to ring the changes:

1. The valve should be closed immediately.
2. The steam ought to be blown-off by opening vent C.
3. The boiler casing is to be drained.
4. The oil supply will be switched off.

Because contrast between words carries meaning, the operator infers a difference between the level of obligation in these four instructions, and may follow some but not others. For these reasons it is best to avoid using modal verbs in instructions.

Use simple imperatives   Problems of authority, repetition and uncertainty are removed by using the simple imperative form of the verb. Problems of choice of person and choice of modal verbs disappear because the structure no longer requires these elements:

1. Close the valve immediately.
2. Open vent C to blow off steam.
3. Drain the boiler casing.
4. Switch off the oil supply.

Notice that variety has been introduced into the instructions by the variety of active verbs, 'close, blow-off, drain, switch'. In each case, the first word in the instruction names the type of action which will be required, and helps to focus users' attention on what they have to *do*. Furthermore, active sentences are easier to read than passive or modal ones. For these reasons, normally use the simple imperative in instructions.

Most of the time, the main instructing verb should start the sentence; but if the activity first requires a decision, then the instruction should start with the 'If . . .' clause, *before* the imperative verb, so that the condition is understood before the action is ordered. If the phrases are the other way round, operators may act before they read about the conditions required. Thus, do not write:

Close the steam valve by turning V4 clockwise, if the temperature reading is over 275°C.

Write instead:

> If the temperature reading is over 275°C, close the steam valve by turning V4 clockwise.

Other preliminary phrases or clauses that should usually appear *before* the imperative verb are:

> Expressions of location: At panel B, switch . . .
> Indications of time: When . . , switch . . .
> Indications of instrument/tool: Using . . ., rotate . . .

Try to avoid negative instructions. Keeping a string of reversals in mind is difficult:

> Pressure must not be lowered until the temperature is not less than 70°C.

Better write positively:

> Keep the pressure constant until temperature is at least 70°C.

A negative is, however, the best choice in a prohibition or warning, where it serves to emphasize that something must *not* be done.

> Do not open valve G24 until the pressure is below 2.4 kg/cm^2.

Instructions which are complete, unambiguous, and written in a clear, imperative style will enable the reader to use them conveniently and correctly.

Negative instructions

12 *Writing descriptions and explanations*

The writing of descriptions needs special tactics. The aim of a description is to create in the reader's mind a clear picture of a process or a piece of equipment. In writing operating instructions, success can be defined as the machine operating properly or the process producing the correct results. The state of understanding or visualising something is less obvious, and less measurable. There are degrees of understanding, from a vague grasp, through a picture held with difficulty in focus, to a detailed and confident knowledge. Because the aim is neither so easily identifiable nor so clearly defined, descriptions are not as restricted in the choice of structures and tactics as are operating instructions, but we can establish useful basic strategies to guide the writer.

Read the following description, which is taken unaltered from an industrial report:

Granulation Plant to silo delivery system

Product from the Granulation Plant is delivered on to the reversible conveyor on the silo North side. No. 1 bay receives product off boom 4T44, fed by the reversible conveyor moving westward. No. 2 bay receives product off boom 4T43 fed off the reversible conveyor running eastwards. No. 3 bay receives product by setting boom 4T43 in an East-pointing rest position and sending product over it to a series of two conveyors running East and South and so delivering on to the No. 3 bay boom. Thus, No. 2 bay boom has to be used for both silo No. 2 and 3 deliveries.

No. 2 bay boom (4T43) has slewing and luffing and belt

drive is by means of a 5 hp gear motor and chain drive to the tail pulley, i.e. the return side of the belt transmits full driving tension. Inherent in the recovery by means of the Goliath crane is the feature that whenever any of the three booms is discharging into its bay it interferes with the crane's long travel and grab operation in its immediate vicinity. In other words, we rely entirely on the skill and attention of crane drivers to avoid any collision of the crane with an operating boom.

The crane cab is totally enclosed and was designed to give extensive window area with few blind spots. A refrigerated and filtered-air supply is provided for the cab. Three-lever systems govern all the crane movements, i.e. long travel, grab traverse, grab lift and lower and the grab open and close. Two built-in hoppers located respectively between the North and South crane legs receive recovered product and discharge out to the North and South recovery conveyors.

Few readers feel a confident grasp of the delivery system after reading this. Yet its organization is quite logical within its own terms; it describes the delivery of product in sequence from the plant to the hoppers, and details the equipment in turn. Why does it fail? Because it offers no overall picture of the layout; we are swamped with detail from the begining. Readers can cope with this complexity only if they have a firm plan in mind on which to hang the details as they come in. Without such an overall plan, the information piles up in a confusing way.

Here is a second description of a complex system:

Operation of factory steam-main pressure-control system

When the machine is standing, the governor sleeve is at its highest position and the speeder sleeve is lowered to a pre-set position found by experience to be three turns, eighteen notches of the hand wheel.

With the lube-oil pump running, control oil flows through the pressure-reducing valve and choke to the relay valve and to the oil-return via the characterised port of the speeder sleeve. The area of the port is restricted in the start-up position of the speeder and governor sleeve so that the control-oil pressure is high and the relay valve opens the main throttle-valve.

The machine is started 'off load' by manual control on the spider valve and run up under controlled conditions to the synchronous speed of 3650 rpm. At this point the alternator is put 'en bars' and becomes a synchronous-speed machine with the governor sleeve in a fixed position.

The 'logic' the writer has applied to this description is the logic of an operating instruction. Faced with a complex and sophisticated network, he or she has decided to describe the sequence in which the system is operated. But this is quite different from the sequence of understanding. Again, we stress that this is a real and complete description from a genuine report. But we doubt if many readers of that report, who did not already know the steam-system, understood it. The reader is given too much detail, too soon, without a framework to fit it on to. It is like a pile of clothes with no pegs. An amorphous mass is left in the reader's mind, from which he or she finds it impossible either to grasp the overall shape of the system, or to understand any part of it. The writer has confused the writing of a description with the writing of an operating instruction. Knowing how to operate a machine is not the same as understanding it, as this example shows only too clearly.

A third example of a description is this:

The light-pen

The light pen is a photo-sensitive device which responds to the very short pulses of ultra violet light emitted by the cathode ray screen as it is struck by the electron beam.

It consists of a short pen-shaped tube containing an optical system which transmits the ultra violet light signals along an optical fibre cable to a photo-multiplier. When switched on, the photo-multiplier generates a corresponding electrical pulse which is fed back to the controller. A foot switch allows the operator to control this feed back by switching the photo-multiplier circuits on or off.

If the controller receives a signal from the pen, it causes a program interrupt and the computer notes the current position of the electron beam and jumps into the light-pen manipulation programs. By holding the pen in front of the screen and depressing the foot switch, the operator indicates points to a running program for relevant action. For example, alpha-numeric data can be input from the screen simply by indicating the required character sequence from a standard character list displayed on some convenient part of the screen.

A computer light-pen is probably a more complex (and less

familiar) piece of equipment than a silo delivery system, or a factory steam-main. But most readers find this description easier to understand. Why? The answer is that the logic of the arrangement is the same as the logic of understanding. The writing follows a clear sequence; first comes a definition of the equipment in the most general terms, which relates it to familiar objects:

The light-pen is a photo-sensitive device . . .

next is a brief statement of what it does:

. . . which responds to very short pulses of ultra-violet light . . .

third comes a short list of its main component parts:

It consists of a short pen-shaped tube containing an optical system . . .

fourth is a brief description of how it works:

When switched on, the photo-multiplier generates a corresponding electrical pulse . . .

and last a brief overview of how it is used:

A foot switch allows the operator to control . . .

Only when these basic points have been established in the first paragraph does the writer go back, in the second paragraph, to deal with the equipment in greater detail.

Write descriptions stage by stage

The previous example is a good model of how to write a description. Like peeling an onion, it gets into the detail layer by layer. Very general statements, overviews, and definitions first orientate the reader's mind. Basic questions are then answered in this order:

- What is it like?
- What is it used for?
- What does it consist of?
- How does it operate?
- How do you use it?

A description of anything can be written in this way. For instance, a car: What is it like?

> A car is a metal structure about 5 m by 2 m by 2 m high, with wheels at each corner.

What is it used for?

> It transports people over distances too great to walk.

What does it consist of?

> It consists of a passenger compartment, with seats and windows, an engine for motive power, and steering, braking and warning systems.

How does it operate?

> The engine burns petrol to produce motive power which is used to drive the wheels forward.

How do you use it?

> One seat is provided with hand and floor controls to guide the car, and to control starting, accelerating and stopping.

These may seem basic and obvious points, but to someone unfamiliar with the equipment they provide useful orientation. Because such basics were left out, the first two descriptions were confusing for the reader. We have seen descriptions of simple items such as an electric kettle where the reader was given a mass of detail about the soldering, insulating, and wiring of the kettle but there was not a single mention of boiling water. Effective descriptions usually start from the outermost layers of purpose, use, general appearance and overall construction before going into detail.

Logical order in description   The 'logical' order for descriptions starts with the familiar and general and moves by stages towards the specific and detailed. Language itself operates on the same principle. Thus a 'light-pen' is not a 'pen', since it does not draw, or use ink; but it looks more like a pen than anything else, and it is used to make the computer draw. So the name 'pen' is used by analogy to describe it. The adjective 'light' distinguishes it from any other type of pen such as a 'fountain pen', or a 'ball pen'. The same principle of analogy and differentiation applies to description as applies to naming. The most convenient way of describing something is to say what familiar object it resembles, and in what ways it differs from that familiar object. Definition is a process of comparison and distinction, which works in stages from a familiar general category, to a specific example.

After the initial general definition, the reader wants a description of what the equipment looks like, and a description of its general function. Finally, the component parts can be specified and described in turn. Within each sub-division, however, the same logic applies. The description of the light-pen was part of a larger document describing an interactive computer terminal. Each element in the system (the video display unit, the light-pen, the key-board, the software) received a separate description. Each description followed the sequence of general definition, appearance, components, functioning and use.

In describing complex equipment or processes, the writer meets one of the limitations of language. Prose is linear; it covers the page in a steady sequence, and contains no loops or repetitions. Nor is it possible, even though we have two eyes, to read two parallel pieces of prose at once. But most machines can do more than one thing at once. Any system of even moderate complexity is likely to have loops, repetitions, and simultaneous activities. Language can never, therefore, reproduce the operation of the system. What it can reproduce, though, is the sequence of the reader's attention as he or she understands the system. Attention, like language, is linear, and we can only fully attend to one thing at once. The writer can therefore sequence his or her language to direct the reader's attention in a comfortable progress. The image to have in mind while writing is not the imitation of the system described, but the imitation of the reader's gradually dawning understanding. A good model is a set of colour slides, moving in sequence from a general view, through middle distance and close ups to X-ray and microscope views. Each picture in itself is complete. Each picture necessarily repeats parts of the previous picture. But taken in sequence they construct a clearer impression of the original object than any single picture, no matter how massive and detailed. Think of descriptions as progressing in layers, from the general to the particular, from the familiar to the new, from the obvious to the surprising, from the distant to the close up.

The IP inductive-loop paging system

The IP 90 is an inductive-loop paging system which allows individual calls to be sent to any of 88 persons equipped with a cordless miniature receiver. A spoken message can be sent out, after initial transmission of a call signal.

The complete system comprises a control panel, one or more transmitters, a number of receivers and one or more loops of copper wire laid around the area in which calls are to be received.

An alternating magnetic field is generated throughout the area contained by the loop and within a narrow zone lying outside that area. A receiver which is within the area of the magnetic field responds to a call signal sent to it by emitting a whistling signal. The person wearing a receiver can listen to a spoken message by holding the receiver to his ear and, at the same time, holding down the small knob on the side of the receiver.

Not only individual but also group calls can be transmitted. The paging system allows the inclusion of either one or two groups, each of which can have up to twelve participants. Any participant recognizes from the rhythm of the call signal whether the call is intended for an individual or for a group.

The paging system can also be connected to an internal telephone exchange if required, in which event calls can be made from any telephone. The paging system comprises the following units:
control panel
one or more transmitters
one or more loops
receivers (maximum 88)
storage racks

The writer then goes on to describe each of the units in turn. This description is comfortable for the reader because it follows the logic of the reader's understanding.

Explanations

Explanations go beyond descriptions. A description focuses on *what* is there: an explanation goes further and says *why* (and perhaps *how* it works). In writing explanations, use the same techniques as in writing descriptions. First give a general definition. In an explanation this will be of the aim, purpose, or result of the process or system. *Why* it is being done is the most helpful explanation, followed by a comparison with some familiar process. Next will come a general statement of the theory which lies behind the process; next a general statement about *how* it is operated; and only then an over-view of the components. Last of all, the details of the individual elements in the system, and the way they operate can be given in order.

It helps the reader grasp a complex system if it is broken down into a manageable number of separate sub-systems, which form a perceivable pattern. A complex software program may have 50 sub-routines, but the human memory cannot grasp 50 separate items readily. It can, however, grasp more easily a structure with about three to seven elements. Try to break the system down in the first place into 3–7 components, each of which has a readily identifiable function within the whole system, and an easily memorized name which reminds the reader of this function. Within each of these major divisions, the operations can be broken down into 3–7 sub-operations. In this way, 50 or so individual actions can be built into an hierarchical structure which can be grasped and remembered by the reader.

In writing explanations, even of the smallest sub-element in a complex system, it is helpful to the reader to stress the sequence the action fits into, and the aim of the individual action within the context of the larger system. The mind can remember detail only if the detail fits into a pattern. Repeated stress of sequence and aim helps to reinforce the mental image of the overall pattern. It assists both understanding and memory.

Keep thinking of the reader

Instructions, descriptions, and explanations are separate writing tasks; much confusion arises for readers if they are unsure which they are reading. Some texts prevaricate, and this confuses readers by confusing the signals which tell them what to do with the information they are processing. Making decisions about aim (operation, visualization, understanding) will improve the text's efficiency as communication. If both understanding and operation are required, write separate sections. A prose description may come first; the next section can be instructions to be worked through with the machine. There is no repetition in this. The two aims are separate, and the reader will find it more convenient to have two separate sections.

In Chapter 4 we said that argument should invert the order of discovery. It should start from the conclusion, and then support it with evidence. The same pattern applies to description. The overall picture comes first; only then can details be absorbed. In our experience, many descriptions fail because they do not start with sufficiently general statements. The writer is familiar with the equipment or he or she would not be writing about it; but what is so obvious to the writer that it does not need saying may well be essential new information to the reader. We advise writers to go one step further into the obvious than their judgement suggests. We know few readers who complain of one or two extra sentences which tactfully remind them of what they already know. But we do know many readers who complain that they can not follow the information because some major point is missing.

Writing letters and 13 memoranda

Letters (and the informal, internal kind of letter we call a memorandum) are the principal day-to-day medium of information exchange. This chapter is not about letter-writing in general, though much of what we say would apply to any letters; it is about letters written to give technical information, the type of letter likely to be written by the scientist or engineer working in an industrial or scientific organization. Other sorts of letters (in particular, sales letters) are not our province.

Every letter carries not only information but also an image of the writer and the organization he or she works for. It is important to be aware of the potency of this image. Consider, for example, the following letter in reply to a customer's query about his account:

Dear Mr Knight,

Re: 55 78 91 99
     38 00 31 00

We are in receipt of your letter received at this Office 14th April 1987 and would advise that according to our records, an exchange of model to colour receiver type 7641 was effected on account 55 78 91 99 from 15th December 1986 and an initial payment of £8.50 was allocated.

However, an annual invoice in respect of previous television was despatched prior to details of exchange of model being completed on the account and a subsequent payment of £72.15 was allocated on 15th December 1986.

It would appear that a further remittance of £179.22 was made 13th January 1987 in respect of annual rental for both television accounts and the sum of £86.02 has been transferred to clear rentals on account 38 00 31 00 until 19th April

1988. Two detailed statements are enclosed to assist in clarification and you will observe that account 55 78 91 99 is in fact clear until 23rd February 1987 with a further credit balance of £79.40.

In the circumstances, would you kindly advise whether this balance is to remain on the account or be refunded.

A pre-paid envelope is enclosed for your convenience.

Yours sincerely,

John W. Hunt
Manager, Subscriber Relations Dept.

We wonder what sort of 'subscriber relations' the writer of this letter presides over. Is he hired to make a point of offending customers? Even a tolerant or resigned reader can hardly sense helpfulness in this letter. The writer seems aloof, impersonal, and probably old, crabbed, and bad-tempered. These reactions are a reader's natural response to the tone created by the wording of the letter. But many of the words and phrases are traditional and conventional usage in business correspondence. The writer may be a young, friendly man with a genuine concern for the comfort of his customers, but we cannot, however hard we try, ignore the overtones of aloof detachment.

People often argue that letters such as this belong to the age of Dickens; yet this example is real. Admittedly, it is an extreme example, but many of the features of this letter can be found in the less monstrous, but very numerous, examples we all receive. Here is a re-written version of the same letter:

Dear Mr Knight,
                    Balance of your television rental

Your television rental account is in fact paid until 23rd February 1987. We exchanged the television for a colour set on 15th December 1986, but our invoice was unfortunately sent out before this.

We have received three payments from you:

15th December, 1986	£8.50
15th December, 1986	£72.15
13th January, 1987	£179.22

Because the rentals for the first set were more than covered by these payments, we transferred the balance (£86.02) to the other rental account. This still leaves a credit balance of £79.40. Would you like us to refund this, or will you leave it in credit for future rentals?

To help you follow this rather complicated situation, we are sending copies of the two accounts, that is No. 55 78 91 99 and No. 38 00 31 00. We are sorry for the confusion.

Yours sincerely,

John W Hunt
Manager, Subscriber Relations Department.

The success of this letter derives not just from the friendly tone but also from the directness of style and the clarity of the information. There are no tortuous structures or pompous words, no stylised phrases such as are never spoken aloud by a real person. There is also a careful re-thinking of the information needed. The reader is not overloaded with a mass of detail which may or may not be relevant. The letter is short and to the point, but we do not feel it to be abrupt, unfriendly, or stingy with information. The truth is that the over-elaborate courtesies of the first version (such as 'I trust that this information will suffice') strike readers as hollow and hypocritical.

We learn an important point from the original letter. It was probably not indifference that created the unfortunate tone; rather, it was probably helpfulness which failed to think. No letter-writer actually *wants* to create the impression that this letter creates, but many letter-writers, naturally friendly people in themselves, *do* create just this impression by lack of thought.

Communication is a relationship

When we communicate, we are forming a relationship. Even if we transmit and receive only neutral information, we cannot help making judgements about the other person, and his or her likely intentions. Because there is a residual unease in person-to-person interactions, inherited from rougher and more insecure times, we have evolved elaborate rituals to reassure each other of good intentions. Thus, in a normal spoken interaction, a great deal of information about attitude and intention is transmitted non-verbally, by facial expression and movement, gesture, position of the body, distance away, use of the eyes, and many other signals. This non-verbal component of the message is vitally important in forming the communicative link.

In a letter there is no face and no smile. Without non-verbal signals to confirm good intentions, the *tone* of the letter is especially important. Judgement of the other person's intentions, of his or her confidence and assurance about what he or she is saying, is a vital part of communication. We perceive the *senders* of messages as well as their information. The research on credibility we reported at the end of Chapter 1 confirms this. The perceptions which led 1580 scientists to make judgements about the personal qualities of the report-writer after reading only a few paragraphs also operate when reading a letter. Readers cannot stop themselves making continual judgements of writers' intention and competence, as well as of the information they are receiving. Nor can writers prevent these normal human perceptions coming into play. That was why the example a few pages ago was so disturbing.

Being careful about tone does not mean that letters should be full of racy mateyness, or crammed with lugubrious reassurances. It *does* mean you must select from the resources of the language code very carefully, to guard against possibilities of misinterpretation. Use the language of everyday human contact. Overformality and impersonal constructions have no associations of friendliness, no familiar context of helpful human interaction. We meet them only in the cold impersonal environments of administrative writing, and they open a door to chilly drafts of indifference.

Helpful clarity
Choice of language affects the way readers respond to letters. If writers wish to convey the impression of being friendly and helpful, the simple natural rhythms of everyday serious conversation are best. Why, then, do some writers choose a high-flown style? The answer is, we think, that the artificiality of writing to a face they have not seen is as upsetting for the writer as for the reader. Writers feel they must be careful not to offend; finding it difficult to judge the reactions of a silent and invisible reader, they protect themselves by being over-formal. Writers also feel that they must be more explicit in writing, and they reach for the longer, more formalized words. It is true that the absence of non-verbal signals means letters must be clear; but clarity does not come from long-windedness. Writing needs precision and detail, but it does not need a roundabout, pompous, and over-formalized style. The aim should be to create the impression of an efficient but human organization, which is interested in the reader's problems, and wants to help.

Use personal pronouns
Avoid impersonal constructions; they give the atmosphere of distant formality which upsets readers. Write 'I suppose', not 'it

is apprehended that'. You may feel that using 'I' lays you open to personal responsibility for the information you give; but use of the first person does not increase your responsibility, especially if you write on headed notepaper as an organization's agent. Equally, roundabout, impersonal phrases will not decrease your responsibility, but they will reduce clarity.

Writers are afraid of sounding self-centred if they continually use 'I' or 'we'. So they use a variety of alternatives such as 'the writer', or 'the undersigned', or 'this office'; the reader translates all these as 'I' with the added connotations of impersonality. 'The writer' means, for the reader, 'I, the distant and indifferent writer . . .'. Use 'we' for communal work or decisions, or write active sentences with the object under discussion as subject. Thus do not always write: 'I have the parts you ordered ready for collection'. Sometimes write instead: 'The parts you ordered are ready for collection'. Similarly, it is often possible to turn the sentence round so that 'You' becomes the subject of an active sentence. Thus do not write, where there are already several sentences starting with 'I', yet another one: 'I am pleased to tell you that the tests were negative'. Write instead, 'You will be pleased to know that the tests are negative'.

A skilful choice from these resources can make a letter varied and interesting, and avoid chilling impersonality.

Avoid long, formal words

The temptation to reach out for the long word seems more irresistible than ever in letters. Words and phrases long out of use in normal conversation are dusted off, and ancient formalities are dragged out. Often, writers seem to climb up on to ancient, Dickensian high stools and desks, straighten their backs, clear their throats, and with much dipping and chewing of their quills, scratch and blot their way through copious and fawning formalities. Try to use simple, familiar words instead. They are easier to read, more economical in time and space, but most importantly they have the atmosphere of efficiency and friendliness. Remember the advice of Sir Ernest Gowers:

> Every entrant into the civil service comes equipped with a vocabulary of common words of precise meaning adequate for all ordinary purposes. But when he begins to write as an official he has a queer trick of forgetting them and relying mainly on a smaller vocabulary of less common words with a less precise meaning.[1]

The English language is rich in verbose and unwieldy phrases to replace the plain and serviceable everyday word. Instead of 'about' the writer can say 'in regard to' or 'referring to' or 'in connection with'. We think writers choose these longer phrases because they feel such wording adds variety and elegance; perhaps they feel that these ceremonious circumlocutions convey a timeless old-world courtesy; perhaps also they hope that if they linger politely over these words, their reader will think they have taken care and trouble over the letter. But whatever the motive, the tactics are mistaken. Such long phrases do not convey respect and courtesy; the simple phrase conveys real helpfulness by sensibly getting on with the job.

Layout of the letter

As we said in Chapter 4, the layout of a document is part of a system of signs, a code which reader and writer use more successfully when it is familiar to both of them. For these reasons, letters should follow the standard format which the reader is conditioned to expect. The writer's address, if it is not printed, will be expected in the top right-hand corner. The name and address of the reader will be expected slightly lower down on the left. The references will usually be either below or above the receiver's address; they can also be put in the title line of the letter. Within simple conventions, a letter can follow any form which is a convenient and effective way of communicating the information.

The first impact of the letter is created by the greeting. Many writers always put 'Dear Sir', or even worse 'Dear Sir or Madam', even if they know the name of the person they are writing to. But using first names has become the norm in personal contacts, and is becoming the norm in business letters. If you are not on first-name terms, the best policy is to address your reader by surname. A name is a personal thing, and to use it is a sign of respect. The convention of addressing even friends with a peremptory and military 'Sir!' died with the First World War; to start letters with a uniform 'Dear Sir' suggests indifference to people and their names.

Some companies state that all letters must be addressed to the company. This is an antiquated restriction, and we meet it less and less; but in replying to one of their letters, the sensible thing to do is to accept their requirements, since there is no point in irritating your reader gratuitously. But show that you are replying to the person who wrote to you by clearly marking your letter for the attention of that person. When you are writing to someone whose name you do not know, 'Dear Sir or Madam' is acceptable as a polite form of address, but only then.

When addressing the letter, put the addressee's position in the company as the next line after his or her name. There are two reasons for this. First, if no official position is in the address, the office may think the letter is personal, and leave it unopened when the addressee is away. Second, if the addressee has left, the new holder of the job may send your letter on. This confusion is avoided if the addressee's status is given after his or her name.

In most letters, some sort of heading or title-line should come immediately after the greeting. Most people in offices deal with many letters on widely different topics every day, and it helps them to focus their attention on the subject of any particular letter quickly if the topic is clearly stated in a title line. But do not write 'Re: Cotton wool swabs'. The *Re* adds nothing, and most people do not even know what it means (it is in fact Latin for 'the thing' and was used by mediaeval lawyers to give formality to their writing). Just as informative, and simpler is: 'Cotton Wool Swabs'. The title line may also contain the references, if they are informative. Thus the title might be 'Cotton-Wool Swabs : Order C.59487'. It could also contain the date of the letter you are replying to: 'Diesel Generator : your letter of 21st April'. In this way, cumbersome references are kept out of the first sentence.

Your first sentence should contain the main point of the letter. Many writers seem to find it difficult to start. They write:

Start with the important point

> Dear Sir,
>
> Thank you for your letter of 27th April, which we have received. Turning to the matter you mention in your first paragraph, you will be pleased to know that the Diesel Generators are ready . . .

The opening phrases of this letter are redundant; they have little function other than to clear the writer's throat. Readers must skip over them to get to the meat of the letter, and this is wasteful for reader and writer alike. More importantly, it blunts the impact of the message. Such an opening gives an apologetic and hesitant tone. Start letters, instead, with the key point:

Dear Mr Smith,

The diesel generators are ready . . .

Many of the stilted phrases of the ugly 'correspondence' style are redundant opening lines:

With reference to your enquiry please find attached . . .
I am writing to tell you that . . .

No one could write 'I am not writing to tell you that . . .' or even 'I am writing not to tell you that . . .'. Equally silly is the opening:

We have received your letter . . .

The phrase is meaningless because its opposite is unlikely.

Much awkwardness in opening sentences is created by the feeling that it is essential to refer at the outset to the date of the letter to which you are replying. We have already suggested that the date is better in the reference or in the title line; but if you must refer, in the first sentence, to the date of the letter to which you are replying, put it in a more comfortable position, not highlighted at the beginning. Do not write:

Thank you for your order of 21st April for diesel generators, which are now ready.

But write:

The diesel generators, which you ordered on 21st April, are now ready.

The old habit of using Latin in the first sentences of letters is dying out. Writers used to refer to 'yours of 21st. ult.' or 'prox.' or 'inst'. Many readers are not certain what the abbreviations mean, and in any case such Latin tags give an air of stuffy pomposity to a letter. Write clearly by always stating the month itself.

Sometimes a letter is little more than a cover-note for something you are sending. The traditional openings for this are stilted and formal. Do not write 'Please find enclosed . . .'; it has an unnatural ring to it, and most of the variations of this phrase are not much better. It is simpler and more natural to write: 'Here is the plan you wanted . . .'

Organization   Before ending a letter, make sure all the necessary points are covered. Give information clearly, and in an order which makes it easy for the reader to follow the points through. Do not be afraid to use sub-headings in a letter. They are very helpful to the reader as a signal that he or she is moving to a different topic. If the letter is more than a page long, it can have sub-headings, exactly as in a report. Check that you have dealt with all the questions you must answer by making brief notes in the margin of the enquirer's letter, and going through them while writing.

At the end of your letter, stop. This is obvious advice, perhaps, but many writers add pious and empty courtesies. A customary flourish, by its very weary familiarity, adds nothing; indeed, it detracts from the impression of sincerity. Consider this ending:

Ending

> Meanwhile we should be pleased to have your assurance of immediate delivery of a replacement supply and look forward to being advised of delivery on Monday or Tuesday of next week,
>
> Yours faithfully,

The ending has a genuine point to make, but does so in such a verbose way that it is unlikely to succeed. A more effective ending is:

> Please will you tell us by Tuesday next week when you can deliver.

A second example of a verbose ending which struggles to say something simple, at great length, is:

> We should be pleased to have confirmation of your understanding of this purchasing agreement between us, which we are sure will be to our mutual advantage.

Such an ending leaves a bad taste: 'We should be pleased to . . .' sounds pompous. 'Confirmation of your understanding . . .' means simply 'confirmation'. 'Agreement between us' means simply 'agreement'. 'We are sure will be to our mutual advantage . . .' sounds like the bland re-assurances of the con-man. A better ending is:

> Please confirm this agreement.

Many absurd and uncomfortable phrases are used to end letters. Such endings should be cut out; the best way to finish a letter is with the last factual statement. If an early reply is genuinely needed, then give both a date, and a reason.

Not:

> The favour of a response in the near future would be appreciated.

but:

> Please reply by the 25th because we make up our monthly orders then.

The signature
It is polite to type your name, or write it in block capitals below the signature. The range and variety of English surnames is amazing. We all feel upset if our name is mis-spelt; we all feel embarrassed if we are unsure about the spelling of a name. To save your reader puzzling over a signature, try also to acquire a legible and neat signature.

Finally, it is off-hand to end 'Dictated and signed in his absence by . . .' It suggests the writer is too busy to deal with letters personally. We know it is sometimes done for legal reasons, but the secretary is as much the organization's agent in law as the manager is. If your letter has to be signed by someone else, the simple explanation 'for' is clearest and politest. When signing letters, it is also polite to put your position or status after the signature. Everyone in the office may know who you are, but the reader may not. It is always courteous to tell your reader in what capacity the letter is written.

Tactics for letters
Not all letters merely report information. In many cases they have to explain failure, repeat requests, refuse information or confess to not having done something. If you have to fulfil one of these tasks, try to report first what you *have* been able to do, then report what you have not been able to do. Reflect on the impression this reply makes:

> We have searched our files for the test reports on Batch C467. We think this report must be held at the New York office, and if you write direct to them you may be able to get a copy of it. We are sorry not to be able to help you this time.

This letter reports failure to help, but does so in a strategic way. The impression is that the writer has made an effort to find the information, and he or she has thought of the way forward for the reader. Exactly the same information could have been communicated more clumsily:

> We do not seem to keep copies of the test reports, such as that on Batch C467 which you requested, though we spent time searching our files. You should write to the New York office.

The blame here appears to be put on the reader's shoulders for asking the wrong office. Even the fact that the writer spent time looking for the report sounds like a reproach, whereas previously it sounded like an effort to help. Tactical thinking is vital if you are to convey a good impresion. By using sympathy and understanding for the reader, you can create a good impression and avoid unfortunate misunderstandings.

Writing memoranda

A memorandum may be as long as a short report or as brief as a sentence. The main difference from a letter is the informality and immediacy of the memorandum. Because it is internal, it does not require the apparatus of addresses; because it is informal it does not require a greeting or a farewell; because it is immediate, it does not require a framework of courtesies. But a memorandum cannot be carelessly written. Tone is important; only careful choice of tactics can avoid the threat of misunderstanding. The most important advice is to avoid over-formal language, and to use every-day, clear and direct words and structures. A memo which starts:

> The writer apprehends that difficulty has been experienced in achieving monthly targets . . .

will court failure. It would create a better impression written in simpler language:

> I realize that you have found it hard to meet monthly targets . . .

Elaborate courtesies in memoranda rarely ring true, and in some circumstances invite a cynical reaction. A simple 'please' or 'thank you' is adequate, because its simplicity reinforces rather than detracts from its sincerity. Thus a balanced memorandum to the sales staff might read:

> Our sales quota for the month has again been achieved by the middle of the third week. Head Office have commented favourably on our area's performance. Thank you for your efforts.

The original version was less effective:

> I am very pleased to tell you that our sales quota for the month has already been met, and it is only the middle of the third week. You will be delighted to know that Head Office has commented favourably on this area's performance. Once again, my heartfelt thanks for your very real efforts.

A memorandum is a tool of management, a business device, aiming at convenience and speed. To spin it out with a *multiplicity* of 'pleases' and 'thank-yous' is redundant. Memoranda should briefly state their message, and stop.

Most activities are co-operative; few organizations work for the benefit of one person only. It is therefore usually possible to put any request in a form which makes some benefit for the reader clear, and a little thought will make the writer sensitive to the ways in which such tactics can be used. It is well worth while, in terms of co-operation and efficiency, to make the effort to adjust to a reader-centred way of thinking. As an example, here is a memorandum which does its job less than efficiently:

Use of envelopes

It appears that new envelopes are being used for internal mail and for the London office when, instead, used envelopes, sealed by stapling, would be quite satisfactory or, alternatively, envelopes could be dispensed with and the contents folded and secured by either a paper clip or staple and the recipient's name written on the outside.

In the interests of economy, it is suggested that for internal mail or for London office, where practicable, either of the latter two methods should be adopted, care being taken to avoid any confusion or mis-direction by ensuring that any re-used envelopes are clearly addressed and all previous names and addresses obliterated.

Supplies of used envelopes are normally available from Traffic Department.

The first impression is unfavourable, because the title line is not helpful in focusing attention on the precise subject. A more informative title would be: 'Economical re-use of envelopes', or 'Saving costs by re-using envelopes'. Next, long sentences (only three for the whole memo), and pompous words ('alternatively', 'dispensed with') build up an atmosphere of directive, insensitive fussing over details. There is no attempt to make the instructions in any way to the benefit of the reader. Nor is there any attempt to soften it with a simple 'please'; it remains blunt and impersonal. We would judge that there would be little saving of envelopes as a result of this memo. But it can be re-written in a simpler, more direct and personal style, adopting the tactics of appealing to mutual benefit:

Saving costs by re-using envelopes

Envelopes are costing our organization a great deal of money. Please re-use envelopes for internal mail as much as possible.

Re-used envelopes can also be used for mail for London office; re-stapling old envelopes, or simply folding the message (and stapling or clipping) will do. Please make sure that the old address is crossed out. Traffic Department have plenty of used envelopes.

Simplicity and thoughtfulness transform a poor memo into an effective one.

Many letters are dictated. This is neither as easy nor as time-saving as it appears. Spoken language is very different from written language; in general it does not have the same sentence structures, uses more and simpler words, and relies on intonation as well as syntax for structure and emphasis. Here is an exact transcription of a spoken talk on a technical subject:

Dictating letters

Well if you take one of these animals and put it between two electrical terminals in a laboratory, and create a strong static electricity field, which doesn't hurt the animal at all, it's perfectly lively and unaffected by it, but it will start to discharge electrons; they fan out from the openings of the body, the openings in its external shell, its exoskeleton, and there's an avalanche of electrons moving out and knocking into molecules of gas in the air, nitrogen molecules mostly, and these are excited, and because they're excited, they glow, and so each individual insect, gives out rather a weak light, but if you look at it, in a darkened room, you can see this glow fanning out in all directions.

If you have never seen spoken language written down before, you have probably not thought how radical the differences are. The spoken voice, has an extra 'code', an extra system of signals to communicate with. Intonation, by rising and falling pitch, by varying loudness, and by grouping sounds, is able to communicate the structures and meanings of groups of words. Because of this, spoken language often does not need the same explicit system of grammatical structures which written language uses. Stripped of the ability to use this intonation code, the *writer* has to use the grammar code more fully. It is for this reason that transcribed dictation is often uncomfortable to read. It also tends to be more repetitious (often using the same word with different meanings in the same sentence) and to use long phrases rather than single words.

Simply talking into a dictating machine naturally produces the spoken variety of language. Therefore, when dictating, you must learn to reproduce the grammatical explicitness of written language while speaking. Here are three pieces of advice:

A dictated letter often lacks structure and headings. Therefore make a brief note plan of the main points before dictating. Look through these notes, determining the best order and dictate from them, clearly specifying paragraphs and sub-headings.

Dictate slowly, using deliberately short sentences. Because spoken language tends to make less use of what we would recognize as a sentence boundary, dictated letters often have long sentences. Sentences which seem short when dictating are frequently of the right length when written down.

Try to dictate in a clipped style. Talking is easy and encourages verbosity and repetition. If you say things briefly, and stop before expanding, repeating or embroidering the point, the written result will be economical and effective as written language.

Finally, it is essential to edit dictation. The transcript may have a different tone from that intended. Here is an example of 'raw' dictation, with signs of loquacity and unusual structures in written language. It was unfortunately issued in this form:

Dr Brown used to work with Quintra and has now been appointed Production Manager at this comparatively new plant which so far has not been involved with exterior finishes but is about to do so having developed a range of pre-treatment systems and undercoatings for the industry which is likely to expand very substantially over the next few years. He now wishes to introduce new window re-finishing lines and to this end has been sampled with our products. Evaluation of the other products continues but next week Dr Brown will advise E.C.D. of his requirements. At this stage, demand will certainly be small because in terms of manufacture they have had no previous experience as a company in producing these coatings.

When spoken, the oddities of grammar in structures like 'which so far has not been involved . . . but is about to do so' and 'in terms of manufacture they have had no previous experience . . .' would go unnoticed. Intonation would supply the structure which the grammar confuses. The letter also has very long sentences, and verbose phrases like 'to this end'. Edit dictation to produce written language:

> Dr Brown used to work for Quintra. He has been appointed Production Manager at this new plant. So far it has not produced external finishes, but is about to start. It has developed a range of pretreatment systems and undercoatings for the building industry (which is likely to greatly expand over the next few years). He wants to introduce new window re-finishing lines so I gave him samples of our products. He will continue to evaluate the other products; but he promises to tell us what his requirements will be next week. They have no previous experience in the company of producing these coatings, so orders will be small.

No doubt many readers already follow the suggestions we have made here; but we are still surprised at the number of tortuously phrased and confusing letters we see. If writers are careful about adopting a direct and friendly tone, use simple, clear language, thoughtful tactics and a helpful layout, their letters create a favourable impression.

Clear and useful letters

1. Gowers, Sir Ernest (1954) *The Complete Plain Words*, HMSO, London; reprinted (1969) by Pelican, Harmondsworth, p. 42.

References

14 *Writing minutes and reports of proceedings*

The term 'minutes' is used widely to mean three different things:

- informal notes, usually attached to and commenting on files of papers, much like memoranda;
- brief, formal records of decisions taken at a committee, board or other formal meeting;
- descriptive reports of the proceedings at a meeting, summarizing the discussion and recording the decisions taken.

Minutes as memoranda

Minutes as memoranda are used mainly in national and local government, and in the armed forces. They are informal but official internal documents, used principally to accumulate comments on papers (especially correspondence) in a file. For example, papers relevant to a given topic are assembled within a manilla file. A 'minute sheet' is fastened inside the cover of that file, and people who receive the file write their comments on the minute sheet, before they pass the file to the next person concerned with it. In that way, a dossier of comments builds up on the minute sheet. Readers of the file may record a point of view both on the documents in the file and on other comments on the sheet; they may provide additional information or commentary on a document in the file; or they may record executive decisions.

Minutes as memoranda are usually expressions of opinion, recognized as part of the internal management process of an organization. Since they are informal, usually hand-written, they are often written in a cryptic, abbreviated style; their writers rely on file-readers being familiar with the contents of the file, and on the fact that the topic under discussion is 'in the air' at the moment.

It is admirable to aim at being brief and to the point in such minutes: but it is important to remember that the minute sheet becomes an official record, part of the file itself; the record must be comprehensible not only while the topic is current, but also six months or six years later. Beware, therefore, of a laconic, allusive style that may bewilder readers who were not party to the exchanges in and around the file while the topic was 'hot'.

Attempts to record what went on at a meeting, especially what was decided, can be of three broad types:

Minutes as records of a meeting

1. simple statements of the decisions alone;
2. statements of the decisions, accompanied by a summary of the main points made in discussions at the meeting, with information about who supported the varying points of view;
3. full verbatim transcripts of everything that was said at the meeting.

It is comparatively easy to write the first type (brief records of the decisions alone). It is comparatively easy – albeit tedious – to produce the third type (full transcripts of what was said), provided you have high-quality tape-recorder equipment placed strategically around the meeting-place. It is infernally difficult to write the second type – minutes that are supposed to report not only the decisions taken, but also the gist of the full discussion.

Brief, formal records of decisions

Writing minutes that are to be simple records of decisions at a meeting is a straightforward task: you must record what was decided, no more and no less.

For official bodies, the minutes are the legal records of their meetings. The minutes must reflect exactly the sequence of the meeting, and for each minute, four components are usually necessary:

- a number and subject heading;
- a sentence or short paragraph describing any document(s) on which discussion was based, and *perhaps* mentioning who made an introductory statement;

- a statement of the resolution(s) or decision(s) on the subject, normally without voting figures;
- a reminder to act (if that is not incorporated in the resolution).

For example:

84.17 New Furniture for the Research Building

Dr Brown presented the RB Working Party's report on furnishing (RBWP 17/6).

AGREED that £17 460 be spent on items 4, 9 and 12 in the report's recommendations.

ACTION: Dr Brown

or:

84.3.7 New Furniture for the Research Building   *Action*

Dr Brown presented the RB Working Party's report on furnishing (RBWP 17/6).

RESOLVED: that £17 460 be spent on items 4, 9 and 12 in the report's recommendations.   JB

In addition to these components for each item, formal minutes usually need:

- date, time and place of meeting;
- names of Chairperson and Secretary;
- names of those present (though for large meetings, numbers present will do);
- apologies for absence;
- names of any visitors who attended in special capacities.

Figures 14.1, 14.2 and 14.3 show three ways in which formal minutes can be laid out.

In some organizations, much heat is generated over whether lists of participants should be hierarchichal or alphabetical, and whether they should be based on personal names or on roles within the organization. Many variations are possible.

In general, the form in which a name is expressed, and the

Minutes of the 26th Meeting of the Committee on Chemical and Material Development

25 December, 1988
Cardiff Works

PRESENT Mr G. Pearl, Cardiff (Chairman), Mr J. Black, Manchester, Dr I. Brown, Cardiff, Dr B. Diamond, Cardiff, Mrs V. Emerald, Birmingham, Mr R. Green, Manchester, Ms L. White, Cardiff, Mr A. Grey, Cardiff (Secretary).

APOLOGIES FOR ABSENCE Mr M. Ruby

26.1 MINUTES OF 25th MEETING, 25th September 1988

It was agreed that the words 'electronic components' in minute 25.4, line 4, be altered to read 'resistors and fixed capacitors'. The minutes were then accepted.

26.2 MATTERS ARISING

25.3 Puretex Paper

Mr Pearl reported that no good substitute had been found to date. He was asked to continue to search.

ACTION: Mr Pearl.

25.7 Life Tests on Line Output Transformers (Report PR 793)

AGREED: that £1500 be spent on modifying test-cabinets.
ACTION: Mr Grey.

26.3 APPLICATION OF PVC SIMULATED-WOOD FILM

AGREED: that £1780 be spent on large-scale pilot-plant trials of PVC simulated-wood film
ACTION: Dr Brown.

26.4 REPRESENTATION ON NEW GROUP PLANNING ORGANIZATION

AGREED: that representatives on the new committee should rotate

: that the period of representation should be one year

: that Mr Grey and Mr Pearl should be the representatives from 1st January 1989

ACTION: Mr Pearl and Mr Grey.

26.5 ANY OTHER BUSINESS

26.5.1 Trials with bright-tin plating

AGREED: that Dr Brown should co-ordinate efforts to draw up plating standards on behalf of the C and MD Committee.

: that Dr Brown report on progress to the next meeting.

ACTION: Dr Brown.

26.5.2 Notice of motions for the next meeting

1. To begin using plated-through holes in PC boards (Ms White).

2. To change the manufacturing specification for winding jibs for deflection coils (Ms White).

ACTION: Ms White and Mr Grey.

Fig. 14.1 A possible layout for minutes, for comparison and contrast with Figs 14.2 and 14.3.

Minutes on 26th Meeting of the C and MD Committee

25th December 1988, Cardiff Works

PRESENT John Black, Production Manager, Manchester
Irene Brown, Research Manager, Cardiff
Brian Diamond, Assistant Research Manager, Cardiff
Valerie Emerald, Manager, Chemical Development Group, Birmingham
Robert Green, Production Supervisor, Manchester
Alan Grey, Research Officer, Polymers, Cardiff (Secretary)
Geoffrey Pearl, Research Director, Cardiff (Chairman)
Leonora White, Research Officer, Plastics, Cardiff

APOLOGIES FOR ABSENCE Michael Ruby, Birmingham

		ACTION
135	**MINUTES OF 25th MEETING, 25th September 1988**	
	The words 'electronic components' in minute 129, line 4, were altered to read 'resistors and fixed capacitors'. The minutes were then adopted.	
136	MATTERS ARISING	ACTION
	127 Puretex Paper	
	Mr Pearl reported that no good substitute had been found to date. He was asked to continue his search	GP
	131 Life Tests on Line Output Transformers (Report PR 793)	
	RESOLVED that £1500 be sent on modifying test-cabinets.	RG
137	APPLICATION OF PVC SIMULATED-WOOD FILM	
	RESOLVED that £1780 be spent on large-scale pilot-plant trials of PVC simulated-wood film.	IB
138	REPRESENTATION ON NEW GROUP PLANNING ORGANIZATION	
	RESOLVED: that representatives on the new committee rotate	
	: that the representation period be one year	
	: that Geoffrey Pearl and Alan Grey be the C and MD representatives from 1 January 1989	GP AG
139	ANY OTHER BUSINESS	ACTION
	139.1 Trials with bright-tin plating	
	RESOLVED: that Irene Brown co-ordinate efforts to draw up plating standards on behalf of the C and MD Committee	IB
	: that Irene Brown report on progress at the next meeting	IB
	139.2 Notice of motions for the next meeting	
	1. To begin using plated-through holes in PC boards.	LW AG
	2. To change the manufacturing specification for winding jibs for deflection coils.	LW AG

Fig. 14.2 A possible layout for minutes, for comparison and contrast with Figs 14.1 and 14.3.

Minutes of the Technical Training Directorate, Technical Writing
Policy Committee, held on Saturday 30th February, 2001

PRESENT   I.M. Superior   HTTD (Chairman)
             T. Hardy   AHTTD
             Miss C. Bronte   MTWG-1
             C. Dickens   MTWG-2
             Mrs E.C. Gaskell   MTWG-3
             R.Burns   AMTWG - Scotland
             R. Llewellyn   TW4 - Wales
             W. Shakespeare   TW3b-3 (Secretary)

1 **MINUTES OF THE MEETING OF 25th DECEMBER, 2000**   ACTION

    Correction to the distributed draft:

    p.8, 5.24.2   'finding' amended to 'funding'.
    p.9, 5.26.3   'computed' amended to 'completed'.
    p.12 5.30.2   'translation' amended to translocation'.

    The corrected draft minutes were accepted.

2 **MATTERS ARISING**

    2.1   Minute 3.19: Revisions of estimates

        HTTD reported that he had received the out-turns and
        revised estimates from TWG - Wales and TWG - Scotland
        and had asked MTWG-1 to co-operate with TW3b-3 in
        drawing up a report to be presented to the TTDTWPC
        at its autumn meeting.   MTWG-1
                                                        TW3b-3

    2.2   Minute 4.7: Projection for 2002

        MTWG-2 reported that copies of the Projections
        Sub-Committee report would be distributed in April.   MTWG-2

3 **PAPER SIZE SUB-COMMITTEE**

    AHTTD presented the Paper Sub-Committee Interim Report
    (TTD/TWPC/9/64A). AGREED that a decision on the
    Sub-Committee's recommendations be deferred until after
    the European Community Directive on Paper Sizes had
    been received.

Fig. 14.3 A possible layout for minutes, for comparison and contrast
with Figs 14.1 and 14.2.

appropriate position in the list of the Chairman, the Secretary
and any senior managers, depends on the atmosphere prevailing in your organization. Rigidly stratified organizations like to
see status revealed in the attendance list; modern, less formal
organizations are happy with alphabetical order. Formal organizations like to see courtesy titles, especially academic titles;
organizations where first-name exchanges are usual, normally

prefer courtesy titles to be dropped. We think this is more a matter of propriety of organizational behaviour than of clear communication. We make no recommendation. We suggest simply that you follow custom in your own organization.

There is more substance to a debate over the use of names or roles in minutes. Some organizations argue that people attend meetings by virtue of the role they play in the organization; meetings are made up of representatives of groups, not of individuals; and since individuals change roles frequently, it might not mean much to later readers of the minutes to learn that 'John Jones presented . . .', whereas it would be informative (and might be significant) to learn that 'The Manager of the Packaging Department presented . . .'.

We think that it is often sensible to give roles or job-titles as well as names in a list of participants, as in Figs 14.2 and 14.3. However, the need to do this on every set of minutes depends on the ease with which names can be fitted to roles by reference to other sources of information. If the membership of a standing committee is fixed for a period, and a list of the members for the period, with information about their roles, is presented at the beginning of the minute book for that period, there is less need for repetition of information on each set of minutes. We recommend strongly, though, that you use names in the minutes, not job titles, especially when the job titles are expressed as acronyms. The text in Figure 14.3 is very uncomfortable reading because of all the lumpy acronyms.

Perhaps the most important point to remember about minutes is that they usually have to be comprehensible not only to those who *were* at the meeting but also to those who *were not*. The minutes of official bodies may serve as more than simple records of decisions: they may also serve to propagate information, and to authorize action. As you write minutes, therefore, it is not enough to rely on allusions to discussion at the meeting: it is essential either to spell out precise information for those who were not at the meeting, or, if agenda papers as well as minutes are circulated to outsiders, to refer to specific items in the agenda papers that are referred to in the minutes (as in Figs 14.1, 14.2 and 14.3).

Summaries of discussion and decisions   Earlier, we described as 'infernally difficult' the task of writing minutes that not only record decisions but also summarize the gist of the discussion during a meeting. We know the frustrations: you have to try to follow, to make notes on, and then to

summarize the rambling, repetitive, often irrelevant, and sometimes incoherent utterances of committee members. We have
yet to find anyone who responds happily to a request to 'just
take the minutes'!

One cause of difficulty is that it is impossible to be a full
contributing member of the committee *and* take notes conscien-
tiously at the same time. The secretary's job should be to listen
to what is being said, to extract the essence of each utterance,
and to record as much as he or she thinks will give a true and
adequate impression of each speaker's contribution. A full participant in the meeting should be doing more than this. His/her
job is not only to listen carefully, and to extract the essence of
each utterance; it is also to evaluate each utterance, to formulate
complementary or contradictory contributions, and to express
them coherently at appropriate moments. It is impossible to
fulfil both the secretarial role and the full participatory role at the
same time. So we urge you to decline to be minute-taker if you
are supposed to be a full participant in the meeting. (We
recognize that it is easier for us to urge this than for you to do it!
Nevertheless, the organizers of meetings should be invited to
consider the efficiency of asking you to do both jobs.)

It is also difficult to sift valuable points from redundancies and
irrelevances. We regret that we know of no magic method or
formula for doing this. And we know of no sure way of ensuring
that you do not offend some committee members by reporting
more of someone else's views than you report of theirs. One tip
we can offer is that, when you write the minutes, you avoid
simply reflecting the sequence and length of contributions from
each member. It is probable that the notes you make will be in
chronological order, and will reflect roughly the amount said by
each member. When you come to write the minutes, you may
find it effective to record the principal points of view, irrespec-
tive of the exact sequence in which they were expressed, and to
add a note of which members supported each point of view (if
that is relevant). Focus on gathering points, not on extracting
something from each contribution.

Another tip is that you might use an adaptation of the 'pat-
terning' technique for note-taking advocated by Tony Buzan[1].
Figure 14.4 shows his recommended general form for note-
taking. He advocates that key words and phrases are all that are
needed to recall information, and these words and phrases can
be related in spider-like shapes or molecular networks. The
names of people supporting particular points of view can be
attached to the key words, if necessary. Practice is needed to use

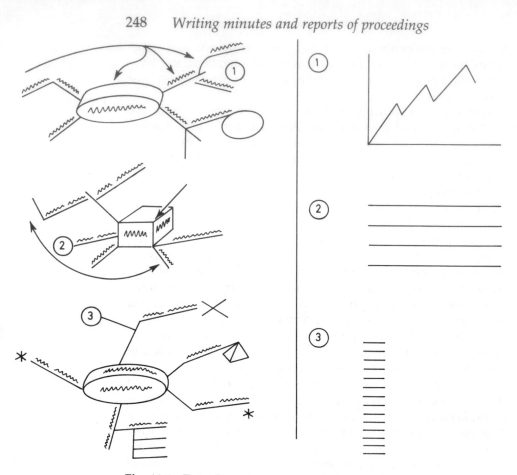

Fig. 14.4 Tony Buzan's recommended general form for note-taking. He recommends that two pages should be used concurrently, one for patterns, the other for graphic or more linear information (reproduced from *Use Your Head* by Tony Buzan, by permission of BBC Enterprises).

this technique efficiently. Your record looks messy, but as Buzan points out 'the word messy refers to the *look* and not to the *content*'.

Another difficulty lies in knowing how much to record of debate that led finally to negative decisions. In minutes of the first type (brief, formal minutes), no record should be made of proposals or amendments that were discussed and rejected. No record need be kept of the vote. All that need be recorded is the positive decisions that were reached by a simple majority vote (or other majority, if a special majority is written in to the organization's constitution). What the organization decided *not* to do is, so runs the theory, irrelevant; and it is irrelevant in the

British democratic system whether the majority in favour or against was large or small.

Such a theory may be acceptable for the formal running of institutional bodies; but it is rarely judged acceptable in business and industry. In large research departments, for example, there is usually considerable value in recording what products, policies or processes were considered and rejected (or left for later action) during a research programme. Though it may seem tiresome to have to record such information 'for the archive', the archive may be vital as a means of preventing waste of time and money on 're-inventing the wheel' in later years. Equally important, your company's culpability for loss or damage may depend heavily on your ability to show the possibilities and contingencies that were considered before a certain positive line of action was chosen.

Consequently, in many organizations, it is important to record in minutes not only enough detail to show why a decision was taken, but also enough detail to explain why other decisions were not. The detail must be comprehensible not only to those who were present at the meeting, but also to those who were not – and especially to those who read the minutes some time after the events/decisions that are recorded.

Yet another problem in writing minutes is ensuring that you record accurately the decisions that are reached. In meetings that lack good leadership, and/or that pride themselves on arriving at decisions by consensus, there is often considerable confusion about the precise wording of what has been decided. A good chairperson will state the proposition clearly before any vote is taken; but where that is not done, and where there is continued discussion after such a statement, we recommend that you establish a practice of reading out to the meeting immediately after each decision the words you have used to record that decision. Train your chairperson to allocate time to this checking activity, or be sure to intervene yourself, so that there can be no argument subsequently about what was agreed.

Style for minutes

Minutes should be written economically but clearly. It is tempting to use a compressed, note-form style, on the grounds that you are simply providing brief reminders for people who were at the meeting. But even for such people, a compressed style may be too cryptic:

> Enhancement request received for console filter to eliminate invalid password logon messages.

Action: John Brown.

Where did the request come from? What action was agreed? Even a week later, participants in the meeting may have difficulty in remembering exact details.

Especially, people who were not at the meeting may be bewildered by a compressed, allusive style:

X reported no peripherals contact yet.

This meant 'X reported that he had not been able to find a suitable supplier of two printers by the time of the meeting'. The phrase 'no peripherals contact' might be an adequate cue for participants in the meeting: they may be able to recall the in-committee discussion of the need for two printers, and Mr X's difficulties in making contact with suitable suppliers of peripheral equipment; but for people who were not at the meeting, 'peripherals contact' does not trigger a memory of precisely what was discussed. Clearer, more exact writing is essential.

In particular, indications of time and place must be made clear. That is, the rules of reported speech must be followed carefully. Not only tenses, but also pronouns, possessive adjectives, and adverbs of time and place may need to be changed. The statement by Miss X, of the Research Department, on Friday 6 May:

My department will not be able to provide this service before next Friday.

must become

Miss X stated that her department would not be able to provide that service before the following Friday.

or

Miss X stated that Research Department would not be able to provide that service (or the service requested) before Friday 13 May.

An outline of the rules for reported speech is given in Appendix B.

Reference   1. Buzan, Tony (1974). *Use Your Head* BBC Publications pp. 104–5.

Writing in 15
examinations

Most of us find examinations stressful, and when our full-time education comes to an end, we vow that we shall avoid being examined in future. But in modern business and industry, the introduction of new technology frequently means that we need to qualify in the use of new skills; and as we become more senior, we find increasing need for further training in management and in business-school studies. So, as our final chapter, for professional readers and for students, here is a review of the tactics for academic writing, especially of writing in examinations.

In Chapter 1 (pages 4 to 5), we emphasized the different objectives in professional writing and academic writing. In professional life, most writing is designed either to transmit information/ideas that you have but others have not, or to elicit information that others have and you need. The objective is genuine movement of knowledge between the parties in the exchange. Academic writing, especially writing in examinations, is different. In an examination, your task is to display to the examiners – who normally know far more than you do about the subject – what you think they think you ought to know about that subject! This task presents real communication problems, but it is a different task from professional communication. It calls for a different definition of 'effective' writing from the one we have used so far.

Above all, effective writing in examinations requires you to give the examiners what they want.

In our advice on professional writing earlier in the book, we have discussed the need to:

Give the examiners what they want

- relate your new information carefully to your readers' existing level(s) of expertise;
- discard information that you have available but that would be irrelevant to your readers' immediate needs;
- avoid jargon or inflated vocabulary that your readers will not know or need.

Now, we have to acknowledge that, when you are writing in examinations:

- your information is rarely new to the examiners;
- you are rarely writing for readers who have a lower level of expertise than you have;
- you are often required to display *how much* you know rather than your ability to select only what will be needed to equip your readers to take a decision or complete a task;
- you are often expected to introduce specialist terminology in order to demonstrate that you understand that terminology, and can manipulate it accurately.

Accordingly, in this part of the book, we have to seem to turn some of our previous advice on its head. But in fact, what we have to say is not really contradictory. We have been saying that to write effectively, you must use just the right tactics of selection, organization and expression to produce the desired response in your audience. That remains true in examination writing. The difference lies not in the approach to writing, but in the decisions you should reach. You should still think carefully about aim and audience, and then select, arrange and express your information skilfully; but your decisions should focus as much on passing the examination as on passing information. You should focus on providing what is expected, rather than on increasing your readers' state of knowledge. Or at least, you should increase the examiners' state of knowledge by showing that you know what they would like you to know, and that you know how to marshal and express that knowledge coherently, in the forms and styles they require.

Simulating real-life situations Of course, some examiners may ask you to simulate real-life situations. If that is the case, focus sharply on what you are asked to do, and do it. Consider, for example, the task presented by this exercise:

Assume that you work for a steel-making company. Your Production Manager has asked you to investigate the potential of a new thermocouple cartridge – the Measurit cartridge – designed for use in analysing the carbon content of steel.

The notes below represent the information you have gathered in your enquiries. SELECT information from these notes and write a memorandum to your Production Manager giving your opinion of the new thermocouple.

The notes accompanying the question gave information about the significance of the carbon content of steel, about how thermocouples work, about the construction of the thermocouple, about the equipment and personnel required to operate the thermocouple, about its accuracy in trials and in routine use, and about its general performance compared with the performance of other analytical equipment.

In writing a memorandum in answer to this exercise, you should recognize that you are writing to the Production Manager of a steel-making company. It would therefore be inappropriate to include in your text a discussion of the significance of the carbon content of steel, or of how thermocouples work. If you were asked to write an academic essay on the use of thermocouples in analysing the carbon content of steel, it might be appropriate to demonstrate your knowledge of the metallurgical background; but such a display would be wasting the time of a Production Manager. He/she would probably have all that knowledge already, and in any case, you have been told that responsibility for evaluating the information provided has been delegated to you. Your memorandum should therefore focus sharply on whether you think the thermocouple would be useful in your steelworks, with a few salient facts to support your opinion. A good memorandum would probably begin like this:

> Use of the Measurit cartridge would increase the efficiency with which we measure the carbon content of steel at intermediate stages in our production process. The cartridge produces results in 10% of the time taken by conventional methods, it can be handled by unskilled personnel, and it requires no special laboratory space . . .

Note the contrast with a characteristic essay-style opening of a document for academic purposes:

> The steel-making process is affected substantially by the carbon content of the steel. All the alloying constituents of the steel affect the temperature at which the solid-to-liquid phase

change occurs, but the element that most significantly affects that temperature is carbon. Therefore, a method of analysing the carbon content is needed, which will give a quick and accurate analysis of carbon content . . .

Most Production Managers would be exceedingly irritated by the patronizing tone of these well-known facts! They would be equally irritated by time-wasting, 'throat-clearing' beginnings such as

As requested by you, I have investigated into the working of the new Measurit Cartridge, and give below my findings and opinion on it.

I hereby give my opinion regarding the new thermocouple for your kind consideration.

In response to your request in connection with the potential of the Measurit cartridge designed for use in analysing the carbon content in steel I have the following information and comments to make.

Analysing the objective of the examination — Your tactics for writing accurately must be dictated by a careful analysis of what the examiners want from you. In a chemistry examination, you may be asked to describe and explain the mode of operation of condensed phosphates such as tetrasodium pyrophosphate or sodium tripolyphosphate in detergents. In such a question, the examiners are chiefly interested in your chemical knowledge. Your ability to marshal and express your knowledge is a secondary – though not *un*important – consideration. In contrast, in an English or Communication Studies paper, you may meet a question such as

Queen Victoria remarked that Mr Gladstone '. . . speaks to me as if I were a public meeting'. Discuss the differences of selection and organization of information, demeanour, delivery and language appropriate to a discussion between individuals and to the presentation of a paper at a large technical conference.

This question clearly wants a theoretical discussion of elements in the communication process, *and* the examiners want to see if you can select, marshal and express your points skilfully.

In all examinations, the examiners' interest is divided between content and expression. At one extreme, the examiners may concentrate almost entirely on your ability to find the right solution to a mathematical problem or a design difficulty. Your ability to write coherently may be a slight consideration, since little writing of prose may be involved. At the other extreme, the examiners' principal focus may be on your skills of organization and expression. The content you express may be a secondary consideration: all necessary information may even be provided for you.

The secret of success is to establish why you are being asked to write. In closed examinations (examinations created, answered and marked within a school, college or university), it is simple – and sensible – to find out the type of answer required by the examiners. It is entirely reasonable to ask the examiners what *sorts* of questions they set, and what *types* of answers they require. It is good practice, too, to study past papers, to get a sense of how the examination is constructed. In open examinations (examinations created by national bodies, answered in many centres, and marked by many examiners), it is more difficult to obtain information directly from the examiners; but past papers are usually available, and examining boards usually publish reports on their examinations, discussing candidates' performances. These reports usually provide evidence of the examiners' objectives, standards and attitudes. You and/or your teachers would be well advised to look at recent reports on any examinations you have to take.

Tactics for writing examination answers

We are not competent to give advice on tactics for writing in the whole range of special-subject examinations on topics ranging from Accountancy to Zoology. For such examinations, we must just exhort you to think carefully about the specialist content required, and to marshal and express that content in accordance with the examiners' requirements. But we can offer advice on what examiners usually want in examinations designed primarily to test communication skills – in examinations with titles such as 'English', 'Communication Studies' or 'Technical Writing'.

In the 'Queen Victoria remarked . . .' question, we have given an example of a question that requires a theoretical discussion of tactics for communication. Such questions elevate 'Communication' to the same status as 'Chemistry': that is, the discussion of communication becomes the content of the question. Tactics for answering such a question are the same as for answering any other special-subject question: analyse carefully the aim, select and arrange appropriate material, express the chosen material accurately and readably.

We have mentioned, too, the decisions you must make in answering such a question. If you are asked to discuss the physical process of reading, should you use terms such as *eye span* or *saccades* (the jumps made by your eye as it moves along the line of print)? And if you do use such terms, should you define them, to show that you know what they mean, or will the examiners expect you to assume that your readers are familiar with the meanings? Regrettably, our experience is that examiners do not always make clear the audience you should assume, even in their statements of examination objectives and in their annual reports. If in doubt, you should explain terms as you go along, to emphasize not only that you know the terms but also that you can handle them competently.

Examinations in Communication or Technical Writing

In some examinations on Communication or Technical Writing, you are asked to demonstrate your ability to fulfil particular communication tasks. For example:

> Summaries for technical papers are usually either *descriptive* or *informative*. A descriptive summary makes no attempt to draw information out of the paper; it merely describes the type of information the paper contains. An informative summary attempts to state succinctly the details of greatest interest to the paper's readers. Write an *informative* summary of the following notes in not more than 150 words. The resulting summary should be designed for a general readership, such as for *The Engineer* or *New Scientist*.

In questions such as this, you are asked to show by your deeds that you know what is wanted in an *informative* summary. The examiners are looking not only at your use of English in writing the text, but also at your understanding of what constitutes an informative summary, and at your sense of what items of information in the full text are worthy of inclusion in a summary for the specified audience.

What advice can we offer on how to answer questions that ask for theoretical discussions of specialist content, or that ask you to demonstrate your ability to fulfil particular tasks like summary-writing or writing business letters? Only advice that you have probably heard before: don't start writing your answer too quickly. Plan before you write. As experienced examiners, we can say that the presence of some pencilled notes at the start of an answer is usually a sign that what follows will be above-average rather than below-average. Plan in advance the proportion of the total time for the examination that you will allot to each question. Plan to spend a proportion of your time for each question on making notes before you begin to construct your answer. Allocate perhaps 10 minutes out of 45 to note-making. Jot down anything that occurs to you that is on or near the subject you are to discuss. Very brief notes will do, in any order. Then, select from the notes the material from which to build a structured answer, and write that answer as clearly and simply as you can.

Examinations in English

The objectives of examinations that focus specifically on English are often not well understood. All too often, we find students mechanically 'doing English' (with attendant examinations) without realising exactly what they are doing, and why. What is an English examination, especially one set by a professional body, designed to do? What do examiners want in answers to traditional types of English questions? What tactics will produce the best response?

Broadly, examiners of English want two things:

1. to know if you can use language skilfully in expressing yourself clearly and coherently;
2. to know if you are sufficiently skilled in interpreting the customary uses of language in your working environment; that is, to see if you will be able to disentangle facts and ideas from other people's writing.

These two objectives lie behind the customary composition and comprehension questions in English examinations.

Questions on vocabulary and idiom. Some of the oldest and simplest types of English questions are aimed at testing the range of vocabulary at your disposal. You may be asked to use given words in appropriate sentences. You may be asked to choose from several words one that would express an exact shade of meaning in a given context. You may be asked to discriminate between words that are similar in form or spelling but that have clear differences in meaning. All these questions are intended as straightforward tests of the range of vocabulary at your disposal.

Similarly, the examiners may ask you to insert a common idiomatic phrase into a sentence, or to correct the way in which a phrase or other group of words is used. Again, such questions are straightforward tests of the range of language at your command.

You may react against questions of this type, because the vocabulary and phrases incorporated seem to have been chosen at random, even whimsically. That is not usually the case. Usually, the items of language tested are included because the examiners know from experience that such language is needed in a particular working environment and/or because they know that such language is commonly misused or missing. They are anxious to ensure that such language is acquired by people aspiring to join the group on whose behalf the examination is set.

How should you prepare for such questions? Mainly, by conscious learning; especially, by frequent reference to a good dictionary. Whenever you come across a word that is new to you, look it up. There is no shame in having to do so. Indeed, constant checking on the accepted meaning of language is a scholarly practice, aimed at precision and appropriateness.

Also, read good writing. Read the more serious daily and Sunday papers; read the more serious journals, so that you become familiar with their vocabulary and style, and so that you become accustomed to careful arrangement of thought and skilful expression.

And when you arrive at your examination, look carefully to see what the question asks for, and give it exactly. Pay attention to the whole answer, not just to the word or words on which you were focusing special attention. Here is a warning from an examiner's report:

> Candidates should remember that when sentences are required containing examples of specific words, attention should always be paid as much to style and grammar as to the correct use of the given word. Marks are lost if there is *anything* faulty in the sentence.

Questions that ask for a precis. In Chapter 9 (pages 129 to 131), we distinguished between a summary and a precis. In summary-writing, you are usually expected to emphasize the information in the original that readers will find most interesting or useful. In precis-writing, you are usually expected to retain the shape and emphasis of the original, but to reduce it substantially.

In precis-writing, you are usually asked for a title, and you are almost always required to work within a specified number of words. The examiners want you to provide a title as an indication that you have identified the essential theme of the text exactly. The limit on length is designed to test your ability to work within constraints. Both are reasonable objectives, intended to assess valuable real-life skills. In professional life, it is frequently important to be able to detect and articulate a central theme in a mass of information. It is almost always important to be able to work within constraints. In modern business life, it seems that there is never enough time, space, money or other resources to work in an ideal way. It is therefore desirable to encourage people to develop an organised 'habit of attack' on common tasks. Teachers and examiners in English are usually looking for a habit of attack on writing tasks that begins by identifying what is wanted, then recognizes the operational constraints, and then composes a coherent utterance that makes the best use of the opportunity provided.

So, recognize what the examiners are asking for in a precis question. They are asking you to summarize essential ideas and facts from a given passage. You are not asked to comment, or to add information from your own experience.

The best approach to precis-writing is to see it as a *building-up* activity, not as a process of pruning or trimming down. Your answer must be a coherent statement, with emphasis and balance. Your sentences and paragraphs must be complete and connected. You are unlikely to produce a comfortably connected text if you simply try to supply new link statements to stretch across gaps left by the chunks you have cut out of the original. Think of precis-writing as a reconstruction procedure, a building-up of a new unit, using the basic materials from the old. Take the original apart, and lay the pieces on one side; then take up the essentials to form a new core, and build back on to the core as many details as fit into the permitted space.

In most precis-writing questions, you will be expected to keep the general sequence and shape of the original, especially if your precis is intended to give a clear reflection of the approach used by the original author. On a few occasions you may be invited to highlight main points and reduce the emphasis on others, especially when your precis is intended to draw attention to the significant outcomes of a debate or a piece of research. Read the rubric carefully, and provide the type of answer the examiners expect.

Questions that ask for an essay. In asking you to write an essay, examiners are trying to assess the ideas and information you can produce, and your ability to compose text yourself (without any prompting from supplied items of vocabulary or an original text to be summarized).

As you think about the content of your essay, try to imagine that yours is the two hundred and forty-fifth essay the examiner will read on the subject. That may help you recognize the depressing effect of banal and platitudinous beginnings such as:

Winter means November, December and January.

Neighbours are the people who live next door to you.

The subject of this essay allows for an immense range of views, ideas and personal objectives that can be placed on paper and produced as the finished article. (*Truly*, this was produced by a sixth-form examination candidate!)

Begin by making your first point. For example:

When you live in a house that is linked or is close to another, inevitably you become aware of the lifestyle of the people who live in the other house. If their patterns of movement, norms of behaviour, and styles of dress are different from yours, there is scope for irritation and discomfort on both sides. Tolerance and consideration are needed if neighbours are to live in reasonable accord . . .

Beware of the temptation to drag in chunks from an essay you wrote some time previously, which fitted in very well on that previous occasion but are irrelevant now. Heed this heart-cry from an examiner of English:

Regularly large numbers of (students) either produce other essays obviously prepared from back papers – we easily recognize these essays – which have little or nothing to do with the chosen subject, or else drag in, willy nilly, chunks of them. Many marks are lost in this way, and also by too long, off-the-point introductions which sometimes continue for several pages before the subject to be discussed is actually reached. Risqué, inappropriate anecdotes are not wanted either, even if they are intended to amuse or placate a jaded examiner.

Ensure that what you write is really relevant to the exact topic you have chosen. If your topic is 'Seen from the top deck of a bus', it is irrelevant to describe your fellow passengers or the song of a thrush in a hedge as you drive past. Similarly, if your topic is 'Inventions that are needed', it is inappropriate to preface your real essay with two pages on the history of inventions from the wheel to Watts' steam engine. Here's another examiner:

> A common tendency (*is for*) the candidate to take a key-word from the essay title and to let an essay develop from it. . . . 'Is sport too commercialized?' tended to become just 'sport' and 'The influence of climate on national character' often turned into 'what sort of climate do I like best' or 'what nations do I dislike'.

Examiners cannot give marks for essays that are not on the subject set. Nor can they give marks for a treatment of a subject that is not the treatment required. Here is a sixth-form candidate who attempted an entirely inappropriate opening to an essay on the effects of the sun's rays on the weather:

> While talking to a friend one Sunday evening about holidays he told me about the time when he was staying in a Norwegian hotel. With plenty of time on his hands and not a cloud in the sky he decided to sunbath: After a short time he found he was becoming sunburnt so he decided to fetch some lotion from his room but as he turned round he noticed that a thermometer said that the air temperature was −11° Centigrade and this he said always amazed him that he could be sunburnt at this temperature.
> 'Ah!' I exclaimed, 'that is easy to explain and no doubt the snow was not melting either.'
> His reply was in the affirmative.
> 'Well,' I continued, 'you know that the amount of heat which is absorbed by a body depends on the type of surface which the heat or sun's rays strike. If it strikes a surface which is smooth or light in colour then little heat is absorbed and thus the tempreture remains low which happens in the case of snow and dry air . . .'

It is particularly important to recognize the type of English expected in a particular examination context. Here is a forthright comment on choice of English, from an examiner for a professional body:

The candidate's use of English is, of course, of great importance. . . . (He/she) . . . should write in good, clear, simple
English, and should never attempt to be 'literary'. Jargon,
colloquialisms, slang, clichés and all those remarks 'worn
smooth by the rippling of innumerable minds' should be
avoided. Many candidates nowadays echo the unctuous, con-
descending manner of the worst film and TV commentators,
while others use a matey, slangy, unpleasantly facetious way
of writing which is out of place in an examination essay (and
is) always highly objectionable to the examiner.

From this discussion of essay-writing, six positive guidelines
emerge:

1. Read the topics carefully, and recognize *precisely* what you
   are invited to write about.
2. Give your personal opinions: be accurate and truthful. Do
   not write what you think you are expected to think. If there is
   room for argument, state both sides of a case and then say
   which you prefer and why.
3. Always jot down notes before you begin. Let your mind
   rove, and make a short pencilled note of everything that
   occurs to you, even if you cannot see its exact relevance.
   Then arrange the notes into groups for paragraphs. (Perhaps
   do this by allocating numbers to your sequence of points.)
   Ruthlessly reject stuff that is not relevant. From the groups of
   points, create a plan or framework that will give your essay
   shape. Select as much as you can use in the time available.
   You will get no marks for what you would have written if you
   had more time. Six complete points briefly made will bring
   you more reward than two points fully discussed, and four
   that you have not been able to include.
4. Keep your introduction short. If you are talking about heating a modern house, do not waste time on a preliminary
   account of how a caveman heated his cave, even if you have
   stupendous knowledge of that subject.
5. Make sure that you keep to a consistent sequence of tenses,
   not only in narrating a story, but also in ordinary speculative
   discussion. This jumble of tenses in writing about what life
   would be like on the moon is very common:

   > Men *would be able* to leap great distances, for their weight
   > *will be* very different, and they *can* also *see* much further
   > than on earth.

6. Allocate five minutes to reading through your essay after writing, to correct careless errors, which may lose you several marks. Examiners will be sympathetic to the fact that you are working under pressure, but carelessness such as this loses marks:

(A complete paragraph) The factor which is the usual cause for the everyday rain showers and the determination of whether the day is likely to be wet or dry is the pressure consideration.

Soliciting and vice increase. We in this country are trying to do something about it. We can only find the offenders very large sums of money.

Our village, which I take as being very typical, comprises one green, one pond, which, to add to the excitement has two ducks on it and five pubs.

Television puts an end to everything that is useful, to children in particular.

A word about punctuation. We have just remarked that examiners will recognize that you are working under pressure; but they will nevertheless expect you to write coherent and manageable text. In particular, they will not be pleased if they have to read part of your text several times simply because you have been careless about punctuation. Punctuation is not an artificial paraphernalia devised by English teachers to help you fail examinations; it is an integral part of the code that we call English. It is a vital means of indicating where boundaries are intended between word-groups; it is a vital means of indicating the relations of word-groups in statements; and it is a vital means of indicating tone and stress in written work. H. W. Fowler, in *The King's English*[1], cannot be bettered on this:

> The work of punctuation is mainly to show, or hint at, the grammatical relation between words, phrases, clauses, and sentences; but it must not be forgotten that stops also serve to regulate pace, to throw emphasis on particular words and give them significance, and to indicate tone. . . . Secondly, it is a sound principle that as few stops should be used as will do the work. . . . Thirdly . . . they are to be regarded as devices, not for saving (the writer) the trouble of putting his words into the order that naturally gives the required meaning, but for saving his reader the moment or two that would

sometimes, without them, be necessarily spent on reading the sentence twice over. . . . Stops are not to alter meaning, but merely to show it up.

Note how punctuation is needed in the following sentences to show up where the meaning-boundaries are intended to be between word-groups (examples 1 and 2), to show up the relations between word-groups (examples 3 and 4), and to show the meaning, tone and emphasis of words and word-groups (examples 5, 6 and 7).

1. To get a clean assembly load the assembled equals table before the assembly is run . . .
   (. . . a clean assembly, load the assembled . . .)
2. Often reported accidents are not investigated fully . . .
   (Often, reported . . .)
3. He draws an analogy between this and the learning process of a new-born child as it develops into maturity and quotes Freud: . . .
   (. . . as it develops into maturity, and quotes Freud: . . .)
4. The workers who were responsible for the fall in production should be dismissed . . .
   (The workers, who were responsible for the fall in production, should be dismissed . . .)
5. . . . a patient with this disorder is said to have a 'lazy' eye . . .
6. . . . valve must *never* be opened before . . .
7. . . . considerable doubt must be cast on this 'definite' sighting of . . .

Questions that ask for a report of direct speech
Some examinations include a test of your ability to give a report of direct speech. When you tell someone what another person has said, you can do so in two ways:

- by recording the speaker's exact words within inverted commas;
- by giving the exact content of the speaker's remarks in indirect or reported form.

For example:

My boss said, 'There are too many people on holiday this week for you to take any time off'.

My boss told me that there were too many people on holiday that week for me to take any time off.

When you write in reported speech, it is usually necessary to change tenses, pronouns, possessive adjectives, and adverbs of time and place. Watch out for the variations that will be necessary according to the precise time and place of reporting. Consider this original:

Before anyone could complain, he said, 'I decided last week to open the meeting to all members of staff'.

If you are reporting that statement in the same week as it was made, your reported-speech version should be:

Before anyone could complain, he said that he decided last week to open the meeting to all members of staff.

but if you are reporting six weeks later, your reported-speech version should be:

Before anyone could complain, he said that he had decided in the previous week to open the meeting to all members of staff.

An outline of the full rules for reported speech is given in Appendix B.

Questions that ask you to write a letter or memorandum

The examiners' objective in asking you to write a letter should be clear – they want to know if you can organize information coherently, express it appropriately, and conform to accepted conventions of layout.

We have discussed correspondence in detail in Chapter 13. We have advised you to write directly, simply, courteously and helpfully – in the way you would probably like to be addressed, and in the way that is approved by most large, modern companies. We have urged you to avoid the colloquialism of casual speech; equally we have urged you to avoid the automaton-like tone created by the mechanical use of clichés, or the disdainful, pompous and sometimes 'slippery' tone that creeps in with impersonal and passive style.

Regrettably, however, we know that there are teachers and examiners who insist that you use formulaic, impersonal style. You will lose marks if you write:

I have asked our Bristol office to arrange . . .

I am investigating your loss . . .

You are expected to write something like:

Our Bristol office has been requested to contact you with a view to arranging . . .

The misplacement you have reported is being actively investigated in this office . . .

In a BBC broadcast in the early sixties on *Our Living Language*, A. P. Rossiter summed up the language the businessman wants as one '. . . that is terse and vigorous but not discourteous'. But he added, '. . . His present lingo is none of these things; it is diffuse and flaccid and greasily servile'.

We are confident that the format and style we have advocated in Chapter 13 is widely preferred in business and industry; however, we must return to our slogan at the beginning of this chapter: when you are writing in examinations, give the examiners what they want. In preparing to answer correspondence questions, as in preparing to answer all other questions, seek clear information about the criteria that will be used in assessing your performance. Then, build your policies and tactics so that you meet those criteria.

Reference   1. Fowler, H. W. and Fowler, E. G. (1970) *The King's English*. Oxford University Press, Oxford, pp. 233–4.

Appendix A
Readability
formulae

Many formulae have been produced from readability research for assessing the readability of a piece of writing. Some are long and complex, but one simple formula is the Gunning Fog Index. It gives a good approximation to the readability scores produced by more complex formulae. We suggest that you try using this formula on a piece of your own writing. Use a chunk of text from a report, essay, article, laboratory report, or any other continuous prose on an informative subject. It is important, however, to realise before you use it that this formula is intended only as a rapid, and fairly crude, estimate of readability. The results do not confirm, or deny, the laurels of good style to the writer.

The 'Fog Index' was first published by Robert Gunning in 1952. Here are the steps for the calculation:

The Gunning 'Fog Index'

1. Find the average number of words per sentence. Use a sample at least 100 words long. Divide total number of words by number of sentences. This gives you average sentence length.

2. Count the number of words of three syllables or more per 100 words. Don't count: (a) words that are capitalized; (b) combinations of short easy words – like 'bookkeeper'; (c) verbs that are made three syllables by adding 'ed' or 'es' – like 'created' or 'trespasses'.

3. Add the two factors above and multiply by 0.4. This will give you the Fog Index. It corresponds roughly with the number of years of schooling a person would require to read a passage with ease and understanding.

4. Check the result against this scale:

5	fairly easy
7 or 8	standard
9 to 11	fairly difficult
12 to 15	difficult
17 or above	very difficult

(Adapted from Robert Gunning, *More Effective Writing in Business and Industry* (Industrial Education International, 1962), pp. 2–15.)

The formula is simplified and not necessarily accurate. In particular, you will notice that the most important factor is the length of the sentence. This is because research shows that sentence length is most closely connected with readability. It will always be possible to get an easy readability rating on the formula simply by using very short sentences, but this would produce writing that sounded like a children's book. So use common sense in applying the formula. Never write with one eye on the formula hoping to get a good readability rating; this would distort the style and make the writing worse, not better. But it is useful when you have written something to check it against the formula, as a quick guide to whether the writing is too difficult. If the examples of your own writing, which you test with the formula, show that your writing is unduly difficult, try to see why the formula gives this result. You may find that you have merely used very long sentences, and splitting several of the sentences in half will give you a more favourable result on the readability formula. You may find, on the other hand, that your sentences are of reasonable length but that you tend to use a large number of long words, that you always say 'initiate' when you mean 'start'. Try going through the passage of your own writing which you used as an example, putting simple words in the place of complicated words where this is possible and then see if you get better rating. Remember, though, that formulae are only guides.

Appendix B
Outline of rules for reported (or indirect) speech

If the introductory verb (for example, *say, exclaim, repeat*) is in the present, present perfect, or future tense, no change in tense is needed.

He says, 'The delivery is on its way'.
He says that the delivery is on its way.

He repeats, 'The scheme has worked well'.
He repeats that the scheme has worked well.

He complains, 'The instrument will not be strong enough'.
He complains that the instrument will not be strong enough.

Usually, the introductory verb is in the present tense only when you are making an immediate report – for instance, reporting to a third party the words you have just heard from someone speaking to you on the telephone. Most frequently, the introductory verb is in the past tense. Then, tenses must change.

Direct speech	Indirect speech	
simple present	simple past	The representative said, 'I am sorry but your order is too late'. The representative said he was sorry but our order was too late.

Direct speech	Indirect speech	
present continuous	past continuous	She complained, 'They are asking too much of me'. She complained that they were asking too much of her.
simple past	past perfect	He told me, 'The Finance Director took it yesterday'. He told me the Finance Director had taken it on the previous day.
present perfect	past perfect	We said, 'We have tried to take away the unwanted material, but have not be successful'. We said we had tried to take away the unwanted material, but had not been successful.
past continuous	past perfect continuous	He said, 'They were making special efforts to avoid trouble when I saw them'. He said that they had been making special efforts to avoid trouble when he had seen them.
future	conditional	He said, 'My deputy will attend your meeting'. He said his deputy would attend our meeting.

Note the change of *shall* to *should* with a 1st person report; change of *shall* to *would* with a 3rd person report:

I said, 'I shall ask for leave'.
I said that I should ask for leave.

He said, 'I shall ask for leave'.
He said that he would ask for leave.

Adverbs of time and place must usually be changed.

Tenses, pronouns, possessive adjectives, adverbs of time and **Questions**
place usually change as in statements. The interrogative form of
the verb changes to the affirmative.

> He says, 'Where is the meeting?'
> He enquires where the meeting is.

> He said, 'Can I attend the meeting?'
> He asked if he could attend the meeting.

If the introductory verb is *say*, it must be changed to *ask, enquire,*
wonder, want to know, . . .

Question words (*when, where, who, why* . . .) are repeated in the
indirect question.

> The new group leader asked, 'Where shall I place my equip-
> ment?'
> The new group leader asked where he should place his
> equipment.

If there is no question word, *if* or *whether* is used after the main
verb in the indirect question.

> He asked, 'Will there be anyone to receive us when we
> arrive?'
> He asked if there would be anyone to receive them when they
> arrived.

The main change in reporting a command is that the introduc- **Commands**
tory verb must become a verb of command or request (*tell, order,*
ask, instruct . . .) followed immediately by the person(s) addressed and the infinitive form of a verb.

> He said, 'Take the power off the X and reduce . . .'
> He told us to take the power off the X and to reduce . . .

Add *not* before the infinitive to report a negative command.

> The manager's instruction was: 'Do not remove the X from its
> position on the stand . . .'
> The manager told the operator not to remove the X from its
> position on the stand . . .

Changes of pronouns and possessive adjectives, and adverbs of
place and time are as for statements and questions.

Commands can also be reported using *to be* plus an infinitive construction.

> He said, 'You are to visit Mexico next Friday'.
> He told me that I was to visit Mexico on the following Friday.

Must   In indirect speech, *must* usually changes to *have to* when it expresses necessity or compulsion at the moment of speaking or in the future.

> She said, 'I must practise my speech before I go to the meeting'.
> She said she had to practise her speech before she went to the meeting.

> I said, 'I must go to the Head Office next week to see Mr X'.
> I said I should have to go to the Head Office next week (in the following week) to see Mr X.

But it remains when it expresses a permanent general obligation or when it expresses deduction.

> He said, 'Professional staff must retire at 55'.
> He said that professional staff must retire at 55.

> He said, 'The X must be easier to use than the Y'.
> He said that it must be easier to use the X than the Y.

Say and tell   *Say* is normally used with the actual words spoken. It is never used with the infinitive in reported speech.
Tell is never used with the actual words spoken. A personal object (noun or pronoun) is always present.

Index